THE EUROPEAN UNION SERIES

General Editors: Neill Nugent, William E. Paterson

The European Union series provides an authoritative li[...]
ranging from general introductory texts to definitive assessments of key institutions and
actors, issues, policies and policy processes, and the role of member states.

Books in the series are written by leading scholars in their fields and reflect the most up-
to-date research and debate. Particular attention is paid to accessibility and clear
presentation for a wide audience of students, practitioners and interested general readers.

The series editors are **Neill Nugent**, Professor of Politics and Jean Monnet Professor of
European Integration, Manchester Metropolitan University, and **William E. Paterson**,
Founding Director of the Institute of German Studies, University of Birmingham and
Chairman of the German British Forum. Their co-editor until his death in July 1999,
Vincent Wright, was a Fellow of Nuffield College, Oxford University.

Feedback on the series and book proposals are always welcome and should be sent to
Steven Kennedy, Palgrave Macmillan, Houndmills, Basingstoke, Hampshire RG21 6XS,
UK, or by e-mail to s.kennedy@palgrave.com

General textbooks

Published

Desmond Dinan **Encyclopedia of the
European Union**
[Rights: Europe only]

Desmond Dinan **Europe Recast:
A History of European Union**
[Rights: Europe only]

Desmond Dinan **Ever Closer Union:
An Introduction to European Integration
(3rd edn)**
[Rights: Europe only]

Mette Eilstrup Sangiovanni (ed.)
Debates on European Integration: A Reader

Simon Hix **The Political System of the
European Union (2nd edn)**

Paul Magnette **What Is the European
Union? Nature and Prospects**

John McCormick **Understanding the
European Union: A Concise
Introduction (4th edn)**

Brent F. Nelsen and Alexander Stubb
**The European Union: Readings on the
Theory and Practice of European
Integration (3rd edn)**
[Rights: Europe only]

Neill Nugent (ed.) **European Union
Enlargement**

Neill Nugent **The Government and
Politics of the European Union
(6th edn)**
[Rights: World excluding USA and
dependencies and Canada]

John Peterson and Elizabeth Bomberg
**Decision-Making in the European
Union**

Ben Rosamond **Theories of European
Integration**

Forthcoming

Laurie Buonanno and Neill Nugent
**Policies and Policy Processes of the
European Union**

David Howarth **The Political Economy
of European Integration**

The major institutions and actors

Published

Renaud Dehousse **The European Court of justice**

Justin Greenwood **Interest Representation in the European Union (2nd edn)**

Fiona Hayes-Renshaw and Helen Wallace **The Council of Ministers (2nd edn)**

Simon Hix and Christopher Lord **Political Parties in the European Union**

David Judge and David Earnshaw **The European Parliament**

Neill Nugent **The European Commission**

Anne Stevens with Handley Stevens **Brussels Bureaucrats? The Administration of the European Union**

Forthcoming

Wolfgang Wessels **The European Council**

The main areas of policy

Published

Michelle Cini and Lee McGowan **Competition Policy In the European Union**

Wyn Grant **The Common Agricultural Policy**

Martin Holland **The European Union and the Third World**

Jolyon Howorth **Security and Defence Policy in the European Union**

Stephan Keukeleire and Jennifer MacNaughtan **The Foreign Policy of the European Union**

Brigid Laffan **The Finances of the European Union**

Malcolm Levitt and Christopher Lord **The Political Economy of Monetary Union**

Janne Haaland Matláry **Energy Policy in the European Union**

John McCormick **Environmental Policy In the European Union**

John Peterson and Margaret Sharp **Technology Policy In the European Union**

Handley Stevens **Transport Policy in the European Union**

Forthcoming

Michelle Chang **Monetary Integration In the European Union**

Johanna Kantola **Gender and the European Union**

Bart Kerremans, David Allen and Geoffrey Edwards **The External Economic Relations of the European Union**

Jörg Monar **Justice and Home Affairs In the European Union**

John Vogler, Richard Whitman and Charlotte Bretherton **The External Policies of the European Union**

Also planned

Political Union

Social Policy In the European Union

The member states and the Union

Published

Carlos Closa and Paul Heywood **Spain and the European Union**

Alain Guyomarch, Howard Machin and Ella Ritchie **France in the European Union**

Brigid Laffan and Jane O'Mahoney **Ireland and the European Union**

Forthcoming

Simon Bulmer and William E. Paterson **Germany and the European Union**

Phil Daniels and Ella Ritchie **Britain and the European Union**

Brigid Laffan **The European Union and Its Member States**

Federiga Bindi **Italy and the European Union**

Baldur Thorhallson **Small States in the European Union**

Issues

Published

Derek Beach **The Dynamic of European Integration: Why and When EU Institutions Matter**

Steven McGuire and Michael Smith **The European Union and the United States**

Forthcoming

Thomas Christiansen and Christine Reh **Constitutionalizing the European Union**

Robert Ladrech **Europeanization and National Politics**

Union was both motivated and encouraged to find new security roles. Once it did this, the EU was bound to come into potential competition and conflict with the US, and the result has been a series of more or less successful 'experiments' in the development of EU–US security relations. With the impact of transnational terrorism, and the 'securitization' of new areas of international life such as those relating to energy and the environment, both the EU and the US have faced new challenges in defining their mutual relationships and responding to the opportunities presented by a changing world order.

How have the EU and the US developed their respective policies in these areas of close mutual engagement? Once developed, how have those policies created competition and sometimes open conflict between the EU and the US, while at the same time leading to areas of close cooperation? What are the implications of the EU–US 'adversarial partnership' for the rest of the world, and how might this partnership impact upon the future development of its members and the rest of the world arena? As noted above, these are not purely academic questions; they concern policy-makers not only in the EU and the US but also in a host of other countries and in a wide range of non-governmental bodies, from giant corporations to environmental, humanitarian and other pressure groups. The purpose of this book is to sharpen these questions and to provide the means to work towards at least some of the answers to them.

The nature of the book

The book takes as its key theme the interplay between competition and convergence, basing this on the fact that in every aspect of their relationship the EU and the US are increasingly part of an integrated policy space, but that within this space they are in often intense competition (sometimes formulated as 'competitive interdependence' or 'competitive cooperation'). Though Europe and the US share common understandings about many issues, how they conceptualize – and operationalize – solutions can be quite different. Increasingly also, EU–US relations have close connections with broader issues of world order and the relations between key regions in the world arena. The book deploys a range of approaches from international relations and international political economy to analyse and evaluate both the changing nature of the

relationship and specific areas of policy formation. It draws on the rich tradition of scholarship in EU–US relations, but also looks at work from innovation and management studies as a way of exploring the role of firms and other stakeholders in the relationship. The volume also uses primary data from a variety of sources. We aim to explore the arguments and to reach conclusions not by using one single analytical perspective but rather by deploying the appropriate methods of analysis to deal with specific areas of policy-making and interaction.

Chapter 1 deals with the historical evolution of the relationship, using an approach centred on key points of change or transformation to point out important areas of continuity and discontinuity, and deploying a range of historical evidence such as documents and speeches to illustrate specific phases of change and development. This chapter thus establishes the growth of the 'competition and convergence' which are central to the relationship, and provides the historical context which is vital to an appreciation of current and possible future trends. Chapter 2 deals with the range of frameworks available for analysis of the relationship, and aims to identify the key concerns for analysis and the key approaches that can be utilized. It argues that EU–US relations can be seen as a kind of 'mixed actor system' in which political and economic interactions take place at a number of interconnected levels, and in which the roles of institutions both within and between the key participants have considerable importance. It also puts the relationship in the context of key perspectives on international relations and international political economy, which are then referred to throughout the remainder of the text. Chapters 1 and 2 together can be thought of as the 'source documents' for the book as a whole, since later chapters will refer back to the evidence and frameworks presented in these chapters.

Chapters 3 to 9 deal with specific areas of policy formation and interaction, starting with the longest established areas in EU-US relations, and thus with issues of political economy. Chapters 3 to 6 deal with key aspects of the political economy of EU–US relations, working from trade and monetary relations through to investment and competition and innovation. Chapters 7 to 9 deal with issues not only of political economy but also of diplomacy and security, moving from interregional relations through the 'new Europe' to issues of world order and global governance. This sequence reflects the empirical reality of EU–US relations, in which

as the post-cold war era has unfolded the political and security dimension has become more and more salient and potentially controversial. Chapters 3 to 9 as a whole thus provide a detailed study of the key elements in EU–US relations and also in their links to the rest of the world arena.

The intention in all of these chapters is to identify key areas of development, dispute and convergence and to explore the ways these issues have been managed. Thus these chapters are constructed to a common template: they deal first with policy issues and policy development in the EU and the US, then with issues of competition and convergence and then with mechanisms of management. The rationale for this structure is simple: it is impossible to discuss the relations between the EU and the US unless we are aware of the key ways each of the parties constructs its policies and its roles within the world arena. Each chapter ends with an overall evaluation and a discussion of present and future policy developments cast explicitly in terms of competition and convergence.

Finally, Chapter 10 takes the foundations established in Chapters 1–2 and uses them to construct a comparative evaluation of the present and future 'Euro-American system' centred around the EU and the US. It also reassesses the utility of the analytical frameworks deployed in Chapter 2, which will also have been used within the intervening chapters. The overall conclusion to the book is that the tensions and sometimes open conflicts within the 'Euro-American system' will not be easily resolved, but that the increasing economic and institutional integration, and the continuing political dialogue, that characterize the system will not allow for an easy 'divorce' or a pattern of 'separate development'. The EU and the US have got well under each other's skin, and this will continue to be the source of both competition and convergence in a changing world arena.

Chapter 1

European Integration, Transatlantic Relations and the United States since 1945

The system of relations that has grown up between the European integration project and the United States is dense and complex, and it is one of long standing. Central to the argument in this book is the growth and development of this system of relations, and its impact not only on its members but also on the world as a whole. For much of its life, the system has dominated the global economy and has played a key part in the management of global diplomatic and security issues. It is thus vital to understand the structure and functioning of the system, its central rules and assumptions, and the ways it has changed and developed during more than half a century. This is the focus of the first two chapters in the book.

In a way, as Alfred Grosser has argued, there is no 'year zero' in relations between the United States and Europe (Grosser 1980). The influence of the 'old continent' was central in the establishment and growth of the US, and increasingly from the late nineteenth century onwards, the United States came more and more to play a central part in the European arena. From the beginning of the twentieth century, American investment and economic influence were important to the management of the European economies; nowhere was this more clear than in the aftermath of World War I, when the capacity of the US to contribute to the recovery of Europe, and its willingness or unwillingness to make such a contribution, played a central role in the development of the interwar order. During the 1930s, the American economy and its troubles after the 'great crash' of 1929 fed directly into the increasing instability of Europe, and the uncertainties of US diplomacy in the age of isolationism played a major role in the onset of World War II. The fates of the US and Europe were deeply intertwined even before the great catalytic drama of the war in Europe and beyond (Grosser 1980: Chapter 1; Lundestad 2005: Chapter 1).

This said, detailed analysis of the ways in which the relationship between European integration and the United States was established and evolved should start in the aftermath of the second global conflict. It was at this point that US involvement became structural and in some ways organic, and the growth of European integration itself became a central pillar of the emerging relationship. This chapter sets out to map the historical evolution of the relationship in the sixty years following the end of World War II, and to identify the key forces contributing to the process of historical change. In Chapter 2 we will look more closely at the underlying structures and functioning of the 'Euro-American system' and at the issues and institutions around which it has centred.

The first part of the chapter examines the foundations on which the relationship between European integration and the United States was constructed in the first decade after World War II. In the second part, the focus is on the growth of partnership and rivalry between an integrating Europe and the US. The third and fourth parts of the chapter focus respectively on processes of change and transformation: first, the changes that took place within EC–US relations during the 1970s and early 1980s, and second, the dramatic changes that surrounded the relationship in the late 1980s and after. The key question underlying all of this is simple: How much of what was established during the 1950s and 1960s still survives, and how substantial has the transformation of the relationship been?

Foundations: 1945–58

At the most general level, it could be said that the end of the World War II saw the collapse of Europe and the dominance of the United States. At one time or another, almost all of the European states had been defeated during the war, while even those that had emerged victorious and never been occupied, such as Britain, were exhausted. The European economy had in many respects ceased to exist, because of the divisions and dislocations created by war, while European society was racked by tensions and insecurities. These insecurities emerged partly out of the challenge to governmental legitimacy in almost every European country, but also out of the perceived challenge from Communism represented most clearly by the Soviet Union and the presence of the Red Army in the heart of Europe. At the same time, the US had ended the war in a position of unprecedented strength: its economy had boomed, its military might (bolstered by possession of the 'ultimate weapon' in the shape of the atom bomb) was unchallenged, and American ideas of democracy and progress seemed to be the wave of the future.

This situation was not of course unproblematic. For European governments, particularly those of the western half of the continent, the challenge was not simply one of re-establishing economic and political stability; it was also one of recreating or adapting the European model of statehood in a context where the nature of statehood itself was in question. For their Eastern and Central European counterparts, the challenge was one of resisting or adapting to the fact of Soviet dominance. For the Americans, the challenge was that of coming to terms with international predominance and resolving the clash between isolationism and internationalism – a clash that ran through the heart of US political life. It was out of this complex and unstable mix of political, economic and security problems that the initial 'bargain' between the US and European governments emerged (Grosser 1980: Chapter 1; DePorte 1986; Ellwood 1992; Lundestad 1998: Chapters 1–2; Lundestad 2005: Chapter 1; Sloan 2005: Chapters 1–3).

Between 1945 and 1950, the elements of what later came to be seen as a grand strategic bargain between the United States and Western Europe were put in place. The initial driving forces were a combination of insecurity, the search for governmental legitimacy and the search for a formula to maintain and express US engagement with the international system. For Europeans, the need to counter the Soviet threat and to keep the US committed to European stability rapidly became a central fact of diplomatic life. The Roosevelt administration in Washington had proclaimed at the end of the war that they would aim to withdraw all US forces from Europe within two years, a prospect that fuelled European fears of instability and Soviet opportunism. As a result, a series of European leaders, led by Winston Churchill, the British Prime Minister, expressed their concern about the prospects of instability and threat in the event of a US withdrawal, and this concern itself became part of an extensive debate in Washington about the future of US foreign policy. The working out of this debate thus became crucial to the future of Europe itself, especially after the replacement of Roosevelt by Vice-President Harry Truman in 1945 (Hoffmann and Maier 1984; DePorte 1986; Hogan 1987).

The intersection of European fears and US domestic debate led to a process of incremental commitment between 1945 and 1949 that culminated in the North Atlantic Treaty of April 1949. Before that military 'bargain', however, the key thrust of US commitment had been economic and diplomatic. In 1947, the 'Truman Doctrine' had set out the basis for US commitment to the defence of democracy on a global level, but especially in postwar Europe. This was followed in mid-1947 by the initial moves in what came to be known as the Marshall Plan: in June of that year, General Marshall, the US secretary of state, made a speech at Harvard University in which he set out the terms for continued US economic assistance to Europe (see extract in Box 1.1). His premise was that if Europe was allowed to continue in economic chaos, this would sharpen the political and security threats of Communism, and would increase the power of domestic Communist parties in countries such as France or Italy. While this may not seem radical today, the speech represented a key element in the emerging transatlantic 'bargain' – not least because of the terms on which

Box 1.1   The Marshall Plan speech (extracts)

It is evident . . . that, before the United States Government can proceed much further in its efforts to alleviate the situation and help start the European world on its way to recovery, there must be some agreement among the countries of Europe as to the requirements of the situation and the part those countries themselves will take in order to give proper effect to whatever action might be undertaken by this Government. It would be neither fitting nor efficacious for our Government to undertake to draw up unilaterally a program designed to place Europe on its feet economically. This is the business of the Europeans. The initiative, I think, must come from Europe. The role of this country should consist of friendly aid in the drafting of a European program and of later support of such a program so far as it may be practical for us to do so. The program should be a joint one, agreed to by a number, if not all, of European nations.

Source: Secretary of State George C. Marshall, Address at the Commencement Exercises of Harvard University, Cambridge, Massachusetts, 5 June 1947.

the aid was to be given. These included the establishment or strengthening of 'free institutions' and free markets and, significantly, the construction of a cooperative plan through which the Europeans themselves were to specify the nature and the allocation of the aid itself (DePorte 1986; Hogan 1987; Gann and Duignan 1998; Lundestad 1998, 2005; Sloan 2005).

The Marshall Plan thus can be seen as a keystone of three processes. First, by restricting the aid to 'free' countries, it contributed strongly to the division of Europe that became solidified in the cold war. Although some Central- and East-European governments displayed initial interest in the plan, they were brought rapidly into line by the Soviets, and a political-economic division of Europe was accentuated. At the same time, Communist parties that had aspired to power or in some cases achieved it in some Western-European countries were marginalized through a combination of economic restructuring and associated political realignment. Finally, the requirement that European countries should cooperate to respond to the plan (soon labelled the European Recovery Programme or ERP) can be seen as setting in motion processes that proved fundamental to the European integration process. The plan was to be delivered via the ERP and an associated organization, the Organization for European Economic Cooperation (OEEC), and it is by no means fanciful to see this as the breeding-ground for what became the European Coal and Steel Community, the first institution of European economic integration. In the background, the establishment of the institutional framework that came to be known as the Bretton Woods system, encompassing the International Monetary Fund, the World Bank and the General Agreement on Tariffs and Trade, created a set of multilateral rules that were to be crucial in shaping the development of the European economies and of European integration (Mee 1984; Milward 1984; Hogan 1987).

It can be argued that by 1949, with the signing of the North Atlantic Treaty between the US, Canada and fourteen European countries, the key elements of the 'transatlantic bargain' were in place. The ERP (and in broader terms the Bretton Woods system) expressed the political/economic end of the spectrum, while the North Atlantic Treaty represented the guarantee of continuing US involvement with the security of the continent – and both together had the effect of constructing the boundary between the 'free world' and the Communist bloc that became the centrepiece of the cold war. The ERP also seemed to have contributed to (if not actually having inspired) the proposal made by Monnet and Schuman of France in May 1950 for a European Coal and Steel Community, in which France and Germany would form the core of a new kind of economic and (by implication) political integration. But this process was not without its tensions and divisions. In the first place, the 'new Europe' gradually emerging from the chaos of the postwar period was not a comprehensive Europe: the division between the original six members of the ECSC (France, Germany, Italy and the Benelux countries) and those who were left or chose to remain outside set up a new division within the western half of the continent. Most obviously, Britain, the largest single recipient of Marshall Aid, had declined with almost no hesitation the opportunity to join the ECSC (Grosser 1980: Chapter 3). Second, the process of US commitment to the security of Europe had exposed significant divisions between European governments, particularly between those such as France that saw Europe as a potentially independent 'third force' and those such as Britain that saw the North Atlantic Treaty as a vital strand in the new Atlantic partnership. Finally, in the US, the debate about the nature and extent of US international engagement had served to sharpen the fear of Communism and to set in motion the domestic forces of McCarthyism, which led to a strongly anti-Communist atmosphere. This was only sharpened further by the onset of the Korean War in 1950, which seemed to demonstrate the world-wide threat from the Soviet Union and its allies, including China.

During the 1950s, these coexisting trends towards transatlantic cooperation and tension were perpetuated by a series of events in both Europe and the US. From the European perspective, the period between the establishment of the Coal and Steel Community in 1950 and the signing of the Treaty of Rome in 1957 – the latter establishing the European Economic Community and the European Atomic Energy Community – was one of progress and setbacks. The Coal and Steel Community prospered, partly as the result of natural economic recovery but also as the result of a lowering of barriers and the achievement of economies of scale, and by the mid-1950s this was leading to calls for a decisive extension of the European integration process. But at the same time, attempts to further European integration in the fields of diplomacy and defence were unsuccessful. In 1952, the French had proposed a plan for a European Defence Community, in which there would be substantial integration of military units and military command structures; this was in part a response to American calls for the rearmament of West Germany, and in part a perpetuation of the idea that Europe could be a 'third force' in world politics (Fursdon 1980; DePorte 1986; Winand 1993: Chapters 2–3; Lundestad 1998: Chapter 5; Lundestad 2005: Chapter 3). By 1954, the project lay in ruins, ironically in large part because of its rejection by the French National Assembly, but also because of the abstention of the British and perceptions of a clash with the North Atlantic Treaty Organization (NATO), which had been constructed on the foundations of the North Atlantic Treaty and which now encompassed sixteen European countries. This defeat had two significant implications for the relationship between the US and European integration. First, it meant that for the foreseeable future collective European defence would be conducted through NATO (of which West Germany became a member through joining the Western European Union in 1955). Second, it meant that the European integration project would remain overwhelmingly 'civilian' in character, whatever the attempts by countries such as France to move it in the direction of diplomatic or security coordination.

This was the foundation for the 'relaunching' of European integration in 1955–7 through the negotiations for what became the Treaty of Rome. Because of the defeat of the EDC, the EEC was to be 'civilian' and to be based on a massive extension of economic coordination between the original six member states of the ECSC. Although other countries such as Britain were by this time much more interested in – or worried by – the European project, the prospect of supranational influence over national economic policies was still enough to make them hesitate, thus contributing to the continuing dominance of France and Germany within the project (Lundestad 2005: Chapters 2–3). For the Americans, as might have been expected, the extension of European integration was a two-edged process. On the one hand, it consolidated the economic and social stability of western Europe, and thus contributed to the stabilization of the continent as a whole (DePorte 1986), so many US policymakers were strongly in favour not only of the EEC but also of British membership (Camps 1960; Winand 1993: Chapter 5). On the other hand, those Americans who looked at the aims of the EEC and discerned a threat to US economic interests in areas such as agriculture were less enthusiastic; the fact that one of the first common policies to be adopted by the EEC was the Common

Agricultural Policy (CAP) was to have a shaping – and sharpening - effect on transatlantic relations throughout the 1960s (Krause 1968; Beloff 1976). The ECSC had already attracted the suspicion and in some cases the outright hostility of American steel interests, who saw it as an unfair cartel designed to exclude them from the European market (Diebold 1959), and the EEC looked like a much wider and more dangerous threat.

By the late 1950s, therefore, the tone of relations between the US and the European integration project was in important respects set. In 1958, the major European currencies achieved convertibility into each other and into the US dollar: this was a key indicator of their continuing recovery and consolidation, and of their full participation in the Bretton Woods system of international economic institutions, but it was also surrounded by ambiguities and uncertainties about the future course of transatlantic relations.

Partnership and Rivalry: 1958–71

We have seen that the relationship between European integration and the United States as it had developed by the end of the 1950s contained important coexisting but often conflicting elements of cooperation and competition. The European project on one level was a vital component of the consolidation of the 'west' in the cold war, contributing to stability and to the growth of what Marshall had called 'free institutions'. At another level, it was a source of concern to American economic interests and a focus of aspirations for a European 'third force' that could express a particular identity in the world arena. During the 1960s, these tensions were to multiply, partly for reasons inherent in the European project, partly for reasons reflecting US positions and priorities, and partly because of wider changes in the international system. Ironically, it may seem, the period between 1958 and the beginning of the 1970s was littered with proclamations of 'Atlantic partnership' at the same time as it gave increasing evidence of Atlantic rivalry (Diebold 1960; Cleveland 1966; Pfaltzgraff 1969; Calleo 1970; Diebold 1972; Calleo and Rowland 1973; Winand 1993: Chapters 6–12; Lundestad 1998: Chapter 6; Lundestad 2005: Chapter 4).

From the point of view of European integration, this period was one of consolidation but also of internal tensions and often open conflicts. A number of common policies were initiated, among them two that were to be central to transatlantic relations, the Common Commercial Policy (CCP) and the CAP. Institutional development and consolidation were apparent, especially in the role of the European Commission which became established as a key generator of initiatives on the road to greater integration. At the same time, the economies of EEC member states continued to flourish, led by the West-German economy and the 'economic miracle' it represented. But there were also strong trends in the direction of internal conflict and fragmentation (Camps 1967; Grosser 1980). In the early 1960s, the French tried to set in motion the development of a 'European foreign policy', but this was limited and not supported by key 'Atlanticist' member states; in 1969 there was a further initiative in this direction with the beginnings of what became European Political Cooperation, but the basis remained strongly intergovernmental and diplomatic rather than integrationist and security-related. During the mid-1960s, the implementation of further integrationist measures in agriculture and the development of the 'common market' for goods created sharp perceptions of gains and losses for major member states, and in the case of France led to its declaration of an 'empty chair' policy between 1966 and 1967. As a result, the 'Luxembourg Compromise' of 1967 signalled a retreat from full-blooded integration to a situation in which vital national interests could form the basis for an effective veto of legislation within the EEC. Alongside all of this, the prospect of the EEC's first enlargement continued throughout the 1960s. In 1963, General de Gaulle, the French president, effectively vetoed the first application for membership by Britain (thus also excluding Denmark, Ireland and Norway who had also applied). This veto was repeated in 1967, but by 1970 the installation of a pro-integrationist government in Britain combined with the fall of de Gaulle to produce an agreement on British membership.

The turbulence of developments in European integration during the 1960s was paralleled by problems within American politics and foreign policy. The rich promise of the Kennedy administration installed in 1960 was eroded by the president's assassination, by domestic tensions over such issues as civil rights, by increasing US entanglement in Vietnam and by the continuing threat of Soviet nuclear capability, which led to a major intensification of the arms race. This latter process was reflected in US relations with Europe, leading to the 'nuclearization' of NATO and to the growth of domestic anti-nuclear protest movements. But the tribulations of US administrations were not simply political: the US economy proved sluggish and in some respects uncompetitive, and was increasingly distorted by the focus on military spending and military commitments (Calleo and Rowland 1973). By the end of the 1960s, the Nixon administration installed in 1968 had begun to unwind some of these issues, not without considerable suspicion or difficulty. They had begun the process of 'détente' with the Soviet Union, focusing especially on the control of nuclear weapons, had initiated a broader diplomacy designed to respond to the needs of what they saw as a potentially multipolar world, engaging the Chinese and the Japanese as well as the Soviets and the Europeans, and had begun a reassessment of US economic commitments in the light of the generally poor performance of the economy.

The intersection of these trends in Europe and the US created a series of tensions throughout the 1960s. Even before the Kennedy administration had been installed, General de Gaulle had called for a greater degree of power-sharing in NATO, and had begun to present the EEC as the basis for a new challenge to US dominance (Calleo 1970; Harrison 1982). When in July 1962 President Kennedy made a speech in which he outlined a 'declaration of interdependence' between the United States and a 'uniting Europe' (see Box 1.2), this was greeted in some quarters as a visionary response to the new realities of world politics and in others as an attempt to perpetuate US hegemony over a resurgent Europe in particular (Winand 1993: Chapter 9). Thus it is not surprising that the rhetoric of 'Atlantic partnership' and 'Atlantic community' that arose after Kennedy's speech was accompanied by major efforts to counter it through a discourse of European independence and difference. But not all Europeans were united in this respect: de Gaulle's strident anti-Atlanticism (see Box 1.2), reflected in his veto of British membership in the EEC, and in French withdrawal from the NATO integrated military command in 1966, was balanced not only by British Atlanticism, but also by that of such countries as the Netherlands, Italy and Germany within the EEC itself (Cromwell 1969; Grosser 1980; Harrison 1982; DePorte 1986) . Even such Atlanticist countries were perturbed by the increasing US commitment in Vietnam and by the evidence of US-Soviet diplomacy in the context of 'détente', so the overall picture was a complex one, which could not be reduced to a simple EEC–US partnership or rivalry.

Box 1.2 Kennedy and de Gaulle

The nations of Western Europe, long divided by feuds far more bitter than any which existed among the 13 colonies, are joining together, seeking, as our forefathers sought, to find freedom in diversity and in unity, strength. The United States looks on this vast new enterprise with hope and admiration. We do not regard a strong and united Europe as a rival but as a partner. To aid its progress has been the basic object of our foreign policy for 17 years. We believe that a united Europe will be capable of playing a greater role in the common defense, of responding more generously to the needs of poorer nations, of joining with the United States and others in lowering trade barriers, resolving problems of commerce, commodities, and currency, and developing coordinated policies in all economic, political, and diplomatic areas. We see in such a Europe a partner with whom we can deal on a basis of full equality in all the great and burdensome tasks of building and defending a community of free nations.

. . . I will say here and now, on this Day of Independence, that the United States will be ready for a 'Declaration of Interdependence', that we will be prepared to discuss with a united Europe the ways and means of forming a concrete Atlantic partnership, a mutually beneficial partnership between the new union now emerging in Europe and the old American Union founded here 175 years ago.

Source: President John F. Kennedy, Address on the Goal of an Atlantic Partnership, Philadelphia, 4 July 1962.

[the entry of Great Britain and others] will completely change the whole of the actions, the agreements, the compensation, the rules which have already been established between the Six . . . Then it will be another Common Market whose construction ought to be envisaged . . . Further, this community, increasing in such fashion, would see itself faced with problems of economic relations with all kinds of other States, and first with the United States. It is to be foreseen that the cohesion of its members, who would be very numerous and diverse, would not endure for long, and that ultimately it would appear as a colossal Atlantic community under American dependence and direction, and which would quickly have absorbed the community of Europe.

Source: President Charles de Gaulle, Press Conference, Paris, 14 January 1963.

Alongside this diplomatic complexity, the political economy of EEC–US relations was no less significant. One of the most obvious manifestations of this significance was the growth of all forms of exchange between the United States and the EEC during the early 1960s: trade, investment and travel all experienced a major increase and it is difficult to avoid the conclusion that this was caused by the establishment of a large market among the six EEC member states (Cooper 1968; Diebold 1972). It is also important to note that at this time Britain accounted for much more in all of these areas than the whole of the EEC combined. By the beginning of the 1960s, there was also evidence of the Europeans' increasing capacity to engage collectively with the Americans within the world arena. Most obviously, the Dillon Round of trade negotiations within the General Agreement on Tariffs and Trade (GATT) during 1961 had seen the EEC adopting a collective position. More dramatically, the Kennedy Round of 1963–6, proclaimed by the president as part of his 'declaration of interdependence', saw the creation of a substantive EEC trade diplomacy, which enabled the Europeans to resist US pressure on a number of fronts, particularly agricultural trade (Calleo and Rowland 1973). This set of developments is perhaps best cast in terms of the capacity to resist, rather than the capacity to initiate and lead, but it did signify a distinct set of new directions in international trade diplomacy. There were also the beginnings of European capacity to construct new inter-regional relationships: the most obvious of these were to be found in the framework of the Yaoundé Conventions, which constructed relationships with a set of mainly French ex-colonies in Africa.

Despite this evidence that the EEC was gradually acquiring the ability to exercise collective weight in the context of transatlantic relations and the broader world economy, the 1960s did not provide conclusive evidence of the emergence either of a true transatlantic partnership or of transatlantic rivalry. If anything, they provided evidence that any form of cooperation in the international political economy was hard work, that it would be characterized by disputes as much as by progress, and that it remained fragmented in the continuing absence of Britain and other significant European states from the EEC. By the end of the 1960s, it was clear that this 'gap' was likely to be filled in the near future, but by that time also it was clear that the world economy as a whole was in a state of turbulence and potential chaos. The impact of the war in Vietnam and of conflict in the Middle East, the uncertainties of US–Soviet 'détente' and the unevenness of economic performance in the major western economies created a breeding-ground for uncertainty and instability (Calleo and Rowland 1973; Hanrieder 1974; Shonfield *et al.* 1976; Hanrieder 1982). As a result, the Bretton Woods system of financial institutions, and the rules relating to fixed exchange rates and domestic economic adjustment, were increasingly under pressure. It was apparent that both in the diplomatic and in the economic sphere the 1970s would be challenging to say the least, and that the challenge to the assumptions behind EEC–US relations would be potentially momentous.

Change: 1971–85

On 15 August 1971 in a television broadcast to the American people President Nixon proclaimed what came to be known as his 'New Economic Policy'. At around the same time, in a number of speeches and papers, the administration also enunciated what became known as the 'Nixon Doctrine' relating to its foreign policy and diplomatic commitments, especially to allies. It is no exaggeration to say that these two sets of developments shaped the course of EEC–US relations for at least decade, and that when combined with developments within the EEC itself and in the broader world arena they created a series of significant changes within the transatlantic relationship (Kaiser 1973; Czempiel and Rustow 1976; Kaiser and Schwartz 1977; M. Smith 1978). During the early 1980s, the relationship was given an additional and severe testing by the policies of the Reagan administration, and by the beginnings of a new phase of European integration itself.

Nixon's August 1971 speech (see Box 1.3) rapidly became known as the 'Nixon Shock'. As we have already noted, the US economy had being giving cause for concern for some time, with low growth accompanied by rising unemployment, declining competitiveness and a balance of payments deficit. For some in the US administration this set of conditions as linked closely to the burden the US had been carrying as leader of the 'free world' for the past twenty-five years, and there was a move to declare America an 'ordinary country' in economic affairs, prepared to defend its own interests against all comers (Rosecrance 1976). There is no doubt,

Box 1.3   The 'Nixon Shock'

I have directed secretary [of the Treasury] Connally to suspend temporarily the convertibility of the dollar into gold or other reserve assets, except in amounts and conditions determined to be in the interest of monetary stability and in the best interests of the United States ... To our friends abroad ... I give this assurance: The United States has always been, and will continue to be, a forward-looking and trustworthy trading partner. In full cooperation with the International Monetary Fund and those who trade with us, we will press for the necessary reforms to set up an urgently needed new international monetary system. Stability and equal treatment is in everybody's best interest. I am determined that the American dollar must never again be a hostage in the hands of international speculators ... As a temporary measure, I am today imposing an additional tax of 10 per cent on goods imported into the United States ... At the end of World War II the economies of the major industrial nations of Europe and Asia were shattered ... Today, largely with our help, they have regained their vitality. They have become our strong competitors, and we welcome their success. But now that other nations are economically strong, the time has come for them to bear their fair share of the burden of defending freedom around the world. The time has come for exchange rates to be set straight and for the major nations to compete as equals. There is no longer any need for the United States to compete with one hand tied behind her back.

Source: Address by President Nixon on the Challenge of Peace, 15 August 1971.

as already noted, that the economic problems faced by the US also related to the burden of the Vietnam War, which had created inflationary pressures as well as distorting the balance of the US federal budget. The combination of rising welfare spending with rising external expenditure on foreign and security policy was a potent one (and one that would be seen again in the 1980s). The administration's response, as expressed through the 'Nixon Shock', was to inject a dose of economic nationalism. The dollar was detached from its previous fixed price against gold, resulting in its decline against other leading currencies, while measures were taken to control imports and to boost the competitiveness of US industry. While this might be seen as a logical and rational response to economic difficulties, in the circumstances of the early 1970s it was an explosive set of measures (Calleo and Rowland 1973; Calleo 1981). The administration justified it at least in part by the need for allies to take up the burden of defending democracy, thereby continuing what had been a growing chorus of complaint against the Europeans' unwillingness to either adjust their currencies against the dollar or take up more of the burden of defence spending. But the measures can also be seen –as they were at the time – as an attack on cherished principles of the Bretton Woods system. The effective devaluation of the dollar meant that the USA was asking its allies to pay the price for the loss of US competitiveness, while the imposition of an import surcharge went against one of the central principles of the GATT.

Alongside this set of economic measures, the administration continued its exhortations to its allies – the Nixon Doctrine (Hoffmann 1968; Hanrieder 1974; Hoffman 1978); essentially this consisted of the demand that the allies (whether in Europe or elsewhere) should take up more of the burden of their own defence and stand on their own two feet. As applied to the conflict in Vietnam, this was a means by which the US would eventually disengage and leave the South Vietnamese to fend for themselves. As applied in Europe, it sharpened the pressure on those European allies (now almost all members of the EEC) that had in American eyes grown richer under the protective umbrella provided by America. But the problem was that these demands were coming from an administration which was progressively weakened internally by the Watergate scandal, in which it became entangled after the 1972 presidential election. This erosion of internal legitimacy for the administration, along with the doubts long harboured by Europeans about US involvement in conflicts outside the NATO area, combined to create a new scepticism among EEC member states when it came to US leadership in all of its forms.

By the time Britain along with Denmark and Ireland entered the EEC in January 1973, there was thus a good deal of turbulence in transatlantic economic relations and more broadly in the western alliance. Although in other circumstances this might have seemed like an opportunity for the enlarged Community to assert itself on the world stage, in fact it militated strongly against that kind of initiative. The conditions that had fostered economic progress and the deepening of European integration during the 1960s had actually been short-lived; financial instability, fears of protectionism in world trade and the increasing politicization of economic disputes were to become a key theme of the next fifteen years in transatlantic relations, and thus part of the world with which the Community had to cope (Warnecke 1972).

The year 1973 was in fact symptomatic of the problems. In April, US Secretary of State Henry Kissinger delivered a speech in New York proclaiming this to be the 'year of Europe' and calling for a new transatlantic bargain to express the new balance of influence between the US and its European partners (see Box 1.4). This speech, delivered in the US and not discussed with the Europeans before its delivery, served as a catalyst for European resentment of the Americans' leadership, and among other results prompted the formulation of a 'declaration on European identity' by the Community – a declaration that focused strongly on the need for partnership rather than domination in the relationship with the US (see Box 1.4). By the end of 1973, the October War in the Middle East between Israel and its Arab neighbours had created a double twist to the tension: on the one hand, it fulfilled many Europeans' fears of US domination and risk-taking through the declaration of a nuclear alert by Washington over the heads of the allies, while on the other hand it precipitated a 400 per cent rise in the price of crude oil, creating an energy crisis and stretching the domestic economic management capacities of European countries to breaking-point (Kaiser 1973; Kaiser 1974; Vernon 1973; Lieber 1974; Chase and Ravenal 1976; M. Smith 1978).

The European Community, already absorbing the impact of its new member states and the longer-term effects of the crises of the late 1960s, was ill fitted to respond dynamically to this set of simultaneous crises. Grand plans for the creation of economic and monetary union by 1980, and for the establishment of a European political union, were undermined both by external developments and by the new internal complexities arising especially from British entry into the Community. A period of 'Eurosclerosis' set in, in which it appeared impossible to take significant new initiatives and in which member state governments were unwilling to contemplate the costs of further integration. Indeed, they spent much of their time focusing on the costs of such integration as already existed, with conflicts over the CAP and over the Community budget lasting through the 1970s. There were, however, at least some signs of a more hopeful kind, and some of these were visible in transatlantic relations. Not for the last time, concerns about rela-

Box 1.4   The 'Year of Europe'

The problems in transatlantic relationships are real. They have arisen in part because during the fifties and sixties the Atlantic community organized itself in different ways in the many different dimensions of its common enterprise. In economic relations, the European community has increasingly stressed its regional personality; the United States, at the same time, must act as part of, and be responsible for, a wider trade and monetary system. We must reconcile these two perspectives. In our collective defense, we are still organized on the principle of unity and integration, but in radically different strategic conditions. The full implications of this change have yet to be faced. Diplomacy is the subject of frequent consultation, but is essentially being conducted by traditional nation states. The United States has global interests and responsibilities. Our European allies have regional interests. These are not necessarily in conflict, but in the new era neither are they automatically identical. In short, we deal with each other regionally and even competitively in economic matters, on an integrated basis in defense, and as national states in diplomacy. When the various collective institutions were rudimentary, the potential inconsistency in their modes of operation was not a problem. But after a generation of evolution and with the new weight and strength of our allies, the various parts of the construction are not always in harmony and sometimes obstruct each other.

Source: Secretary of State Henry A. Kissinger, Address to the Associated Press Annual Luncheon, New York, 23 April 1973 – 'The Year of Europe'.

The Europe of the Nine is aware that, as it unites, it takes on new international obligations. European integration is not directed against anyone, nor is it inspired by a desire for power. On the contrary, the Nine are convinced that their union will benefit the whole international community since it will constitute an element of equilibrium and a basis for cooperation with all countries, whatever their size, culture or social system. The Nine intend to play an active role in world affairs and thus to contribute in accordance with the purposes and principles of the United Nations Charter, to insuring that international relations have a more just basis, that prosperity is more equitably shared, and that the security of each country is more effectively guaranteed. In pursuit of these objectives the Nine should progressively define common positions in the sphere of foreign policy ... The close ties between the United States and the Europe of the Nine – who share values and aspirations based on a common heritage – are mutually beneficial and must be preserved; these ties do not conflict with the determination of the Nine to establish themselves as a distinct and original entity. The Nine intend to maintain their constructive dialogue and to develop their cooperation with the United States on the basis of equality and in a spirit of friendship.

Source: Communiqué of European Community Summit Meeting, Copenhagen, 15 December 1973, Annex II: 'Declaration on Europe's Identity.

tions with the US were accompanied by some moves towards greater international coordination among member states. In the 1970s it was the growth of European Political Cooperation (EPC) that promoted greater coordination of diplomacy among member states, albeit on an explicitly intergovernmental basis. Such coordination was apparent in the Community's activities in the Conference on Security and Cooperation in Europe (CSCE, also known as the Helsinki Process) during the mid-1970s, and was also evident increasingly in the growth of a 'European' diplomacy towards conflict in the Middle East during the late 1970s (Allen and Wallace 1977; Allen and Smith 1982; Allen and Pijpers 1984).

The 1970s were thus not an entirely barren period in EC–US relations, although throughout they were fraught with difficulties. Although the Nixon administration, succeeded by the Ford administration after the fall of the president in 1974, did little to bind the wounds created by the events of the early 1970s, the Carter administration (1976–80) was less confrontational and more inclined to seek consensus. By the nature of things, given the economic difficulties faced by the US, the type of international policy coordination favoured by Washington was based on others (now including Japan as well as the Europeans) taking up more of the burden and taking responsibility for world economic growth (Keohane 1979). At the same time, protectionist demands grew in the US itself, especially from industries such as steel or shipbuilding that were feeling the heat of new competition from both Europe and Asia. Resentment over US attempts to get others to adjust was thus persistent, and towards the end of the 1970s it was reinforced by further concerns in the Community about US diplomacy outside the Atlantic area. In particular, European concerns focused on the onset of new tensions with the Soviet Union in Africa, and on the escalation of tensions in the Persian Gulf after the Iranian revolution of 1978–79. By 1980, when the Soviet Union undertook its invasion of Afghanistan and was immediately subjected to sanctions by the Americans, a 'new cold war' was proclaimed, a concept with which many European governments found themselves distinctly uncomfortable (Kolodziej 1980–81; Freedman 1982, 1983; Allen and Smith 1989).

One of the key problems in EC-US relations during the 1970s was that of US leadership. The assumption that America would (and should) lead in all areas of western international life was challenged in a number of dimensions simultaneously. Economically, it was put in doubt by the fragility of the US economy and by the attempt to get others to pay the costs of US economic decline. Politically, it was thrown into question by the internal turmoil surrounding Watergate and by the frailty of successive US administrations in the wake of Vietnam. In terms of security and defence, it was shaken by the 'Vietnam syndrome', which created doubts about the effectiveness of use of force, and by the growth of new tensions leading to the 'new cold war'. For the EC, the issue expressed itself most forcibly in the economic dimension, with the growth of disputes and the threat of protectionism, but the Community was not immune from the impact of the broader diplomatic and military controversies. Indeed, a key development of the time was the increased linkage between economic issues and political or security matters, and this was bound to make the management of relations with the US more challenging for the Community and its member states.

Given these general conditions, the election of Ronald Reagan as US president in 1980 gave an additional twist to already significant tensions. Reagan was committed to the reassertion of US primacy, both globally and in transatlantic relations, and his administration proved troubling for the Community in many ways. Firstly, the practice of what became known as 'Reaganomics' threatened the kind of international economic instability that the Community found profoundly uncomfortable. A series of measures including substantial tax cuts and spending increases, both in welfare and in defence, had the effect of spreading financial instability worldwide, and especially across the Atlantic. The West German chancellor of the time, Helmut Schmidt, once famously accused Reagan of creating the highest interest rates since the death of Christ, as the Americans tried to square the circle of massive tax cuts and spending increases. The US dollar gyrated erratically on the international exchanges, undervalued and overvalued in quick succession as the administration tried to use interest rates to control the money supply. Unilateral US attempts to cure their financial problems intersected with continuing difficulties within the EC over the budget and agriculture to perpetuate 'Eurosclerosis' and to exaggerate economic divergence among the member states. Only in 1985 did some measure of international financial coordination reappear, with the Plaza Agreement on coordination of monetary polices (Oye *et al.*, 1983; Tsoukalis 1986; Woolcock and van der Ven 1986; Oye *et al.*, 1987).

By the mid-1980s therefore, the economic scene resembled a war zone, with instability and fluctuations a central theme of policy-making. Within the EC, however, there had been some progress in the face of considerable difficulties. The European Monetary System, set up in the final year of the Carter administration, had created a level of monetary coordination among its members that provided some insulation from the wilder gyrations of the dollar (Ludlow 1982). In 1984, at the Fontainebleau summit, Community leaders had at least partly resolved the issue of agricultural financing and the Community budget (including the creation of arrangements for Britain that moderated its contribution to the budget for the foreseeable future). And they had begun to move forward on reforms to improve decision-making within the Community and to make possible the completion of what had become known as the 'Single Market' (Pelkmans and Winters 1988; Sandholtz and Zysman 1989). One central theme of these reforms was the need to make the Community competitive in a world economy where both the US and Japan constituted formidable rivals.

The policy impact of Reaganism, however, was not felt only in economic matters. Indeed, for the citizens of the Community in the early 1980s the preoccupation was not so much the economic and financial impact of Reaganite policies as the perception of danger created by US diplomacy and defence policy. Reagan's election had reflected the demand from Americans that the US be made strong again, after the uncertainties of the 1970s, and the administration set out to deliver on this promise with massive increases in defence spending as well as a much more assertive and muscular diplomacy. This was aimed primarily against the Soviet Union, but inevitably had an immediate impact on European perceptions and policy options. As the rhetoric of US policy was ratcheted up during the early 1980s, and European governments were faced with demands that they accept new deployments of nuclear weapons on their territory, popular disquiet grew. At the same time, US responses to Soviet actions in central and eastern Europe, including the imposition of martial law in Poland during 1981, placed additional pressures on European governments to go along with diplomatic and economic sanctions, in circumstances where they almost instinctively would have preferred to negotiate and look for ways out that did not damage the existing European order (Allen and Smith 1989). One of the results of this pressure was an increasing tendency in the Community to explore the possibility of new forms of European foreign policy cooperation, both within the 'civilian' realm of European Political Cooperation and within the distinctly more sensitive area of European security and defence cooperation (Treverton 1985; Joffe 1987).

From change to transformation: 1985 onwards

Up to the mid-1980s, it is persuasive to talk about transatlantic relations in terms of continuity and evolution. Many aspects of the relationship were recognizably the same in the 1980s as in the 1950s, although in a number of important respects the world had changed around them and there had been a clear impact of political and economic change both in the EEC and in the US. A number of the key issues encountered within the system had remained relatively constant since the 1950s: the problems of leadership and followership, the question of burden-sharing in its broadest context, the role of institutions and the questions raised about them. This part of the chapter is based on the perception that since the mid-1980s the changes in and around the transatlantic relationship amount not to a further stage in evolution but to a radical transformation whose implications have not yet been fully realized. In the previous section, we drew attention to the ways in which during the early 1980s the combination of Reaganism in the US and slow but steady resolution of some key issues in the EEC had created a new momentum and arguably a redefinition of US attitudes towards the Community and western European attitudes towards the US. In the US, the globalism of many policies pursued under the Reagan administration from 1980 to 1984 had created a new awareness that American interests encompassed the Pacific as well as the Atlantic, and that the Europeans were less reliable than they might have been as underwriters of an assertive US posture on economic, political and security issues (see Box 1.5). In the EC, the very assertiveness of US policies combined with a consciousness of new developments in European economic and security policies to foster a sense of difference and of divergence.

This means that although 1989 and the fall of the Berlin Wall is often seen as a crucial turning-point in transatlantic relations, it can equally be argued that the turn had been in progress since 1985 at least. From the EC point of view, there were three key ingredients in this process. First, there was the resolution of key institutional and budgetary issues in the Fontainebleau agreement of 1984, rapidly followed by the Single European Act (SEA) of 1985 and in particular by the inception of the Single Market Programme in 1986. The latter was a five-year plan to radically reduce the barriers to a single European market, with the anticipated effect of substantially enhancing the competitiveness of com-

---

Box 1.5 Lawrence Eagleburger on the Transatlantic Relationship, 1984

I have often discussed with European friends the different requirements for a nation with global responsibilities to those with more regional concerns. The use of the word global is not meant in any arrogant fashion. Nor is it to deny the interests that several European nations retain in areas of the world beyond their continent. But the sheer scope of American interests engages us in a different set of perspectives and imperatives. I am persuaded that despite periodic inconsistencies (mainly on our part) and even more frequent crises of policy disagreement (emanating frequently from the European side) members of the alliance can still forge a strong consensus on most issues of importance ... [but] ... now may well be the appropriate moment for all of us – Europeans and Americans – to take a new look at where we should be going together and how we should get there ... The two pillars of a "smarter" relationship, in my opinion, are: increasing respect for the differences in our alliance; and a more coordinated approach – across the board – to all political, economic and security issues with our European allies.

Source: Under Secretary of State for Political Affairs Lawrence Eagleburger, Speech to the National Newpaper Association, Washington, DC, 7 March 1984.

munity industries and enabling the EC to stand on equal terms with the US and Japan in a changing world economy (Hufbauer 1990: Chapter 1; Schwok 1991: Part II; Smith and Woolcock 1993: Chapter 3; Hocking and Smith 1997: Chapters 1–2). As such, it had not only an economic but also a profoundly political set of implications, relating to institutions and regulation in the world economy and to the effective use of market power by the Community to enhance its world role. The SEA underpinned this set of aims by making what appeared to be relatively small institutional changes such as the widespread use of qualified majority voting in the Community legislative process; these changes actually had a major cumulative effect on the capacity of the EC to make decisions in vital areas of political economy (Keohane and Hoffmann 1993). At the same time, the Community completed a new wave of enlargement with the entry of Spain and Portugal in 1986 to follow that of Greece in 1981. One result of all these developments was a distinct wave of confidence in the EC and its institutions during the late 1980s, part of which spilt over into the aspiration for new measures, specifically economic and monetary union (EMU) and further development of foreign and security policy cooperation.

Set against the 'ring of confidence' that began to surround the EC in the late 1980s, US policies and institutions presented a complex and unstable picture. The massive expenditures and the economic fluctuations of the early 1980s created an equally large 'hangover' in the late 1980s, symbolized best by so-called 'Black Monday' in October 1987, when US stock markets nosedived and created world-wide uncertainty about the economic future. The Reagan years had created a very large 'double deficit' in the US economy, affecting both the balance of payments and the federal budget, and it was not entirely fanciful to see the US as being kept afloat by the willingness of the Japanese and the European to buy US government bonds. Although as noted previously there was a return to elements of monetary policy coordination from 1985 onwards, first with the Plaza accords and then in 1987 with the Louvre agreement, the picture remained one of considerable volatility and risk. Diplomacy and defence policy under 'Reagan II' from 1985 onwards were also a source of uncertainty: continued confrontation with the USSR was accompanied by the initiation of the so-called 'Star Wars' (or Strategic Defence Initiative) programme of space defence from 1985 onwards, but in 1986 there began a process of US–Soviet rapprochement which created the possibility of substantial nuclear disarmament. Mikhail Gorbachev, the new Soviet leader, proved open to new and often radical initiatives, but this was not always a source of reassurance for the Europeans, many of whom feared US–Soviet friendship as much as they did confrontation between the superpowers. By the late 1980s, therefore, it appeared that issues of trust and risk in EC–US relations pervaded both the economic and the diplomatic/security spheres (Allen and Smith 1989).

It was against this backdrop that in 1989 the Berlin Wall was first breached and then destroyed, with fundamental implications for the continued existence of the Soviet bloc and the Soviet Union itself. At one level, this is of course best seen as a profound event in superpower diplomacy and security policy: the confrontation between the USSR and the US, which had been heightened by Reaganite policies, had resulted in the collapse of the Soviet sphere, politically, militarily and economically. As such, it was bound to have immediate effects on the relationship between the USA and its key allies in Europe. But it is clear that the events of 1989–91 were also profoundly European in their origins and impact. The collapse of the Soviet bloc, the end of the Soviet Union and the unification of Germany did not of course see the Americans as bystanders, but they did give a new focus to the diplomatic and political evolution of the 'new Europe' which was distinct simply from the superpower game (Allen and Smith 1991–92; Keohane and Hoffmann 1993; Story 1993; Smith and Woolcock 1993: Chapter 1). Another dimension of the events is also central to the story in this chapter: the end of the cold war was as much an economic process as it was a political or military one. Because of this, the EC was thrust almost immediately to the centre of the process, and remained there throughout the 1990s. This much was recognised as early as December 1989 by US Secretary of State James Baker who in a speech delivered in Berlin called upon the EC to play its full role in the stabilization of the new Europe through welcoming membership applications from newly liberated countries of central and eastern Europe (see Box 1.6). The Community was in many respects unable to live up to the expectations of rapid and comprehensive expansion, but the incorporation of East Germany was followed by a broad-ranging aid programme for the Central- and East-European countries (CEECs). While this did not initially come with the promise of membership, by 1993 a process had begun

Box 1.6   James Baker on the Role of the European Community after the cold war

As Europe changes, the instruments for western cooperation have got to adapt. Working together, it is up to us to design and generally to put into place what I refer to as a new architecture for this new era ... The future development of the European Community will also play a central role in shaping the new Europe ... As Europe moves toward its goal of a common internal market, and as its institutions for political and security cooperation evolve, the link between the United States and the European Community will become even more important. We want our transatlantic cooperation to keep pace with European integration and with institutional reform. To this end, we suggest that the United States and the European Community work together to achieve, whether it is in treaty or some other form, a significantly strengthened set of institutional and consultative links ... We propose that our discussions about this idea proceed in parallel with Europe's efforts to achieve by 1992 a common internal market, so that plans for US–EC interaction would evolve along with changes in the Community. The United States also encourages the European Community to continue to expand cooperation with the nations of the east. The promotion of political and economic reform in the east is a natural vocation for the European Community ... We see no conflict between the process of European integration and an expansion of cooperation between the European Community and its neighbors to the east and west. Indeed, we believe that the attraction of the European Community for the countries of the east depends most on its continued vitality. And the vitality of the Economic Community depends in turn on its continued commitment to the goal of a united Europe envisaged by its founders – free, democratic and closely linked to its North American partners.

Source: Secretary of State James A. Baker III, Address to the Berlin Press Club, 12 December 1989.

which led in 2004 to the entry of eight new CEEC member states along with Cyprus and Malta, to be followed in 2007 by Bulgaria and Romania.

The Community was thus earmarked both in the US and in Europe itself for a major role in what became known as the 'new world order'. Its institutional, financial and political capacity to play such a role was tested to the limit throughout the 1990s, and had a fundamental impact both on its internal makeup and on its international role. Beginning with the Maastricht Treaty of 1991, and proceeding through the Amsterdam Treaty of 1997 and the Nice Treaty of 2000 to the unratified Constitutional Treaty of 2004, the European Union (as it became with the implementation of Maastricht in 1993) was continuously faced with the challenge of redefining and 'reinventing' itself in the face of a rapidly changing world arena. Part of this challenge was inextricably bound up with EU–US relations: the EU was seen by many Americans as playing a major supporting role in the redefinition of US foreign policy and its attempts to cope with the disappearance of its superpower rival, as well as forming the basis for a much expanded economic partnership and rivalry. This perception was widely but not completely shared in the EU itself, and fed into the key debates about the EU's appropriate world role that came to characterize much of the 1990s and beyond (Forster and Wallace 2000; Niblett and Wallace 2001; K. Smith 2003; Hill and Smith 2005; Bretherton and Vogler 2006). These debates in turn were greatly sharpened by events both in the European 'neighbourhood' and in the wider world during the early and mid-1990s. The Gulf War of 1990–1 and the series of conflicts in the former Yugoslavia that erupted in 1991 ran alongside and were intertwined with the institutional changes in the EU that established a Common Foreign and Security Policy (CFSP) and then, in the late 1990s, the European Security and Defence Policy (ESDP). But they also accompanied the progress of most EU member states towards Economic and Monetary Union, and the attempts by the Union as a whole to wrestle with the economic adjustments necessitated by simultaneous processes of enlargement and domestic economic management in a globalizing world.

It is basic to an analysis of what happened in EU–US relations during the 1990s to understand that economics, diplomacy and security issues were mutually entangled and highly demanding, and to be aware of the ways in which these issues engaged both the external policies and the internal politics of the EU and the US (Haftendorn and Tuschhoff 1993). At the same time as the 'adversarial partners' were immersed in processes of self-definition and adjustment to new realities, they were also locked together in a number of much more wide-ranging global processes. Among these were the negotiations within the GATT for a new global trade agreement that led in 1993 to the conclusion of the Uruguay Round, to be followed by a series of key sectoral trade negotiations and then in the late 1990s by renewed demands for a new global negotiating round. At the same time, the approach of EMU and the introduction of the euro as the new single currency for eleven EU member states fed into the wider need for international monetary management in a turbulent world, where global conflicts and global currencies were often closely linked. In all of these processes, the EU and the US were inevitably at centre-stage, and were equally inevitably assailed by a mass of domestic and external demands. Whereas in the economic field, it might plausibly be claimed that the EU and the US were engaged on equal terms in key global management processes, this was not the picture in global diplomacy and security policy, despite the progress made in the EU towards foreign and defence policy coordination during the late 1990s (Featherstone and Ginsberg 1993; Peterson 1996b; M. Smith 1998; Howorth 2003; Smith and Steffenson 2005; see also Chapter 9 below).

Around these shifting EU–US relations, there grew up during the 1990s a network of institutional arrangements that for some achieved the status of 'transatlantic governance' (Philippart and Winand 2001; Pollack and Shaffer 2001; Petersmann and Pollack 2003; Steffenson 2005: Chapters 1, 2) . In 1990, the EC, its member states and the US signed the Transatlantic Declaration (TAD) which set out in very general terms the needs for intensified consultation and cooperation. In December 1995, the EU and the US signed the New Transatlantic Agenda (NTA), which set out in more detail the mechanisms of cooperation and specified a wide range of areas for 'joint action', including the creation of a New Transatlantic Marketplace (NTM). Alongside the NTA was created a series of transatlantic dialogues, for business, for legislators, for trades unions and for others in specific sectors such as environmental cooperation. And in 1998 the EU and the US concluded a more focused agreement for a Transatlantic Economic Partnership, designed to create concrete mechanisms for mutual recognition and other policy initiatives. By the end of the 1990s, therefore, there had been created a wide-ranging set of institutions and mechanisms for communication and consultation, especially in economic and social policy matters, that seemed to set the framework for new processes of cooperation across the Atlantic.

These frameworks – and the very foundations of EU–US cooperation – came under intense and sustained pressure in the early years of the new millennium. While there had been tensions and disputes during the 1990s, in areas as diverse as conflict in the former Yugoslavia, global environmental policies and global currency management, these seemed to have been largely contained. After the election of George W. Bush as US president in November 2000, tensions were ratcheted up by a series of policy initiatives from Washington that seemed to express a new unilateralism and a willingness to disregard existing international commitments in the cause of US national security (Peterson and Pollack 2003; Gordon and Shapiro 2004; M. Smith 2004; Andrews 2005; M. Smith 2005a). These initiatives were such as to link together the economic, the diplomatic and the security aspects of international policies, and as such they directly attacked some central assumptions of EU–US relations, at a time when the EU was preoccupied with the implementation of EMU, the continuing attempt to reform the European institutions and the wide-ranging challenge of enlargement. They were greatly intensified in the aftermath of the terrorist attacks which Islamists associated with the Al-Qaeda network carried out on the US on 11 September 2001, by the subsequent US declaration of a global 'war on terror' and by the attack on Iraq in spring 2003. For some commentators, this expressed a radical new attack on the foundations of the transatlantic system and presaged its possible dissolution (Lieven 2002, Lindstrom 2003; Peterson 2004a, 2005; Pond 2004). Alongside the military and security challenges this posed to EU–US relations, there went a series of tensions and recriminations in new or newly-politicized policy areas such as those of human rights and the environment, and an intensification of disputes and differences in global trade and development policies. At the same time, however, there was an expansion of EU–US cooperation in areas of 'soft security' relating to the challenge of terrorism, and a continuation of day-to-day economic cooperation (alongside continuing disputes) in the context of a wide range of bilateral and multilateral institutions (Petersmann and Pollack 2003; Dannreuther and Peterson 2006; Rees 2006). Thus although during the later years of the George W. Bush presidency, after his re-election in November 2004, it was possible to discern a new flexibility and willingness to cooperate in US policies, there is no doubt that during the previous five years the EU–US 'partnership' had been shaken to its core (Zabarowski 2006a).

Overview and conclusion

This chapter has set out to provide a broad understanding of the historical forces and current pressures that have shaped the relationship between European integration and the United States. A number of key phases have been used as the means of organizing what is a complex and often strongly debated historical process, leading to the following overall conclusions:

- First, the 'foundation' period between 1945 and the late 1950s put in place many policies, institutions and practices of which the traces can still be seen, and raised questions about the operation of the transatlantic relationship that remain key to its development.
- Second, during the 1960s a series of tensions emerged within transatlantic relations as the European Communities grew and as the focus of power and interests within the system was contested from a variety of sources.
- Third, between 1971 and the mid-1980s there was a continued process of change, in which relationships were intensified but also conflicted, and during which the impact of external forces from the world arena became more apparent.
- Finally, between the mid-1980s and the present, the coming together of radical international changes with intensified change in the European integration process and significant fluctuations in US policy has created a process of substantial transformation, which is unfinished yet profoundly important both for the EU and for the US.

It is thus important to remember that many of the tensions and pressures that came to a head in 2000–4 had been fermenting since the end of the cold war and the radical changes of the early 1990s. In turn, many of the issues on which attention focused in the 1990s can be seen as radically intensified versions of issues that had been characteristic of transatlantic relations since the early days, and which give rise to the central theme of this book: competition and convergence. Much of the rest of this book is dedicated to the systematic exploration of the ways in which these pressures and tensions have been defined, analysed, managed and – in some cases – mismanaged, but this chapter has attempted to set out the broad historical sweep of the evolution of transatlantic relations as the backdrop against which this exploration can be set. In the next chapter, we will look successively at the components, the structure and the functioning of what can be conceptualized as the 'Euro-American system', as a means of further setting the scene for detailed policy analysis.

Chapter 2

Analysing the 'Euro-American System'

In Chapter 1 we provided an account of the evolution of the relationship between European integration and the United States since the end of World War II. Naturally, the emphasis there was on processes of historical continuity and change, and on the ways the relationships between the United States and the European integration process have been surrounded by other forces of broad continuity and change in the world arena. In this chapter the focus shifts: we are concerned here to identify the key components of the 'Euro-American system', to show how they work together and the ways in which they produce issues for policy and policymakers, and to show how analysts have approached the problem of explaining such a 'complex and messy' set of relations. In providing this more analytical focus, we shall of course be making use of the 'historical' information around which Chapter 1 was centred, and also of further case-study material to demonstrate the application of the ideas that will be discussed.

In conducting this analysis, we are making the assumption that there is a 'Euro-American system' which has persisted over more than half a century, which has a characteristic size and scope, and which has generated characteristic patterns of behaviour (for related approaches, see Czempiel and Rustow 1976; Peterson 1996b; Philippart and Winand 2001). This does not mean that such an approach rules out change: it means merely that we are able to locate changes that take place as part of the system, and also to understand in a more precise way the impact of particular processes of change within and beyond the system. In short, for analytical purposes we conceive of the 'Euro-American system' as the patterns of relations that have grown up and persisted between the societies of the North Atlantic area since 1945 and (initially Western) Europe, and we are concerned to identify the key participants, processes and outcomes of activity within this changing system. In this system, the European integration process has been a central component, and we are naturally concerned to show the ways the significance and impact of this component has altered over time. But we must not lose sight of the fact that European integration, although central, is only one major component of the system, and this is key to assessing the current relationship between the EU and the United States. Our argument will be that in the current period the 'EU–US system' has become largely identical with the 'Euro-American system' and that this has important policy consequences.

The first part of the chapter deals with the key components of the 'Euro-American system': the actors and their interests, the key sub-systems within the system, and the key levels of interaction between the participants. In undertaking this analysis, the chapter looks at the range and diversity of participants, at the ways they are arranged in markets, hierarchies and networks, and the several levels within which 'Euro-American politics' takes place. We argue that the politics of EU–US relations are carried out within an increasingly interconnected and multi-level policy space, within which national governments are still of major importance, but within which they have been joined by a variety of other actors in a 'mixed actor system'.

In the second part of the chapter, the focus is more on the dynamics of the system and the ways they can be characterized for the purposes of analysis. The argument focuses first on the policy processes that characterize the system, both within the European Union and within the United States. It moves on to look at the ways distinctive policy processes at transatlantic level have emerged and been consolidated during the past twenty years and more, and at the ways in which they have reflected the end of the cold war (as introduced in Chapter 1). The chapter then goes on to explore the characteristic institutions and processes of governance that have emerged between the EU and the US, arguing that there is strong evidence of a process of 'transatlantic governance' in a growing number of policy areas. Finally this part of the chapter focuses on how change in a set of overlapping and often interlocking policy arenas has characterized the 'Euro-American system' and especially EU–US relations.

The final part of the chapter deals with the ways analysis of the 'Euro-American system' relates to central frameworks for the analysis of international politics and international political economy. We will present four widely supported perspectives on the 'Euro-American system': the politics of power and security, of dominance and resistance, of interdependence and integration, and cooperation and institutionalization. We argue that in the analysis of the 'Euro-American system' and especially of EU-US relations, elements of each of these four frameworks have important insights to contribute, and that they are particularly important to understanding the key theme of this book: the coexistence of competition and convergence between the EU and the US. This discussion will be reflected throughout the subsequent chapters dealing with key policy areas in EU-US relations.

Components of the 'Euro-American system'

Actors and interests

At one level, the 'Euro-American system' is an example of a key phenomenon in classical and contemporary international relations: a system of states. As noted in Chapter 1, at the end of World War II the United States, Canada and a number of western European countries came together to form and then consolidate the 'Atlantic alliance' centred initially on the North Atlantic Treaty Organization (NATO). These states – winners and losers in the war – came together for classical reasons: partly because of the dominant influence of one country (the US) and partly because of an external threat (from the Soviet Union). In doing so, they did not sacrifice their external sovereignty, since they had entered an alliance of sovereign states with the aim explicitly of preserving their independence and national security. Since the 1940s, this system of states has expanded dramatically – first with the acceptance of former enemy states and those who had initially remained outside the alliance (for example, West Germany, Greece, Turkey, Spain and Portugal) and then, after the end of the cold war, with the entry into the system of ten countries which had formerly been part either of the Soviet bloc or of the Soviet Union itself, along with two Mediterranean countries. In these terms the boundaries and membership of the system have expanded to encompass almost all of the 'Euro-Atlantic area', with the promise of perhaps three or four additional members in the near future. In a similar way, the diversity of the system has also increased, to include members with varied national histories, levels of economic and social development and geopolitical sensitivities.

Alongside this expansion and diversification of the 'Euro-American state system' however has gone another trend the growth of new forms of institution and alignment which have challenged the idea that Euro-American relations are solely about the relations between states. Mention has already been made of NATO, which is distinctive among alliances for its longevity and for the level of joint planning and commitment that it has extracted from its member states. A number of other international organizations, such as the Organisation for Economic Co-operation and Development (OECD) and the Organization for Security and Cooperation in Europe (OSCE), have been established as means of expanding cooperation between states within the system. But the crucial development in this area has of course been the establishment first of the European Economic Community and its accompanying European institutions (Euratom and the Coal and Steel Community), and then of the amalgamated European Community and finally the European Union. These organizations are special, because they go beyond the normal level of commitments among members of an alliance or an international organization such as the OECD: the Member States of the EU and its predecessor organizations have formally yielded a portion of their sovereignty and national independence to the larger organization, giving it the power to represent them on the international stage in a number of key policy areas. As noted in Chapter 1, by the beginning of the twenty-first century these policy areas included trade and broader commercial policy, monetary relations (for about half of the EU member states), key aspects of regulatory policy such as competition policy, and some areas (much debated) of foreign and security policy. To put it simply, this is why this book is about EU–US relations: the expansion of European integration, and its impact on a growing number of policy areas, means that the EU has become a central pillar of the 'Euro-American system'. Indeed, as we will argue later, the 'EU–US system' has become almost identical with the 'Euro-American system' in a number of important areas of politics and policy.

This is not the end of the story, though. The 'Euro-American system' can be conceived of as a state system, or as a system of EU–US relations with a mix of intergovernmental and 'supranational' participation, but it is also a system in which there is a strong and flourishing element of private relations between a range of non-governmental actors. From the beginning of the European integration process, there has been a notable involvement of private investors, producers and others with essentially commercial interests in the development of the 'Euro-American system'. As noted in Chapter 1, the deepening of this essentially private form of participation was strongly stimulated by the establishment of the EEC in the late 1950s, and has responded to successive waves of 'deepening' within the EC and then the EU during the past fifty years. In a very concrete sense, the engagement of multinational corporations in European integration has been vital to the progress achieved by the European project throughout its life. In addition, there has grown up a wide range of transatlantic bodies with cultural, humanitarian and other purposes, which have been said at times to constitute the building-blocks of a kind of 'Atlantic community' going far beyond the simple interactions of states and their governments.

The diversity of participants in the 'Euro-American system' has therefore grown continuously during its existence – and so quite naturally has the diversity of their interests. One way of characterizing this – and one highly significant for later parts of this chapter – is in terms of the types of political aims espoused and pursued by this diverse range of participants. At the level of what is often called 'high politics', the 'Euro-American system encompasses a wide range of interests in national and international security, and in the survival and prosperity of its member states. At the same time, there has been a continuing development of interests in what is often termed 'low politics': the social, economic and cultural concerns that exist among member states but also among the wide range of non-state actors present in the system. Finally, there has been intense development of what can be termed 'sectoral politics', with political activity and preferences centred on specific areas of activity that often carry high stakes and the potential for significant costs and/or benefits to both states and non-state groupings. For the EU and the US, it is clear that interests and activities encompass all of these dimensions, and that one of the key elements in their relationship is the pursuit of coexisting and often competing aims at each of the three levels – high, low and sectoral. As the EU has expanded and extended its policy activities, it has also become clear that the balance of attention and interest between the EU, its member states and the US has shifted, in complex and challenging ways.

Markets, hierarchies and networks

Given that the range of participants and interests within the 'Euro-American system' has developed and diversified over its lifespan, it is important to analyse the ways those participants and interests are distributed and arranged within the system. We have already noted that the impact of European integration on the system has been profound, and that the end of the cold war has had extensive political and economic consequences, but here we need to say more about the types of sub-systems that exist within the system, and the ways they relate to each other.

One key type of sub-system is *markets*. Indeed, it could be argued that for a large part of its existence, the 'Euro-American system' has largely been about markets, their extension and deepening and the ways they are regulated. In the immediate post-1945 period, the need to recover the European market, both as a source of political and social stability and as a source of demand, was a key element in many US policies. Likewise, the foundation of the European Coal and Steel Community and then the EEC during the 1950s was explicitly about the need to instil economic recovery and to do it by re-establishing strong and developing markets in western Europe. Here, as elsewhere, the establishment of markets and their regulation was always linked closely to political and security objectives in the context of the cold war. As the European integration project prospered and deepened during the 1970s and 1980s, it also became apparent that competition between different types of market economies and regulatory structures could emerge within the 'Euro-American system'. By the early 1990s, there was widespread discussion of the frictions between the so-called 'Anglo-Saxon' model of free market, deregulated economies and the 'social market system' said to be characteristic of continental European economies within the EC, with its higher levels of social provision and its pursuit of social solidarity (Albert 1992; see also Smith and Woolcock 1993: Chapter 3). This social market model, sometimes also called 'Rhineland capitalism', was also seen to be characteristic of many EC policy initiatives and activities, a fact that was linked to tensions between different groups of EU member states. By the end of the 1990s, this tension had eased, in the eyes of some observers because the 'neoliberal' model espoused by the US and the British had prevailed and was now being pursued through the EU itself (Cafruny and Ryner 2003: Part 1), but it had not altogether disappeared.

So the 'Euro-American system' is in part a market system, engaging those with economic interests to pursue and linking the regulatory and social systems of those involved on both sides of the Atlantic. At the same time, however, it is possible to see the system as embodying a different type of relations: those of *hierarchy*. The most obvious place to look for these relations is between the member states of the system, where there is often a profound gap between the resources and interests of those at the top of the hierarchy and those at the bottom. As noted in Chapter 1, this imbalance has been evident throughout the post-1945 period, especially in areas to do with 'high politics' and security. The military dominance of the United States (and of US-Soviet relations) during the cold war had deep and long-lasting effects on the ability and inclination of western European governments to assume the burden of their own defence, either individually of collectively, and this in turn still has echoes today in the limitations of European foreign and defence policies, despite significant developments at the EU level (see Chapters 8 and 9 especially). The end of the cold war and the collapse of the USSR served only to accentuate this divide: the idea of the US as the 'only superpower' has had a profound effect both on US policies and on the collective responses of EU Member States, within the EU itself, within NATO and at the national level.

But the impact of hierarchy does not end with security and defence. In the political economy of the 'Euro-American system', the key role of the US dollar as the predominant medium of exchange was cemented into the Bretton Woods system of post-1945 multilateral institutions, and found its expression in a wide range of areas of commercial and industrial activity (Foot *et al.* 2003). The freeing up of trade within the North Atlantic area, the later impact of globalization and the general intensification of patterns of international exchange and production were all affected by the background of US predominance and what has been termed 'structural power'. The development of the European integration project has gradually modified this picture, most obviously in the area of trade relations (see Chapter 5) and to lesser degrees in the realms of technology and monetary relations (see Chapters 6 and 7), and the result has been a series of frictions as the foundations of the system have adjusted to the new reality. Last but not least, the impact of hierarchy has been experienced within a range of social and cultural areas, as the impact of US popular culture and related phenomena has intensified. As will be seen later in the chapter, this has not been a uniform or even impact, and areas of resistance have not been unknown within the EU, but it is important to note the pervasive and continuing impact of hierarchy within the 'Euro-American system'.

Finally in this section, we can point to the importance alongside markets and hierarchy of *networks*. We have already pointed to the ways the 'Euro-American system' has experienced intensive development of private patterns of commercial exchange, and this has generated a wide-ranging set of commercial networks spanning the Atlantic. While one key component of these is clearly the multinational corporation, with its networks of internal trade, investment and production, this is not the only commercial networking that can be seen within the system. Transatlantic alliances of companies, through licensing arrangements or strategic partnerships fortified by cross-investment, have been a key part of the commercial developments within the system, to such an extent that is sometimes difficult to say with certainty what is a 'European' or an 'American' company or product. Alongside these private commercial arrangements, there has also grown up a set of networks sponsored by governmental authorities on both sides of the Atlantic, and engaging business, non-governmental organizations and regulatory bodies in the oversight and monitoring of developments within their areas of concern. A number of these have grown up around EU–US partnership agreements reached in the 1990s, such as the New Transatlantic Agenda or the Transatlantic Economic Partnership (see Chapter 1 and below), and they well represent the desire of many organizations to establish networks of communication and influence in the 'Euro-American system' (Cowles 1996; Peterson 1996b; Cowles 2001a; Pollack and Shaffer 2001; Steffenson 2005). A third type of network is rather less public and accessible: the range of contacts between the US and individual EU member states' policymakers in areas of security and intelligence cooperation. While there has been some extension of this to the EU–US level in the wake of '9/11', and there is increasing collaboration on intelligence between the US and overall EU bodies in the field, there is clearly a strong legacy of past 'special relationships' between the US and countries such as the UK, which has been evident in such episodes as the Iraq conflict from 2003 onwards.

What does the proliferation of relations based on markets, hierarchies and networks in the 'Euro-American system' tell us about the nature of the system itself? One conclusion that can be drawn at this stage is that there are several different 'maps' of the system, depending on the precise focus of any mapping process. These maps overlap: sometimes they come into collision with each other, sometimes they reinforce each other and often they can also be manipulated for political or other purposes by key participants within the system. But they also mean that it is impossible to generalize about 'who runs the system', since in each of the many overlapping and conflicting or complementary areas there are different distributions of power, resources and leverage. As we shall see in later chapters, this has major implications for policymaking and for the management of relations.

Multilevel politics in a 'mixed actor' system

The expansion and diversification of the actors in the system, their coexisting and often competing interests, and the ways in which they enter into markets, hierarchies and networks, imply a 'Euro-American system' in which politics can take place at several different but interconnected levels, with direct and significant consequences for policymaking and policy implementation. Mark Pollack and Greg Shaffer (2001; see also Steffenson 2005) have identified three levels of action and interaction, which they relate to the demand for and supply of transatlantic governance mechanisms: intergovernmental, transgovernmental and transnational. A brief exploration of these three levels can help to complete our picture of the key components in the 'Euro-American system'.

First, as is clear from much of the preceding discussion, the 'Euro-American system' embodies a strong element of *intergovernmental relations* between the member states of an admittedly expanding and diverse system. In this process of intergovernmental relations, we can include certain activities of the EU itself, particularly those conducted through the European Community in such areas as trade and commercial relations. In doing so, we need to be aware that EC policies are themselves often the product of intergovernmental processes at the European level, with member states negotiating and exerting influence to determine the shape of EC policies. In other areas of EU activity, there is even more of an intergovernmental tinge, since when it comes (for example) to the EU's foreign and security policies, Member States have retained a great deal of the initiative, albeit within an increasingly

'Europeanized' or 'Brusselized' policy process (Hill 1995; Hill and Smith 2005). Alongside the activities of the EU or its component parts, there is still a very important intergovernmental dimension to many areas of transatlantic convergence or competition, particularly those dealing with issues of security or defence – where NATO often enters into the picture – or those dealing with matters such as the regulation of investment where there is no definitive allocation of powers to the European Community. As noted earlier, the strong persistence of states and governments as actors within the system means inevitably that intergovernmental relations will remain central to the system for any foreseeable future.

Second, despite what has just been said about the persistence of intergovernmentalism both at the European and at the transatlantic level, there has also been strong growth of *transgovernmental relations* within the 'Euro-American system'. These are relations between officials and departments within national governments (sometimes including elements of sub-national or regional governments as well), which come to constitute semi-permanent networks and which shape the behaviour of their members both at the transatlantic (or EU) level and at the level of their national governments. To put it simply, the increasing intensification of contacts between officials of national governments in areas as diverse as agriculture, environmental policy, policing policy and defence has created a set of transgovernmental networks in which the participants do not always act predictably as agents of their national governments. They can develop – and feed back into national policy – distinctive perspectives and policy prescriptions specific to their sector of policy, and they can thus 'Europeanize' or 'Atlanticize' the responses of their national authorities. It can readily be seen that this transgovernmental image subverts the apparent tidiness of an intergovernmental image where national governments are united and act as one on all areas of national concern. The intensification of transgovernmental contacts, when added to the expansion and diversification of the 'Euro-American system', becomes an essential component of policymaking and what some have termed 'transatlantic governance' (Pollack and Shaffer 2001: Steffenson 2005).

Finally, the 'Euro-American system' has seen a growth and intensification of *transnational relations* – that is to say, of relations that spill across national boundaries and often ignore the influence of national authorities. As noted above, the most frequently used term to describe such relations is that of the network, implying the development of a spider's web of relations that develop largely independent of national influences as a response to problems that are essentially transnational or global in nature. In terms of our earlier discussion, such networks can often be seen as essentially subversive, although some of them are actually closely linked to the interests and activities of national governments or EU institutions. They can generate perceptions of interest and values that are more rooted in the overall stability and development of the 'Euro-American system' than in the national preferences of governments or even in the preferences of EU institutions. As such, they raise issues of regulation for national and European authorities, and within the transatlantic arena these problems have become both time-consuming and often fraught with difficulties.

In addition to the three levels of relations emphasized by Pollack and Shaffer, though, it is necessary here to introduce a fourth category: *multilateral relations*. By this is meant the range of interactions between actors within the 'Euro-American system' in other contexts, often those of a global scope. Although it is clear that a huge range of relevant interactions are essentially contained within the system, there are those that inevitably spill over onto the global stage. Perhaps the longest established of the settings within which such European-American interactions take place is that of the World Trade Organization (WTO) and its predecessor the General Agreement on Tariffs and Trade (GATT). Chapter 1 described the process whereby since the late 1950s there has been continuing and intensifying contact between the EC and the US in this set of institutions, and it is clear that over a period of nearly fifty years this has generated its own distinctive momentum and set of constraints. But this is only one of many global and/or multilateral settings in which the 'Euro-American system' is implanted; many of these are economic, but a growing number are cultural, social, humanitarian, environmental and now security-related. The expansion of the collective action undertaken by the EC and the EU is clearly part of this story, but it is also clear that the expansion of the multilateral institutions themselves has been a key shift in the context within which EU–US relations occur.

It is apparent from the discussion so far in this chapter that the 'Euro-American system' is complex and multidimensional. This complexity and multidimensionality reflect the ways in which over a period of at least fifty years, successive layers of activity and interaction have been laid down within the system. As noted in Chapter 1, this can be seen in essentially historical terms, but here the aim has been to identify the key components of the system in a more analytical fashion. Table 2.1 summarizes what has been argued so far, and from this the complexity is readily apparent. It seems clear that the 'Euro-American system' complies with what

Table 2.1 *Key components of the 'Euro-American system'*

Actors	Sub-systems	Relationships
States: increasing number and variety; spread of 'Euro-American system' after the cold war	Markets: mix of participants, focus on economic exchange	Intergovernmental: channelled through state authorities, expressed in IGOs; focus on 'high politics'
Intergovernmental organizations: coexisting and overlapping, e.g. NATO, OSCE, OECD	Hierarchies: state and other; centred on power and resources; shifts in hierarchies and focus	
	Networks: diversity of participants, lack of hierarchy, focus on communication	Transgovernmental: contacts between government agencies, generation of coalitions and distinctive interests; focus on 'sectoral politics'
Supranational Organizations: chiefly the EU, creating common policies and rules		Transnational: Contacts across societies, focused on networks and 'low politics'
Non-governmental organizations: private, commercial, social/humanitarian		Multilateral: contacts in the world arena, through institutions such as the WTO etc; focus on range of types of issues and politics

Oran Young once described as a 'mixed actor system', within which a multiplicity of actors interact with no necessary of permanent assumption about hierarchy or the use of power resources (Young 1972). Up to now, though, the emphasis has been on the components of the system at the most general level. The chapter now turns to what might be termed the dynamics of the system, in terms of policy processes and policy outcomes.

Processes, institutions and policies

Policy processes

When considering the dynamics of the 'Euro-American system' and within it those of EU-US relations, it is clearly important to explore the mechanisms and processes of policymaking that characterize the system. For the purposes of the analysis here, we can discern two key levels of policymaking: first, the processes that occur within the EU on the one hand and the United States on the other, and second, the processes that occur at transatlantic level and which relate both to EU-US relations strictly defined and to the broader policymaking framework of the 'Euro-American system' broadly defined. The latter distinction is important, since as we have already pointed out on a number of occasions, the EU–US system of relations is not wholly identical to the broader system of transatlantic interactions, and this has significant impacts on the policymaking process in a number of key areas. This two-level approach to analysis of EU–US policy issues – focusing on EU policies, then on US policies and then on their interaction - will be a key organizing theme for Chapters 3 to 9 of this book.

The EU's 'US policy'

It was said as early as the mid-1970s that if the European Community developed a foreign policy, the first target of such a policy would have to be the US (M. Smith 1978). The status of the United States as the 'significant other' of the European integration process was by then already well established, reflecting the forces at work during the cold war and within the international political economy from the late 1950s onwards (see Chapter 1). However, it is rather easier to identify the US as the prime target than it is to develop a coherent and coordinated 'European' policy towards

Washington. From the outset, the European Communities and then the EU have had to take account of the USA in the field of political economy, both as a key external force facing European trade and related policies, and as a key – if not *the* key – shaping force in the broader global economy. The earliest 'European' policy targeted on the USA was thus almost inevitably the Common Commercial Policy, together with the EEC's activities in the multilateral trade institutions, primarily the GATT. This remains, in the context of the WTO, perhaps the EU's most concentrated and coherent 'US policy'. It is also clear, however, that many of the 'internal' policies of the EC have an inescapable American dimension. If the policy discussion is about agriculture, competition policy or research and development, the Americans are often not only the key external point of reference but also to some extent an 'insider' group through the activities of US companies and broader commercial groupings. This tendency is of course as evident in the politics of the Euro as is has been in more long established policy areas, where the 'European voice' is more concerted and audible: the dollar has always been a key point of reference not only for external European monetary policies but also for internal policy-making and implementation, since it affects the policy environment in a pervasive way.

If one moves away from the political economy, it is clear that the USA is equally if not more significant in the development of EU policies in the diplomatic and security fields. The diplomatic coordination that lies at the heart of the CFSP is strongly conditioned by the positions of the United States, not only because they affect the environment within which CFSP emerges but also because they strongly shape the policies of key EU member states (Vanhoonacker, 2001). The existence of 'special relationships', of which the most celebrated or notorious is that between the US and the UK, is thus a key element of transatlantic politics. The achievement of diplomatic coordination and consistency has always been an issue for the EU, and the United States has the potential both to promote it and to erode it – often both at the same time. The end of the cold war, and the United States's position as the 'only superpower' has thus fundamentally reshaped the possibilities for European diplomatic coordination, and this has of course been further underlined by the policies of successive US administrations (see Chapter 9). The more recent elaboration of a European security and defence policy has of course made the issues even sharper (Howorth 2005,

2007): is the EU through collective action in defence likely to mount a challenge or present an alternative to US positions, or is it more likely to be disrupted by the Washington policy process? Here we can see not only that the EU-US relationship is one between two politically influential actors, but also that in some ways they are part of each other's policy processes (more of this and its implications below).

Above all, it is clear from both historical experience and contemporary policy issues that for the EU, the development of a 'US policy' is both uniquely necessary and uniquely challenging. It is uniquely necessary because the US as the 'most significant other' of European integration and as a global power is there in all areas of EU policymaking. This means that the US is not only a material factor in policy formation but also a key shaping force in the development of a 'European identity' within the world arena. The development of a 'US policy' is uniquely challenging because it demands internal coordination within the EU, between and across European institutions and between the European and the national levels on a continuous basis across all areas of policy development. As students of the EU in general and of 'European foreign policy' in particular have pointed out (K. Smith 2003; Bretherton and Vogler 2006; Hill and Smith 2005), these challenges of consistency, coordination and balance across different levels and sectors of policymaking are a key aspect of the European integration process in general: in respect of the US, the challenge is underlined and sharpened on a daily basis as well as on the more strategic level of policymaking. At the same time, as generations of foreign-policymakers have discovered, the shifting policymaking balance between institutions in Washington, complicated by the different levels of government in the US federal system and by the fluctuating effects of US domestic politics, make the formation of a 'US policy' by the EU and its Member States a complex and demanding process at other levels (see for example Smith and Woolcock 1993; Winand 1993; M. Smith 2006a).

The United States's 'EU policy'

In many ways, the problems for the USA in dealing with the European Union are a mirror image of those for the EU in dealing with Washington – with some crucial differences. The EU presents a policymaking challenge because of its internal complexity, the shifting nature and continuous evolution of its institutional and policy frameworks, and because it is a factor in most if not all of the key areas in which US policy is made. So policymakers in Washington as in Brussels and European capitals have to confront the problems of making policy towards a 'moving target' and one in which significant policy developments can be prompted by influences coming from a number of levels within the system. We have seen in Chapter 1 that the development of a consistent set of policies towards European integration has always been a challenge for US administrations, since although they have been broadly consistent in their support for the European project, they have found all sorts of reasons to be concerned about it at anything but the broad strategic level. In the late 1950s and 1960s, this concern was predominantly focused on political economy, with the emergence of trade disputes and the complexity of adjustment to the 'new Europe' (Krause 1968; Diebold 1971). Even at the level of political economy, though, the Americans have found that the policymaking calculus is formidably complicated. Nothing demonstrates this more clearly than US responses to the Single Market Programme of the late 1980s and early 1990s, which had to reconcile the interests of almost every department and agency in the US administration, and which required negotiations not only at the EC–US level but also at subnational and global multilateral levels (Calingaert 1996; Hocking and Smith 1997; Hufbauer 1990). The challenge of achieving policy consistency across the full range of EU–US relations in political economy remains, and if anything has become more complex with the introduction of the euro and the continuing extension of EC policy competence in areas such as competition policy during the past few years (see Chapters 3 to 6 below).

Since the late 1980s, the US has also had to address the issues arising from the concrete development of European policies in the diplomatic, security and defence spheres. While the emergence of European Political Cooperation during the 1980s caused momentary concern for US policymakers, it could largely be viewed as 'procedure as a substitute for policy' (Allen and Wallace 1977) with little concrete or immediate effect. The development of CFSP in the early 1990s, and the later emergence of ESDP as a security and defence arm for the EU, was more challenging, coinciding as it did with the removal of the 'cold war overlay' in security relations between the US and Europe as a whole. If a 'European foreign and defence policy' was to become a reality, it had to raise important questions about US leadership and the capacity of Washington to define the foreign policy consensus in the Atlantic area (M. Smith 1992; Smith and Woolcock 1993). So there was a challenge to some key assumptions in US foreign policy that had been present in the cold war and that had been given additional force by the disappearance of the Soviet Union.

Not only this, but the challenge was also one to institutions and policymaking processes at the more restricted level, since it raised in a new and more concentrated form the question 'Who speaks for Europe?' first raised for the Americans during the 1970s (Allen 1998). Washington had to adjust to a situation in which on an increasing number of diplomatic and even defence issues the first point of call was not key national capitals or NATO headquarters, but the European institutions. Even if they were not the first port of call, these institutions increasingly framed the national policies of growing numbers of European states and also their positions within NATO (a trend only accentuated by the enlargement of the EU to twenty-seven members in the early 2000s). But the reality of 'European foreign and defence policy' was characterized even after the turn of the millennium by an often wide and always fluctuating 'capability-expectations gap' which meant that US policies had to cope with the mismatch of rhetoric and reality (Hill 1998, Howorth 2005). A tendency to revert to 'special relationships' with key partners within the EU is both understandable and could often be seen as desirable in US policy terms.

The framing of a coherent and consistent 'EU policy' by the USA is thus challenging in many of the same ways as the framing of a 'US policy' by the European Union. As in the case of the EU, there is a continuing and often pressing need for American administrations to recognize and respond to important pressures from within the EU's multi-level policymaking process, and a continuing difficulty in taking into account the multiple sources of policymaking. A key area of difference, though, is that the US possesses a full federal government that can mobilize the resources of US society over the full range of external action – a claim that the EU is no position to make or to fulfil. This arguably means that the policymaking relationship between the EU and the US is a mismatch, exhibiting a gap in resources and capacity to mobilize them that can never (and perhaps should never) be bridged. We shall investigate the consequences of this gap in many of the chapters that follow.

Policymaking at the transatlantic level

Given the complexities and unevenness in EU and US policymaking processes, it might be expected that little in the way of coherent policymaking would take place at the transatlantic level itself. As we shall see shortly, despite the development of a range of institutional frameworks for the better conduct of transatlantic (and particularly EU–US) relations, it remains the case that there is no consistent mechanism for the coordination of policies at a comprehensive level between the EU and the US. The open and fluctuating nature of many of the relationships that make up the 'Euro-American system' makes it inevitable that no single centre of authoritative decision-making can be contemplated. But this does not mean that there are no mechanisms for the management of policies within the system. In this section, we explore three possible such mechanisms: transatlantic governance, hard and soft balancing, and crisis management.

We have already noted that the growth of institutions and interactions within the 'Euro-American system' since the 1960s has created conditions in which mechanisms of governance are both necessary and possible. On the basis of mutual benefit, or the limitation of mutual damage, highly interdependent entities such as the EU and the US can develop both formal and informal means of regulating common problems and achieving policy convergence. Indeed, John Pinder argued as far back as the early 1980s that the mismatch between intensifying transatlantic issue interdependence and the lack of policy interdependence was so striking that ways of dealing with it would have to be found if there was not to be a damaging outcome for all concerned (Pinder 1983). Recognition of this problem, at least in the area of political economy, has led to continuous efforts on the part of both the US and the EC/EU to increase mutual communication and sensitivity, short of creating any authoritative transatlantic body. Policy convergence and adaptation has taken place in a number of sectors, such as competition policy or environmental policy, but without curtailing the independence of either party in a formal way (Pollack and Shaffer 2001; Peterson and Pollack 2003; see also Chapters 3 to 6 below). In this way, a degree of transatlantic governance has been achieved, including the development of limited formal institutions (see below). It has to be remembered also, as noted earlier, that this transatlantic level of governance is embedded in many respects in broader structures of global governance, which also produce convergence (and the recognition of common interests) between the two sides of the Atlantic. In the area of security and defence policy, there have also emerged, over a very long period, the structure and habits of 'security governance' at the transatlantic level, but as noted above these are often more fragile and the challenges to them more severe than those of governance in the political economy (Mahnke *et al.* 2004).

Alongside mechanisms of governance, it is also possible to discern a second type of transatlantic policymaking mechanism: balancing. Implicit in much of what has been said both in Chapter 1 and in this chapter is that there has been a long-term shift in the transatlantic balance: first, in the area of political economy and then – and less profoundly, perhaps – in diplomacy, security and defence. In this process, the EC and then the EU have played a major role, since they have created at least the possibility of sustained collective action by the members of the European integration project. Indeed, one way of viewing the entire integration process is as a means of producing 'political economies of scale' in the international arena, and thus making the combined weight of the EU and its member states more effective, not least against the USA (Ginsberg 1989). If this balancing process is viewed as what has been termed 'hard balancing', based on material power and particularly on military capabilities, then the Europeans despite the EU have no really effective means of countering the US as long as Washington pursues a consistent and united course. But if the process is seen as one of 'soft balancing' in which negotiation, policy coordination and the use of 'soft power' is more characteristic, then it is clear that the Europeans have more to say for themselves (Pape 2005; McCormick 2007; see also Posen 2006). Their experience of policy coordination and their enforced reliance on negotiation and persuasion rather than on imposition or coercion might be seen as giving them a comparative advantage not only in transatlantic relations but also in the broader global arena. Recent evidence for the efficacy of 'soft balancing' is often contestable, but that does not mean that this is not a significant dimension of policymaking in the 'Euro-American system' and one that applies to the US in some respects as well as to the Europeans.

A final mechanism that can be identified in policymaking within the 'Euro-American system' is that of crisis management. The system has been characterized by periodic internal crises, in which the possibility of a 'transatlantic divorce' or a 'transatlantic rift' has been discussed, and yet the system has persisted. Partly this may reflect the impact of perceived common interests and the need for governance mechanisms to handle both policy convergence and policy competition. Partly also it may reflect the impact of balancing strategies as outlined above, and the growing impact of the EC/EU on those strategies at the transatlantic level. But the process may also reflect the growth of mechanisms of crisis management, in which the members of the 'Euro-American system' have developed conventions or habits of adjustment and the management of risk, thus avoiding fundamental breakdown of the system. As was seen in Chapter 1, the 'Euro-American system' has generated crises on a regular basis: in the 1960s with the disputes over 'Atlantic Community', in the 1970s with the impact of the 'Nixon Shock' and conflict in the Middle East, in the 1980s with Reaganism and greater European assertiveness, in the 1990s with the series of adjustments needed after the end of the cold war, and in the early years of the new millennium with the impact of the 'war on terror' and the invasion of Iraq. Yet the system has persisted, not only through recognition of the risks inherent in its breakdown but also because certain conventions of crisis management have been developed and have themselves persisted (M. Smith 2005d). In this process, the development of European integration has played a significant part, particularly since the end of the cold war, since it has enabled the Europeans to concert their positions and provided an increasingly authoritative interlocutor for Washington at a continental level. This is not to say that there have not been crises within the EU, often precisely because of the attempt to coordinate a position *vis-à-vis* the USA (see Chapter 9 especially), but it does mean that the EU provides a means of crisis management at the European level in diplomatic terms, which then in its turn facilitates the operation of the mechanisms at transatlantic level. We will explore this more fully in later chapters.

Institutional development

In what has gone before, this chapter has touched often on the nature and impact of institutions within the 'Euro-American system'. We have seen that there are many such institutions, covering a growing range of interactions within the system, and that they can be both formal and informal in nature (see also Frelleson 2001; Gardner 2001). The general proposition to be explored in this section is that the 'Euro-American system' has become increasingly institutionalized, and that this process of institutionalization has contributed to the ways the system works in the early years of the twenty-first century. Along with this central proposition, the argument is that the specifically EU–US institutions within the system have become the predominant ones, and that other competing institutions have been reduced to a supporting role, albeit an often highly significant one. We can explore these general propositions by focusing on three key issue areas in the system: economic, diplomatic and security/defence.

In the economic sphere, as has been noted already, the EU-US relationship is both heavily institutionalized in itself and part of a broader framework of institutions for global regulation and governance. The institutionalization of EU–US relations has been especially intensive and progressive since the end of the cold war, prior to which there were few formal mechanisms for the management of EC–US relations *per se*. During the 1980s, mechanisms of coordination centred not so much around EC–US relations as around the multilateral system represented especially by the GATT and the International Monetary Fund, and around the Group of Seven (G-7) of major industrial countries. During the 1990s, however, mechanisms for bringing together policymakers in the EU and the US, and formal institutional agreements, multiplied (Peterson 1996b; Pollack and Shaffer 2001; Steffenson 2005). First, there was the 1990 Transatlantic Declaration, whose purpose was as much diplomatic as economic: it set out the broad framework for EC–US cooperation based on annual summits, the development of sectoral working groups and the exchange of information about a range of international concerns (Schwok 1991; Peterson 1996b). Second, in 1995 came the New Transatlantic Agenda (NTA) and accompanying Action Plan. While based on the same presumptions as the TAD, the NTA went further in specifying concrete areas for joint action and in setting up monitoring mechanisms, specifically the so-called Senior Level Group of EU and US officials (for details see Pollack and Shaffer 2001: Chapter 1; Steffenson 2005: Chapters 2–3). Tellingly, whereas the TAD was an agreement between the US and 'The European Community and its Member States', the NTA was concluded between the US and the EU. One of the key elements of the NTA was the project for a New Transatlantic Marketplace, in which barriers to trade and exchange would be reduced if not eliminated. While this was not achieved in the short term, it was followed up by the Transatlantic Economic Partnership agreement of 1998, which made much more specific commitments to such processes as mutual recognition of product standards. In 2005, a major review of the NTA concluded that yet more needed to be done in order to reduce barriers to transatlantic economic partnership, but this represented a further step in the evolution of these institutions rather than a revolutionary break (European Commission 2005b, 2005c; Pollack 2005).

Alongside the formal large-scale agreements on economic issues went transatlantic efforts to build up non-governmental networks in the economic domain. Most notable among these was the Transatlantic Business Dialogue, which was established at the same time as the NTA and which has persisted for a decade with fluctuating levels of activity and impact (Cowles 2001a, 2001b). Other dialogues were established on legislative issues, in environmental and consumer affairs and in labour issues, again with variable success. These initiatives were important in a diplomatic sense as well as the practical sense, but in a way they only scratched the surface of other institutional links that have intensified within the transatlantic political economy. Most obviously, the vast range of economic and commercial groupings that have profited from the intensification of transatlantic interdependence constitute a major institutional network at the private level that has profound implications for the management of the 'Euro-American system'. Trade associations and similar groupings on both sides of the Atlantic spend a lot of their time trying to influence policies as they emerge both in Brussels and in Washington, and by so doing they contribute to the flows of information and ideas that are key to the development of the system more broadly (see for example Cowles 1996). They shape the need for 'early-warning mechanisms' on trade disputes, or on competition policy issues, and they support the use of such mechanisms both by the EU and by Washington, thus constituting a major point of resistance to fundamental splits in the transatlantic political economy.

The 'Euro-American system' has also witnessed a major growth of institutions for diplomatic coordination. Perhaps most obviously, the commitment to annual EU–US summit meetings engaging the key officials on both sides of the Atlantic has seen the emergence of new expectations and habits of consultation. The NTA itself, as noted above, has had an impact on broader diplomatic issues as well as on the management of the transatlantic political economy. Consultation between the EU and the US in international institutions such as the United Nations has grown in intensity, assisted by the intensification of coordination between EU member states in such multilateral contexts (Laatikainen and K. Smith 2006). Within the EU, the institutional changes that have brought forth the office of the high representative for foreign and security policy, as well as the establishment of special representatives for particular areas of conflict, has provided a more secure basis for transatlantic policy coordination. But there are severe limits to this coordination, primarily because of the persistence of strong national diplomatic relations between EU Member States and the US. In other words, here we can see an area of institutional competition, in which on many issues there are choices to be made about which channels are most useful and most secure for the pursuit of national or European policies. The aftermath of '9/11' itself produced an intensification of diplomatic coordination, accompanied by the growth of new links in areas such as intelligence and policing (Rees and Aldrich 2005; Dannreuther and Peterson 2006; Rees 2006). But here again the intensification of activity at the EU–US level was accompanied by parallel and sometimes conflicting developments at the bilateral level between EU member states and the US. While it is quite appropriate to point to an intensification of EU–US diplomatic institutions, both formal and informal, it is not possible to see these as the consistently predominant mode of institutional coordination on transatlantic diplomatic concerns.

In security and defence policy, inevitably, the institutionalization of EU–US coordination is most recent and most challenged. The growth of ESDP in the late 1990s and early 2000s created concerns in the US that there might ensue the 'three Ds': decoupling, duplication and discrimination (Albright 1998). From the US point of view (and from that of a number of EU member states, most notably the UK) the danger was that a new institutional competitor might be created for NATO, an organization whose continued existence was under question in the aftermath of the cold war. Despite the fact that in all EU treaties it was explicit that ESDP would not undermine NATO, the concern has not been banished. It has, though, been muted by the development of arrangements for the sharing of NATO assets under the so-called 'Berlin Plus' agreements, and by the way in which a division of labour has grown up around successive NATO and EU peacekeeping operations in the Balkans (Howorth 2005, 2007; Webber 2007; see also Chapters 8 and 9 below). While these issues will be dealt with more fully later, the point here is that in areas of security and defence policy, the institutional development of the 'Euro-American system' has not been based on the centrality of the EU–US relationship. As compared with the political economy of the system, there is a higher degree of institutional competition and overlap, with greater uncertainty about the ways in which institutions interlock on specific policy issues.

Change

The discussion in Chapter 1, with its 'historical' focus, dealt inevitably with processes of change, in both the long and the medium term, within the 'Euro-American system'. The purpose here is not to repeat that discussion, but to point out in more analytical terms what has been the impact of change on the system and on the ways it operates. The discussion centres on the ways differential patterns of change can be seen in three key areas of Euro-American relations; incidentally, and importantly, it also uncovers important variations in the impact of the European Union and of EU–US relations in the three areas.

The first area – or arena – of change is the political economy. We have seen that since the establishment of the EEC in the 1950s this has been an area of persistent and perhaps fundamental change. The range of actors involved in this area has multiplied, its scope has expanded and the boundaries of the policy arena have shifted sometimes in dramatic ways. Not only this, but here is an area in which the establishment and development of the EU has had profound consequences: first for policymaking both in Europe and in the US and second for the ways the policy area is managed. The 'balance of power' in this area has shifted inexorably towards the collective EU position, though it has not of course created a position of EU dominance. Rather, it has created a twofold process: on the one side of policy convergence under the pressure of interdependence and common concerns, and on the other of competition between public and private actors for influence and advantage. This has in turn led to the elaboration of institutional arrangements both in the EU and in the US and at the transatlantic level with the aim of managing and profiting from this process of 'competitive cooperation' (M. Smith 1998), such that the density of transatlantic institutions and of what has been termed 'transatlantic governance' is intense and highly significant in terms of the global political economy. The result is a situation of intense but still uneven interdependence, in which the EU and the US operate as 'adversarial partners' at both the transatlantic and the global level.

In the second arena – that of diplomacy – the picture is more mixed. This is an area in which initial analysis shows the USA still to be in a leading position and able to take the initiative both at the transatlantic level and – more tellingly – at the global one. The range of participants here is more restricted than in the political economy, and more of those that do participate are governmental in the broad sense. A crucial element in this arena is the relative underdevelopment until the end of the 1990s of the EU's diplomatic apparatus, and the continuing influence in EU positions of strongly held and independently pursued national policies. The boundaries of this area have been expanded greatly with EU enlargement and the new fluidity following the end of the cold war, but this has in many cases produced new uncertainties about EU collective action and its consolidation. Institutions to manage this area have been developed, but they are still subject to fluctuations in salience and effectiveness and to the possibility of defection by those with 'special relationships' of various kinds within the system. Here, the EU is not alone on the diplomatic or the transatlantic stage, but there has been a significant move towards policies of 'soft balancing' by EU member states in respect of the US, facilitated by the development of the EU's diplomatic machinery and practices.

The third area – security and defence – shows a balance skewed even more firmly in favour of the US – not only in favour of the US, in fact, but in favour of institutional mechanisms that are not necessarily associated with EU–US relations. There is a long history in this area of institutional arrangements that have been deliberately kept separate from European integration processes, specifically of course NATO. The participants here are almost entirely governmental, and the mechanisms for their coordination or competition are almost exclusively intergovernmental in nature – even within the EU, where ESDP remains robustly intergovernmental in character, at least for the time being (Mahnke *et al.* 2004; Howorth 2007; Webber 2007). The impact of '9/11' and the 'war on terror' has changed this position at the margins, but not fundamentally. For EU–US relations, this means that the advantage held by the US in terms of 'hard power' and its capacity to mobilize it remains a trump card, although the EU has begun to infringe on this predominance in certain tightly specified areas of activity. Given the institutional competition between the EU and other bodies within Europe itself, and the predominance of American 'hard power', it might be suggested that this is an area that for the foreseeable future will remain contested and uncertain for the Europeans themselves, let alone for the 'Euro-American system' in general.

Table 2.2 attempts to summarize the arguments about processes within the 'Euro-American system' that have been advanced in this section of the chapter, by bringing together the four elements outlined above: policymaking in the EU and the US, transatlantic policymaking, institutional development and change. Many of the chapters that follow will pursue the general arguments raised here. The important conclusion at this stage is that the development of EU–US relations within the context of the 'Euro-American system' is essentially uneven and in some areas strongly contested. This differential picture of development and contestation is fundamental to the evolution of the boundaries, scope and rules of the system, to the institutions operating within it and to the political patterns produced within it.

Four images of the 'Euro-American System'

This chapter so far has focused tightly on the components of the 'Euro-American system', how the system operates and what significant variations in patterns of institutions and policymaking can be discerned within it. The complexity of the system, its politically charged nature and its significance within the broader international arena mean that it is also important to take note of the ways in which the system might be analysed by competing approaches to international relations and international political economy more generally. By doing this, we can put the relationship in the perspective of broader IR and IPE scholarship, and demonstrate the ways the 'Euro-American system' can be linked to them.

Table 2.3 shows how the 'Euro-American system' can be viewed, using four different images or perspectives (for a similar approach using slightly different third and fourth perspectives, see Little and

Table 2.2   Processes, institutions and policies in the
'Euro-American system'

Policymaking	Institutions	Change
The EU's US policy: US as most significant 'other' Linkage of political economy, diplomacy, security Challenge to collective action	*Formal institutional frameworks:* Transatlantic Declaration New Transatlantic Agenda Transatlantic Economic Partnership	*In political economy:* shifts in balance of power, emergence of competition and convergence on traditional agenda and 'new agenda'; impact of globalization
The US's EU policy: Cross-departmental, multi-level Moving Target Linkage of political economy, diplomacy, security	*Non-governmental frameworks:* Transatlantic Business Dialogue Transatlantic Legislative Dialogue Transatlantic Consumer Dialogue etc.	*In diplomacy:* impact of CFSP, development of collective 'European' diplomacy targeted inter alia on the US, but limitations of solidarity; impact of the end of the cold war
Policymaking at the transatlantic level: Governance Balancing Crisis Management	*Multilateral frameworks:* EU–US relations in global organisations: UN, WTO, etc	*In security and defence:* predominance of the US; roles of security institutions e.g. NATO; impact of 9/11 and 'war on terror'; new security roles for the EU

Table 2.3 Four Images of the 'Euro-American System'

Images	Participation	Processes	Issues	Change	Example
Power and Security	States and Governments	Balance, alliance, competition	Security, 'High Politics'	Shifts in balance, threats	Cold war and after; US power, alliance politics
Dominance and Resistance	Hegemonic forces	Structural power, subordination	Economic and other forms of inequality	Overthrow of hegemon; struggle	Role of US economic power; 'empire by integration'
Inter-dependence and Integration	Transnational and trans-governmental actors	Multilevel political and economic processes	Wide range of social and economic issues	Growth of interpenetration, integration	Growth of transactions, exchange; trade, people, culture
Institutions and Co-operation	Institutions and 'governing bodies'	Management through rules and negotiation	Rule Making, adaptation of institutions	Reconfiguration of institutions and rules	Institutional density of trans-atlantic arena; trans-atlantic agendas, agreements

Smith 2005; for related approaches see Guay 1999: conclusion; Peterson 1996b; Mowle 2004: Chapter 2). The approaches are: the politics of power and security; the politics of dominance and resistance; the politics of interdependence and integration; and the politics of cooperation and institution-building. They are not in reality mutually exclusive, but they are presented separately here so that a clear view of their different implications can be formed. They will also form part of the background to the analysis throughout the chapters that follow, and in the conclusions to the volume they will be actively reviewed.

Each of the four images emphasizes specific aspects or constellations of the participants, policy processes and processes of change dealt with in this chapter. Thus, the 'power and security' image produces a focus on states as the key participants, the distribution of power and preferences as key elements of the system's structure, the pursuit of security and 'high politics' as the central issue of the system, and the changing balance of power as a motor of change; a focus which was reflected in several parts of this chapter. This is in contrast to the 'dominance and resistance' image, which emphasizes the existence of hegemonic forces: these in turn create a process in which key elements are the presence of structural power and systematic subordination, central issues that reflect economic and other forms of inequality, and mechanisms of change that emphasize the struggle for hegemony and the possibility of systematic conflict. In turn, the 'interdependence and integration' image focuses strongly on the existence of transnational and transgovernmental groups, on the presence of multilevel political and economic processes, on economic and social issues and on the growth of interpenetration and integration that produces change in the direction of policy and political interdependence; thus it raises issues key to our earlier focus on markets and networks. Finally, the 'institutions and cooperation' perspective focuses particularly on the presence of institutions and governance mechanisms, and thus on the growth of institutional density in the 'Euro-American system'; it then moves on to emphasize the management of interdependence and the negotiation of rules and networks as the central process, and rule-making and institution-building as the key issues around which the system revolves, finally focusing on the reconfiguration of institutions through negotiation as the key motor of change in the system.

Table 2.3 also provides brief examples of the four images, drawing on the material presented in Chapters 1 and 2. An important point to underline here, though, is that although the Table separates the four images and their characteristic participants, processes and change patterns, the reality is that the 'Euro-American system' contains strong elements of all four images, often in an unstable combination. It is thus essentially a mixed system of relations, conforming to but in some ways going beyond the notion of a 'mixed actor system' outlined earlier in this chapter. A second and equally important point that has emerged from Chapter 2 is that the 'Euro-American system' is implanted in and strongly influenced by the broader world arena, and shaped by the changes that have characterized that arena for the past sixty years and more. This is what gives rise to many of the key challenges of EU–US relations, as we shall see in the following chapters.

Overview and conclusion

This chapter has set out to deal with the 'Euro-American system' in an analytical manner, in contrast to the 'historical' narrative presented in Chapter 1. The two chapters are of course complementary, and this chapter has made use of many of the examples noted in chapter 1. The chapter has dealt with:

- The key components of the 'Euro-American system' and how they relate to each other. In doing so, it has uncovered a system of mixed participation in which strong elements of state and governmental power coexist with the development of transgovernmental and transnational relations in a 'mixed actor' system.
- The dynamics of the 'Euro-American system' and their implications for policies and institutions within the system. This exploration has revealed many dimensions of the competition and convergence that lie at the heart of this book, and that create key issues of policy formulation and management.
- The broad images that can be used to explore the 'Euro-American system' and relate it to the broader study of the global arena. These connect the study of the 'Euro-American system' to the broader study of world politics and international political economy, and provide a set of conceptual tools to which we will return at many points in what follows.

The overall conclusion from the chapter is that the 'Euro-American system' demonstrates many of the key characteristics of a 'mixed actor system', in which there are coexisting and often competing tendencies towards competition and convergence, and in which the study of different policy areas produces different impressions of the key institutions and processes of change within the system. EU–US relations have become a central if not a predominant part of the system, and this means that the study of EU–US relations must form a predominant part of our understanding of the system as a whole. But EU–US relations are not yet identical with the system itself, and this is an important consideration in analysis of policy areas relating to defence and security in particular. The following chapters take this starting-point as given, and will go on to explore in detail a range of issues within the 'Euro-American system' with the aim of testing and illustrating these broad conclusions.

Chapter 3

Trade

This chapter is the first in this book to deal with a specific policy area and with the trends and issues that have occurred within it. Whereas Chapters 1 and 2 have covered broad trends and the changing nature of the relations between European integration and the United States, here the focus is much more on the particular characteristics of the policy area and of EU and US policies, on the ways in which these have generated tendencies towards competition or convergence, and on the ways in which the relationships has been managed. The chapter thus draws upon Chapters 1 and 2 for broad background, but focuses strongly on recent and current policy developments and their implications. It begins by exploring some of the main features of the trade relationship, proceeds by assessing EU and US trade policies, and then moves on to deal with some of the issues of management that have emerged within the relationship.

Though the growth of China, India and other developing states has eroded the dominance of the Euro-American partnership in international trade, the US and the EU remain key markets and players in the conduct of international commercial relations. Indeed, the economic weight of the European Union in trade terms makes it a central player in the conduct of international trade negotiations. The US remains central as the world's largest national economy, with a gross domestic product of over $12 trillion. For both actors much of this trade is, in fact, intra-firm trade between foreign affiliates of European or American multinationals (OECD 2005). In the US, for example, 60 per cent of goods produced for export by foreign firms located in America is destined for another business unit of the same firm (OECD 2005). The European Union is the world's largest trading entity, with strong trade positions across merchandise (goods) and services trade. The EU's merchandise trade (excluding intra-EU trade) was worth over $2.7 trillion in 2005 (WTO, 2006: table 1, p. 11). Germany is the world's largest exporter of goods, worth $971 billion in 2005, based on soaring demand for capital goods from developing and developed states alike (WTO ibid.). The US remains the world's most important and largest single-country consumer market and makes the largest single country contribution to international services trade. The US imported $1.7 trillion worth of goods in 2005, comfortably the largest importer in the world (WTO ibid). In services trade, the US is both the largest single-country consumer and producer of services, worth $642 billion in 2005. The European Union accounts for approximately $2 trillion over global services trade. Though much attention has been focused on trade in cross-border services (quite correctly), international trade remains mainly about the movement of goods, which five times greater by value. Nor is services trade expanding faster than merchandise trade: both grew by about 10 per cent from 2000 to 2005 (WTO 2006: ibid). As can be seen from Figure 3.1, the EU runs a trade surplus with the United States.

In sum, though China, India and other developing states are growing rapidly, America and Europe remain the pre-eminent actors in the global trade system. However, international commerce is expanding rapidly in the non-OECD area, and this will have implications for the centrality of the EU–US relationship in world trade. Moreover, the tendency towards regionalization of world trade also means that trade flows can follow a marked regional pattern, where intra-regional trade intensifies. For example, Figure 3.2 illustrates how most of Europe and North America's merchandise trade is essentially internal trade. This regional aspect of trade creates incentives for firms to either locate in major regions or else lobby their government to secure access via a regional trade agree-

Figure 3.1   Europe's trade with the United States

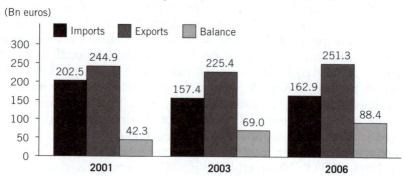

Source: European Commission (2005c) Bilateral Relations – USA, http://wto.org/english/res_e/its2006_e/its06_general_overview_e.pdf, accessed 30 August 2007.

Figure 3.2 Comparison of American and European trade by region, 2005

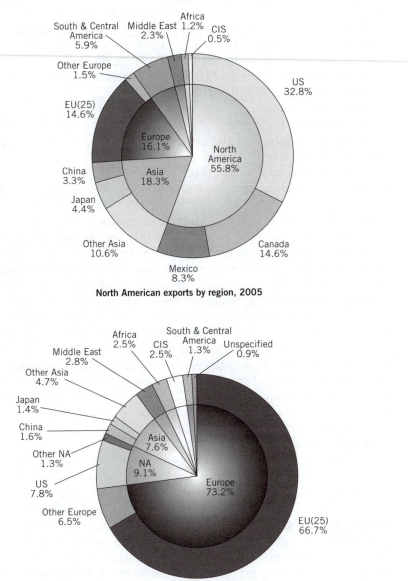

Africa 1.2%
CIS 0.5%
Middle East 2.3%
South & Central America 5.9%
Other Europe 1.5%
EU(25) 14.6%
US 32.8%
Europe 16.1%
North America 55.8%
China 3.3%
Asia 18.3%
Japan 4.4%
Other Asia 10.6%
Canada 14.6%
Mexico 8.3%

North American exports by region, 2005

Africa 2.5%
South & Central America 1.3%
CIS 2.5%
Unspecified 0.9%
Middle East 2.8%
Other Asia 4.7%
Japan 1.4%
China 1.6%
Other NA 1.3%
US 7.8%
Other Europe 6.5%
Asia 7.6%
NA 9.1%
Europe 73.2%
EU(25) 66.7%

European exports by region, 2005

Source: World Trade Organization, International Trade Statistics, 2006, http://wto.org/ english/res_e/ste/rls2006_e/its06_general_overview_p.pdf, accessed 30 August 2007.

ment. As we will see in Chapter 7, regional trade agreements like NAFTA can create obstacles for firms whose countries are not part of the agreement, hence not necessarily entitled to whatever standard of liberalized trade agreed. European firms were worried that NAFTA would create barriers and in response invested into Mexico, effectively jumping the NAFTA wall; they also pressed the Commission to negotiate an EU–Mexico bilateral agreement, which came into force in 2000 (Busse *et al.*, 2000)

Among all economic issue areas within the Euro-American system, arguably trade relations have the greatest political salience. This is partly because of the intrinsic importance of the area but that is not the entire explanation. In contrast to relations in antitrust or monetary policy, trade relations have become the most clearly 'politicized', with a large number of stakeholders and a significant public profile. Whereas monetary – and even more so, antitrust – sectors remain the domain of experts and policymakers, the development of trade policy is notable for the significant and deep involvement of firms and, at least in the EU, the active participation of non-governmental organizations. For almost sixty years, the US and the EU participated in an international trade system characterized by the expansion of trade, which grew more quickly than GDP. The GATT process of negotiated, reciprocal trade liberalization worked very well for some four decades and succeeded in dramatically lowering tariffs in the developed world. GATT, often derided as an ineffectual organization, actually succeeded spectacularly and its successor the World Trade Organization now has a membership of around 150 states. This institutionalization of liberalized trade owes much to the leadership of Washington and Brussels and is reflective of what the two powers are able to achieve working together.

Yet, with the uncertain outcome of the Doha Round negotiations, the United States and the European Union confront a dramatically changing trade policy environment, and one in which politicization is at much higher levels. The current malaise in the international trading system arises partly from the exhaustion of governance structures that dominated the postwar trading system. The changes include: the erosion of the dominance of the EU–US axis in the WTO; the increasing pressure on agriculture; WTO disputes that are reducing room to manoeuvre; and an increasing number of stakeholders. Finally, the renewal of a security dimension to trade issues (and more directly investment ones) is weakening political support for multilateral liberalization. These pressures have led the United States to pursue regional or bilateral pacts that, to an extent, undermine its commitment to multilateralism. The EU already had a considerable number of regional pacts, but finds itself under increasing pressure to adjust internally, thanks largely to the increasing influence of developing states in the WTO process, as well as several WTO disputes decisions. The EU has come under pressure in the more judicialized disputes process and these 'defeats' come at a delicate time for the European economy, with sluggish growth fuelling resentment at outside influences.

These features share common roots. The first may be described as the return to multipolarity; the rise of China, India and Brazil to economic prominence is challenging long-held assumptions about who, exactly, governs international trade. In the early years of the Euro-American system, American dominance was taken for granted; in the 1950s, the American economy accounted for half of total world output. However, the US is increasingly challenged across a range of policy areas not just by the EU but also China and to a lesser extent India and Brazil. This political reality reflects important changes in the direction of trade in the international economy. EU–US literature traditionally began by noting how the EU–US relationship was the most important trading relationship in the world. This is changing. China now barely trails the US as the main exporter to the Eurozone countries, and the US too has become much more bound up in China trade, at least in merchandise trade. As the European–American economic relationship becomes one of several dense and complex economic partnerships, its political salience *vis-à-vis* others becomes more problematic.

There is also a second and related root to the current features of the global trading system, and one that particularly affects EU–US relations. The multipolarity outlined above is linked increasingly to an important security element, where economic policy is developed and implemented with security considerations in mind. Congressmen and senators in Washington face increased calls for tougher vetting of foreign investment in the United States, with rationales for such calls being a complex mix of protectionist desires and security concerns. At the same time, in the EU, the increasing salience of concerns with energy and environmental security also has strong repercussions on the shaping of external trade policies. Finally, the judicialization and increasing institutionalization of the global economy also presents challenges. The

European Union (like other actors) is increasingly constrained in the types of policies that can be effectively developed and implemented: this arises mainly from the increased importance of trade for both economies.

The combination outlined here, of increased multipolarity in world trade, linked with growing politicization and judicialization, is a potent one. For the EU and the US, it means that the days when trade could be dealt with in a relatively 'technical' way among experts are going if not already gone, and this has implications both for their trade-policymaking processes and for the management of their mutual trade relations.

European Union trade policymaking and trends

As we noted in Chapter 2, the EU is something of a 'moving target' for its policymaking partners, as its institutions develop and evolve and its member states' preferences shift in response to domestic and international pressures. The elaboration and consolidation of the Common Commercial Policy from the 1960s onwards has gone alongside a continual growth in the European Community's (and then the EU's) role in the global trading system. The enlargement of the Community and then the Union has played an important part in this growth, and has also given the EU a distinctive set of international trading relationships, reflecting the influence of its diverse membership and the members' historical links with different parts of the world. The articulation of common rules for the EU's internal market has made the Union even more important in international trade, as foreign firms see the creation of a generally affluent and growing common economic space (Young and Peterson 2006: 797). The European Union is now the largest exporter to China, and its attractiveness as an export market has increased as the Eurozone countries – particularly Germany – experienced renewed economic growth from 2006 after years of stagnation. This gives the Union considerable leverage in international negotiations, and makes other states keenly interested in both EU commercial policy and the process by which the Union formulates its positions. This process is complex and highly institutionalized, and not surprisingly the academic literature on EU trade policy pays considerable attention to the internal constraints on the effective development of EU trade policy. Voting rules within the

Council of Ministers matter decisively for international trade negotiations; the unanimity requirement makes it relatively easy for the
EU to resist external pressures for change, but also constrains its
ability to offer policy changes (Meunier 2005: 166). This internal
division is a key element of the EU's trade power: 'The EU has
been able to obtain more in international trade negotiations than it
might have if all decisions had been made through strict majority
voting and with lots of flexibility granted to European negotiators'
(Meunier and Nicolaïdis, 2006: 909).

Another important internal feature with implications for international negotiations is the competence question: whether member
states or the Commission (acting on behalf of the Community)
have the legal authority to negotiate international trade agreements
on behalf of the Union, particularly in the area of services trade,
which was not a significant element of international commerce
when the Treaty of Rome was signed. The competence issue
seemed to have been settled with the Treaty of Nice, which
extended the Community's competence into the areas of services
and intellectual property (WTO 2004: viii). Leaving aside the legal
issues, it is also true that the EU is a fractured polity, with many
deep and longstanding institutional differences among member
states. Traditionally, this has been portrayed as a simple cleavage
between the more free-trading northern European members (UK,
Netherlands and Germany) and the protectionist 'south' led by
France. The addition of new members and the rise of new issues on
the trade agenda have made this simple division rather outmoded.

The focus on internal constraints helps us a great deal but can
take us only so far. Much of the literature on EU trade is written as
if the EU didn't trade with anyone, so tight is the focus on internal
processes and norms. This is perhaps an inevitable result of the
focus on the EU as a regional integration process. Yet, it can be
suggested that the EU is increasingly constrained internationally;
and if one wants to understand the internal dynamics of (for
example) state aid policy or agricultural policy in the Union, one
needs to grasp how the international environment is influencing
events. The WTO gets its influence on the EU in two ways: first, it
fosters the adoption of certain modes of behaviour; and second, the
dispute settlement understanding is sufficiently robust to alter
WTO member behaviour. The WTO has caused 'broad institutional change' in the European Union, as the norms and expectations of the multilateral institution diffuse down to Brussels (Knodt

2004). This argument, while situated in the multilevel governance tradition, owes much to regime theory, with its emphasis on actor expectations and the development of an enlightened self-interest among parties to a multistate cooperative arrangement. The important contribution of Knodt's work to the discussion here is that it moves the emphasis away from WTO as arena to WTO as actor. For the EU and its trade policymaking, this constitutes a major shift in the global context.

In recent years, most major states have opted for some form of multi-track approach to trade negotiations that blends participation in the WTO with efforts to gain preferential access to one or more foreign markets through preferential trade agreements. Japan and South Korea were about the last major trading nations to adopt this approach and each has sought to sign PTAs with key trade partners. They have done so for two reasons. First, like other states, they are frustrated by the increasingly complex and fruitless multilateral track at the WTO. Second, their firms have lobbied each government to negotiate preferential trade deals so as to neutralise the gains made by competing firms whose governments have already signed such agreements (Manger 2005). The European Union, by contrast, has always adopted a multi-track approach to commercial policy negotiations. This should not surprise us, as the Common Market itself is a preferential trade agreement, one that operates under art. 24 of the GATT relating to plurilateral agreements negotiated among GATT (now WTO) members.

Regulation and EU trade policy

Where the EU does differ from other WTO members, not least the US, is the degree to which it places international regulatory matters at the heart of its trade strategy. Regulation as a trade issue differs from the 'classic' trade defence instruments such as anti-dumping and quotas; the latter are 'at-the-border' issues whereas regulation refers to how a product or service is developed and delivered. As such, regulatory issues push trade politics well behind national borders and make national laws and procedures topics for negotiation. The successive rounds of GATT negotiations effectively removed tariffs as barriers to entry, but the reduction of tariffs does not automatically make the market more contestable. As we explore further in Chapter 5, internal regulations can hamper effective market access for foreign firms. Thus, there is a logic to the extension of trade liberalization negotiations to the issue of regulation (McGuire 2004; De Bièvre 2006). The interesting question is why the EU has pursued this with so much more vigour than other parties. One line of explanation would locate the reason in the existence of the Commission itself; it should not surprise anyone that a supranational bureaucracy – which is exactly what the Commission is – develops a preference for regulation. The Commission thus sees an opportunity to turn the WTO 'into a regulatory agency in its own image' (Young 2004; Jones 2006; Sally 2004: 114). This process arguably reached its zenith in the early stages of the Doha Round negotiations, with the European Union officials being the staunchest advocates of the inclusion of a range of regulatory areas (trade facilitation, competition policy, investor protection and government procurement). These 'Singapore issues', so called because they were first agreed as an agenda item at the WTO's Singapore ministerial in 1996, presented a particular problem for developing states; all these issue areas are complex regulatory areas requiring significant legal and bureaucratic infrastructure. For these states, the EU's position represented an attempt to impose on them a model of governance suitable for an already affluent and stable polity. In the event, the Commission agreed to drop all but trade facilitation from its Doha negotiating stance.

Though it has largely failed through multilateral negotiations, the Commission showed no signs of retreating from an interest in regulatory issues and international trade. The EU remained keen to use regulatory standards for food and other products, both to protect EU consumers and, perhaps, to restrict access to the European market. Europe had been at the forefront of these new types of trade disputes thanks to its long-running battle with the United States (and latterly other countries including Canada) in respect of the export of hormone-fed beef and genetically modified soybeans and other crops to Europe. However, Europe is hardly alone in using product standards in this way. Indeed, according to one study, the United States has the largest number of notifications to the WTO of product standards that appear stricter than prevailing international levels (Gallagher 2007). The EU has also pursued the regulatory agenda through its regional trade agreements. It is now commonplace for the EU to include competition policy, investment protection and a raft of other issues in any negotiation with a prospective trade partner. Though these efforts can be resisted, the EU's emphasis on institution-building, and on the cultivation of norms and values associated with democracy can be attractive to developing states, more so than the American approach that pays much less attention to the normative element of relations (Doctor 2007).

Erosion of preferences

The EU has long made extensive use of the desire of states to gain access to the European market to construct its 'pyramid of privilege'. Developing states, particularly former colonies, gained preferential access to Europe's markets for their goods – mainly agriculture. Developed states had to content themselves with the Union's most-favoured nation (MFN) tariff rates, but the WTO process has gradually eroded these. Aside from some sectors with tariff peaks, average EU tariffs are low, at about 5 per cent, and no longer represent a barrier for most firms.

Trade policy in the European context has always been more than the export and imports of goods and services. Historic links that member states have with former colonies give trade policy a significant and long-established link to development policy. Successive preferential trade agreements with African, Caribbean and Pacific island states have had, at their heart, an intention to use easier access to the Union's consumers as a means of economic development. The Lomé and now Cotonou Conventions have provided the legal and political basis for these policies.

However, policy trends have eroded the historical basis of development policy as trade policy. First, the expansion of the WTO, in terms both of membership and scope, has eroded the special treatment afforded to developing states. The Uruguay Round agreements comprised a 'single undertaking' where all WTO signatories, regardless of their stage of development, were bound by the same rules. The concession to developing states lay in the phase-in period for the agreement; after Uruguay, developing states were afforded far less special treatment. This had implications for the future of the European Union's elaborate construct of development-oriented trade policies, which, since they applied only to certain countries, were inherently discriminatory. Neither were they reciprocal, as ACP states did not have to offer significant concessions to gain access to the European market. EU development policies thus violated two principles of the WTO – non-discrimination and reciprocity – and with the entering into force of the WTO agreements in 1995 a new approach would be needed to avoid costly WTO litigation. The EU succeeded in gaining breathing room. The Cotonou Agreement, for example, operates under a WTO waiver that expires in 2008; the EU and its developing country partners are urgently trying to conclude a set of WTO-compliant Economic Partnership Agreements (EPAs) ahead of this expiration (Perez 2006). Second, the more judicialized disputes process in the WTO has curtailed the privileges offered by development agreements. WTO cases involving sugar – and the more famous 'banana' case, which centred on the EU and the US (see below) – have forced the EU to restructure its preferential agreements, offering better access to all WTO-member developing states. Here, the WTO non-discrimination principle pushes the EU to adopt a common approach to all developing states, regardless of their previous political relationship with the EU. In response, the EU has rather 'internalized' some aspects of development policies into both its WTO processes and negotiations with prospective PTA partners. For example, the European Partnership Agreements, aimed at replacing the EU's current set of preferential trade relationships with developing states under the Cotonou Agreement, will be designed to be more congruent with WTO regulations (European Commission 2007a).

The changing nature of American trade policy

The United States has long been ambivalent about the international political economy but has none the less led developments that sought to develop an international regime to regulate trade. In 1945, the charter of the International Trade Organization (ITO) was drawn up as part of an American-led effort to create post-war economic institutions capable of avoiding the economic catastrophe that had in the view of many contributed to the slide towards war in 1939 (Wilkinson 2005: 15). Though ITO was effectively killed off by a threatened Senate veto in 1948, American presidents got around that setback and were instrumental in the creation of the General Agreement on Tariffs and Trade (GATT). Designed only as a stop-gap institution until the ITO was resurrected, GATT nevertheless overcame this handicap to become a remarkably successful organization. Though American impatience with GATT eventually told, GATT worked effectively for many

Box 3.1   The EU and the banana trade

Few trade disputes are as long-running or as complicated as the European Union's dispute with several states over the importation of bananas. The case shows how difficult it can be to reconcile the conflicting demands of liberalized international trade with development policies and internal Union politics. The dispute traces its origins back to market access preferences for fruit from the African, Caribbean and Pacific (ACP) states. The effect of the banana import regime was to favour fruit imported from former European colonies and discriminate against other producers, mainly those in Central and South America. The United States, at the urging of American firms with investments in the Central and South American banana industry, took the EU to the WTO in 1996, along with Ecuador, Guatemala, Honduras and Mexico. The WTO disputes panel agreed that the EU was unfairly discriminating against non-ACP producers, and required the Commission to develop a new scheme for banana imports. Reflecting strong disagreement among member states, the Commission made only modest changes to its regime, and so soon found itself back at the WTO. Again, the dispute process found that the import regime discriminated against non-ACP bananas. The EU failed to comply with this judgement, and in 1999 the United States retaliated by placing trade sanctions on European goods worth $191 million per year (that is, the amount of money US firms claim to have lost because of the EU's banana import rules).

The Commission needed a solution that would expand market access for Latin American fruit, while maintaining market share for ACP producers. WTO rules generally do not allow for discrimination of this type: WTO member states are to be treated equally. The EU, with American support none the less negotiated a WTO waiver in 2001 that would allow Europe to maintain some preference for ACP bananas. The waiver, however, is only a temporary solution. Eventually, the EU would have to move toward a 'tariff-only' system where ACP fruit was not guaranteed a specific quota. In mid-2007, the US, again supported by several Latin-American states, placed renewed pressure on the EU by requesting that the WTO create a 'compliance panel' to assess Europe's progress in transforming its banana regime.

The banana dispute illustrates nicely the complex interplay between the US and the EU. While the US strongly opposed the banana regime, it did work closely with the EU in developing the waiver

➡

necessary to maintaining at least some preference for ACP fruit. The outcome also demonstrates how the WTO process affects the evolution of development policies.

Sources: http://search.crownpeak.com/cpt_search/result_1?account=1003&q=bananas; http://www.ustr.gov/Document_Library/Press_Releases/2001/April/The_US-EU_ Banana_Agreement.html?ht=;http://trade.ec.europa.eu/wtodispute/show.cfm?id= 239&code=2, all accessed 10 July 2007. http://www.wto.org/english/news_e/news07_e/dsb_12july07_e.htm, accessed 12 July 2007.

years thanks to its congruence with American trade interests and its organizational structure (Goldstein 2000; Lindeque and McGuire 2007). Much of the GATT's rules and regulations derived from American practice and custom. US rules on injury and anti-dumping were important influences on the eventual wording of the GATT equivalents (Sen 2003). GATT thus enjoyed American support for many years: it helped deliver dramatic reductions in tariff levels and so catalysed increased global trade in the post-war period. However, by the time of the Kennedy Round in the early 1960s, increased import pressures started eroding what had been broad support for GATT. American managers found it more convenient to blame the unfair practices of foreigners rather than look at their own companies' performance.

In addition, the perception grew that the American market was substantially more open than the markets of other countries, and so was allowing foreign firms access without reciprocal US access to overseas markets (Shaffer 2003: 20). Criticism began to focus on the political process that led to this situation. US business blamed the Kennedy Round outcome on a trade policy process too dominated by professional diplomats and technical experts unused to the business world. Changes to the policymaking process included statutory requirements for private sector consultations, thus ensuring that business has a powerful role in the shaping of US trade policy. A complex network of private interests, agency officials at the office of the US trade representative (USTR), Congress and other government departments ensures that American trade policy is a contested process. However, successive reorganizations of agencies have strengthened the hand of USTR relative to other units of the executive. Originally designated as an agency under the president's office, USTR has gradually developed into a full 'member' of the executive branch alongside departments like Commerce and State. Congress urged this building up of USTR authority as part of its desire to make the protection of US trade interests more central to a president's economic policy. The more independence it gained, the more USTR found itself depending on private interests for political support.

The active support of the United States was key to the creation of the World Trade Organization during the Uruguay Round negotiations. None the less, American support for multilateralism has always been contested. The United States maintains a relatively open economy with comparatively few restrictions on foreign firms seeking to do business; subsidies to industry are not used extensively and foreign firms operate in a robust legal and regulatory environment. American leadership has at times been severely undermined by domestic political pressures and a suspicion that sovereignty was being surrendered to international organizations. Congressmen and congresswomen, facing election every two years, are especially sensitive to constituency pressures for trade protection. Elaborate legislative arrangements designed to facilitate trade negotiations in spite of this handicap include trade promotion authority (formerly fast-track authority), by presenting the Congress with a take-it-or-leave-it package, these aim to frustrate attempts to unpick agreements via concessions to constituency lobbies. American trade politics is thus characterized by both considerable protectionism and aggressive efforts to liberalize. In the case of low-skill industrial sectors and agriculture, the Congress has turned to US trade remedies to offset increased international pressures. Where American firms are technologically advanced or represent service-based sectors, US policy has been to use multilateralism as a means of opening markets (Porter 2005).

American support for multilateralism was dealt a severe blow, however, with the failure of the WTO's Cancún ministerial meeting in September 2003. This meeting reflected not only the 'traditional' tensions between the EU and the US over agriculture, but also a new set of pressures from major emerging economies, including notably China, India and Brazil, and it made both the EU and the US reassess their strategies. Competitive liberalization, based on bilateral and regional trade agreements, became the operative policy in the wake of this setback; it was seen both as a mechanism to retrieve something from the stalled liberalization process and also an opportunity for the US to revitalize that process, since foreign states would worry that a full-scale move to regional trade by the US would present unique dangers for market access. Robert Zoellick (the USTR at the time) outlined the essential characteristics of the new policy shortly after the Cancun meeting. Rather than wait for all WTO members to agree a new round of trade liberalization, the US would work with 'can-do' states willing to liberalize on a bilateral basis. The danger with the competitive liberalization is the asymmetry in power it represents. The US used regional trade agreements as an easy way to gain particularly good deals for American-based firms, since the partner state was almost always more dependent on access to the US market than the reverse (Feinberg 2004). The negotiations between the United States and the South African Customs Union, for example, were criticized for the extent to which areas like insurance and banking – areas of American competitive strength – were liberalized to a greater degree than other sectors (Whalley and Leith 2003: 7). The Central American Free Trade Agreement (CAFTA) came in for similar criticism, namely that it did little to open US markets but did more to throw open developing country markets to American firms. This perception was hardly dispelled by the then acting USTR Robert Allgeier, as he sold the benefits of the CAFTA to Congress: 'The chief effect of CAFTA is not to further open our market, but rather to tear down barriers to our products and services in Central America and the Dominican Republic' (Allgeier 2005).

The Bush administration negotiated in the Doha Round in the context of decreased political support for multilateral trade in Congress. As with the EU, the increased judicialization of the WTO disputes process played its part. The controversy surrounding the Byrd Amendment was the best illustration. The measure, designed to allow petitioning firms to share in revenues generated by anti-dumping duties, was found non-compliant by a disputes panel in 2004. Trade partners (including the EU) were eager to see this measure rescinded on the back of this judgement, but Congress was not so keen. The Byrd Amendment stayed on the statute books, with congressmen and congresswomen complaining that the American legislature should not have its powers circumscribed by an international agreement. The effect of the WTO disputes process is to have a 'chilling effect' on the use of trade instruments and there is evidence to suggest that the process is indeed used to help forestall the initiation of trade disputes processes by partners. This is because the cumulative effect of the disputes process raises the cost of initiating trade conflict. However, in the American case, a Congress increasingly worried about the alleged impact of globalization on American workers may decide that the costs of compliance with WTO rules and norms exceed the benefits.

As with the EU, it is clear from this discussion that the US role in world trade is ambivalent, and beset by a number of internal and external pressures. The complexity of internal trade policy making, with Congress in a strong position to champion 'parochial' interests, and the cultural predisposition to resist attack on US sovereignty, have lent a distinctive flavour to US trade policies, and this has been given an additional twist by the recent tendency to look for bilateral or interregional trade agreements which are seen as better serving US interests than global rules and negotiations. Not surprisingly, the EU has been sensitive to these features and quick to respond to perceived challenges.

The Brussels–Washington Axis

For decades, the transatlantic relationship was the foundation-stone of EU trade policy. In the wake of World War II, American determination not to repeat the errors of trade protectionism and economic strife that generated such disastrous consequences helped forge the post-war economic architecture of multilateral institutions and forums to govern international commercial relations. The General Agreement on Tariffs and Trade was the trade-related component, though because of American concerns the GATT did not become the true third pillar alongside the IMF and World Bank until the body attained full treaty status with the approval of the Uruguay Round agreements in 1994. From 1947 to 1994 it ran as a – surprisingly effective – agreement among contracting parties. Eventually, this arrangement had run its course and consensus grew that a more formal and robust organization was required. The World Trade Organization subsumed the GATT and significantly expanded its remit beyond trade in goods; it now covers trade in services as well as the treatment of intellectual property.

From 1947 to 1957 European members of the GATT negotiated tariff concessions with other contracting parties as individual states. During the early years of GATT, the policy focus was firmly on tariff reductions but this changed over decades, in part because the evolution of European cooperation began to raise issues for American policymakers in respect of sectors like agriculture. The Kennedy Round of GATT negotiations was prompted by American concerns about the impact the formation of the Common Market – and particularly the Common Agricultural Policy – would have on international trade (Meunier 2005: 75). In language that prefigured debates decades later, American politicians voiced concern about the creation of a single European economy more or less the same size as that of the US (Meunier ibid.) and the resultant need to ensure that this new creation – valuable though it was – nonetheless maintained a commitment to open markets and trade. Thus, virtually from the outset of the Community in 1957, American trade policy has been deeply informed by the perception that Europe is both a key market and home to internationally competitive firms.

In the subsequent decades the American–European trade relationship has deepened, and two aspects stand out in this evolution. The first has been the emergence of the EU as a fully established negotiating partner with Washington; the second the dramatic expansion of the trade agenda to encompass a growing variety of commercial activities. In respect of the former, the Commission assumed negotiations on behalf of all six members of the Common Market with the signing of the Treaty of Rome. Rather like competition policy, the development of a common external commercial policy was an absolute requirement for the construction of a viable and credible marketplace in Europe. But legal competence is no guarantee of negotiating effectiveness, and early EC negotiators' hands were weakened as national governments kept tight control over the GATT process. Member states did not wish to imperil their new European venture through reckless commitments at the multilateral level (Meunier 2005: 74). Another reason, however, was the simple need for EC negotiators to develop the expertise required to be effective negotiators. This took time and even in the Tokyo Round negotiations during the 1970s some national governments doubted whether Brussels bureaucrats adequately understood the technical aspects of some negotiating areas (McGuire 1997).

As noted above, the evolution of American trade policy has been much less significant than Europe's since the 1950s, but two structural aspects of the US process deserve mention. First, the separation of powers in the US constitutional system means that the president is less able to make credible commitments on trade (or many other matters) than is a prime-ministerial counterpart in a parliament. Though Congress delegated negotiating authority to the president under the 1934 Reciprocal Trade Agreements Acts, its oversight is assured by the requirement that any trade agreement receive congressional assent. In some respects then, Congress plays the same role of 'veto point' as individual member states do in Europe. Both European and American negotiators are adept at employing 'tied hands' negotiating strategies, where the difficulty of gaining internal approval is used as a mechanism to force trade partners to make more concessions.

Traditionally, there has been a remarkable symmetry in the trade flows between the two partners, with the EU typically enjoying only a small, politically uncontentious trade surplus. The United States took 21.3 per cent of EU imports in 1998 and 22 per cent of exports (WTO 2000: 11); though recent figures show that Europe is becoming somewhat less important as a destination for US trade. In 2005, the US was the destination of 24 per cent of EU exports but America's share of EU imports has declined from 20 per cent in 2001 to 14 per cent in 2005 (European Commission 2006). Aside from value, the breadth of the trade is also remarkable; European and American firms sell virtually everything to one another and to consumers – everything from cars, appliances and designer goods to insurance and legal services. In a world of rapid but recent globalization the transatlantic zone has been well integrated for decades and the depth of this relationship is revealed in the extent to which European and American firms have ceased to be 'foreign' in each other's economies. Opel (GM) and Ford of Europe have sold cars for so long in Europe that their affiliation with their American parent causes not the slightest notice. The same is now true for the banks, lawyers, household appliance, and consumer goods retailers.

Competition is based on the high degree of intra-industry trade between Europe and America. This might explain the number of significant EU–US trade disputes, ranging from areas such as subsidies to government procurement policies to safeguard and anti-dumping policies. European and American firms compete with each other in most markets – and occasional trade disputes are to be expected. The major 'growth area' for disputes is not in traditional trade areas like anti-dumping, however, but in regulatory policies, such as technical standards, taxation and issues relating to human and animal health (Pollack 2003b; Young and Peterson 2006). As tariffs and other formal trade barriers are removed, how commercial exchange is regulated comes to be contested. Thus, Brussels and Washington have had disputes over the export of hormone-fed US beef and genetically modified crops (as already mentioned) and the tax treatment of US exports. However, these disputes must be put in perspective: European–American trade disputes in 2000 were worth less than 5 per cent of trans-Atlantic trade (Hufbauer and Neumann 2002). Nonetheless given the importance of trade across the Atlantic, European–America disputes tend to be large relative to cases involving other states. American–European trade conflict serves as an important legal and procedural guide for other WTO members (Petersmann 2003: 7; Busch and Reinhardt 2006). Since the US and the EU account for the bulk of the WTO's case-load – and bilateral disputes are an important element in this – trade conflict between the two offers guidance to other WTO members on developing trade law (Lindeque and McGuire, 2007). In the terms used in Chapter 2, this would seem to be evidence of the growing interdependence and integration that has taken place within the transatlantic 'economic space'; neither interdependence nor integration eliminates disputes, but each of them can generate ways of resolving or managing the inevitable disputes that do occur.

The areas where the EU and the US agree are at least as important as the disputes. Though disagreements generate better headlines, it should not come as a surprise that two large advanced economies should to a large extent have similar policy preferences. For example, both Brussels and Washington advocated the significant extension of intellectual property rights during the Uruguay Round. Though the United States began the process of bringing intellectual property issues under the aegis of the WTO (then GATT) in the Uruguay Round, the European Union quickly grasped the potential significance; Europe was the home base of a vast number of firms rich in intellectual property (IP) in sectors as varied as electronics and perfumes and these corporations were keen to protect their innovations from piracy (Capling 2004). Enforcement of WTO intellectual property provisions has remained a mainstay of EU–US summits. Thus, the Vienna meeting in June 2006 reaffirmed both partners' willingness to implement the joint Action Strategy on the Enforcement of Intellectual Property Rights, which works through the WTO process and capacity-building with third countries (European Commission, 2006b). Financial services liberalization was another area where Brussels and Washington shared interests. The US had pressed other GATT members for significant commitments on financial services but had withdrawn from the talks in frustration when faced with recalcitrant partners (Sell 2003: 167). The European Union, backed by support from national governments – particularly the UK – and business groups, restarted the talks in the absence of the US and was crucial to brokering a solution acceptable to Washington. In both Europe and America there was a widespread desire for more robust, pro-market financial services regulation and in both governments views were influenced by the financial services industry.

Managing the relationship

Trade relations illustrate a central theme in this book: that European–American relations are conducted through a dense network of stakeholders. It should not be assumed that power was held by states, or even coalitions of them, but was rather diffusing among a wider variety of actors – most notably firms – but also international institutions and NGOs. 'Institutions, by providing a venue for the ongoing, systematic exchange of information and ideas, foster consensus formation' (Eichengreen and Ghironi 1998: 71). The TransAtlantic Business Dialogue (TABD) is one important firm-based actor, as is the American Chamber of Commerce in Brussels. In the 1990s, both these actors were important in the development of, among other items, mutual recognition treaties which helped facilitate trans-Atlantic trade. The organization has also been important in the area of standards harmonization in the automobile sector, particularly with regard to curbing emissions (Shiroyama, 2007). TABD's precise influence can be overstated; its influence has waned noticeably in recent years in the absence of strong corporate leadership. However, this hardly signals the diminishing role of business in trade policy. Both the US and the EU have developed mechanisms to consult with business on various trade issues at all stages in the negotiations, as well as with disputes process at the WTO.

What is remarkable today is the sheer number and variety of participants in economic governance. The steel trade dispute of 2001, for example, saw the US, Germany, the UK and Belgium (among others) intimately involved as states, but the European Commission was a key actor, as were steel trade associations on either side of the Atlantic. It does not stop there. As for forums where a solution to the dispute is negotiated, the World Trade Organization is the most important and prominent, but not alone. The Organisation for Economic Co-operation and Development (OECD) has assumed a key role as a negotiating arena owing to the existence of its steel industry committee and previous experience in developing plurilateral agreements in areas such as government corruption and export credit finance. Talks are also held on a bilateral basis – either by special arrangement or as part of the usual cycle of summit meetings held between Washington and European capitals.

The myriad actors engaged in EU–US trade relations might suggest a policymaking process closer to chaos than management, but this would be unfair. While managing the relationship will never approach the textbook flow charts and management models of academia, in fact the process of 'managed muddling-along' does not work so badly. More precisely, the trade relationship demonstrates that in the area of business–government relationships firms to have an important role to play in the provision of expertise and from time to time do exert more influence than some observers are comfortable with. Firms are can also be important in forcing an end to trade disputes, as it is they not governments that actually suffer financial and reputational effects from disputes (Busch and Reinhardt 2006).

Losing control – the move to a multipolar WTO

As noted above, the Doha Round talks were suspended in the summer of 2006 after negotiations broke down. As trade diplomats attempted to revive the round, both the US and the EU faced considerable international pressures: the EU on agriculture and the US on intellectual property and anti-dumping. As with other policy areas, the transatlantic relationship, while very important, is no longer as central to the global trading system as it once was. The Uruguay Round settlement may be seen as the last time Brussels and Washington were able to catalyse international agreement around their policy preferences. The Marrakech agreements (the formal outcome of the Uruguay Round) reflected the EU and US's (and, to a lesser extent, other industrialized states') concerns for trade in technologically sophisticated manufactures or services: hence the emphasis on intellectual property provisions and language in subsidies that favoured research intensive sectors like aerospace and pharmaceuticals (McGuire 2004; Wilkinson 2005). Developing countries expected two things in return: market access for primary products and technology transfer from the developed world. As for the latter, the process takes time and may yet come about; what is clear to developing states, however, is that market access promises have not been kept (Cannady 2004).

The mere fact that the alternate name for the Doha Round is the 'Development Round' suggests just how far the balance of power in the WTO has swung. The changing balance can be understood in this way: some 85 members of the GATT launched the Uruguay Round in 1986, and in Seattle in 1999 some 130 national delegations participated. On the eve of the Doha meeting, the WTO could boast some 144 members and by the end of the ministerial both China and Taiwan had been admitted as members. Strong though they are, both the US and the EU participate in an organization where their influence has been diluted, both by an expanding membership and by procedures that do not favour large trading members. Unlike the IMF, for example, with its weighted voting, the WTO works on a one-member, one-vote system. To a much greater extent than in some other international organizations, both the US and the EU must work diplomatically to get their preferences accepted: simply outvoting other members is not an option.

But deeper structural changes are at work. Cancún's failed ministerial meeting was a watershed for international economic governance. Not all observers agree, of course, and see in the collapse of these negotiations a strong lineage with earlier breakdowns such as those during the Uruguay Round. The adjournment of the Montreal ministerial meeting in 1998 was seen publicly as a failure, but professional diplomats regard it as a clever tactic that saved the talks for further trauma. By implication, the failure to make progress at the Seattle ministerial meeting of 1999 was a similar bump in the road for the WTO. But that is to miss the structural changes. Montreal's collapse did not spark a realignment of political power within the then GATT: the same key players at Montreal – the US and the EC, as well as Japan, Canada and Brazil – were the same players central to the eventual agreement. The process remained 'pyramidal', where the US-EU relationship developed the key positions which cascaded down to the wider GATT membership (Winham in Wiener 2005: 150). By contrast, the failure of the Cancún ministerial meeting in 2003 spawned (or perhaps catalysed) significant new groupings within the organization. The pyramid has been destroyed, but there is no agreement on what has replaced it. The accession of China in 2001 was of course absolutely key to this fracturing of the negotiating order.

None the less, China continues to feature prominently in EU and US trade policy. Both actors target Chinese products with anti-dumping duties and press Beijing to honour its commitments to crack down on intellectual property violations. The tone of US–Chinese economic relations is increasingly shrill, with US politicians and political commentators calling for tougher action. The tone of EU–Chinese relations is noticeable for its lack of public interface, though many of the irritants are common. The US political system gives elected politicians in the Congress powerful incentives to speak out strongly on trade issues; this structural feature of American politics does not have an equivalent in Europe, where trade policy remains more technocratic and consultative. Two member states in particular have a keen interest in open trade policies: the United Kingdom because of its trade surplus in services trade due to London's status as a financial hub; and Germany, which is the world's largest exporter of goods, many of which find their way to the rising and increasingly affluent markets of Asia, China and Latin America.

The emergence of the G-20 (or G-30, or G-80) as a relatively coherent bloc probably spells the end to American–European dominance of the final stages of WTO negotiating rounds. For many observers, WTO governance was synonymous with the 'Quad' made up of the four more important traders in the WTO system: Canada, the EU, Japan and the United States. The real importance of the Quad can be questioned, however; during the Uruguay Round, American and European diplomats essentially used their bilateral relationship to hammer out agreements in the final contentious areas. The rest of the membership was confined largely to the sidelines. This bilateral dominance has been under pressure for some time: the Seattle breakdown was a precursor. Between the Seattle meeting and the Cancún failure, the Quad was quietly but effectively supplanted by a mini-ministerial process where developing countries were much more prominent. Pascal Lamy drew attention to this in his final report as EU trade commissioner:

The so-called Quad (EU, US, Japan, Canada) has met for precisely 20 minutes in the last five years . . . In its place has come a flexible feast of mini and micro Ministerials, ad hoc small groupings, always with the EU, US, Brazil and India at the core. (Lamy 2004)

Narlikar notes that the increasing prominence of the ministerial meetings was designed to enhance the legitimacy of the WTO in the eyes of member states by offering a greater opportunity to exercise voice (Narlikar 2004: 417). At Cancun, this voice was used powerfully to block what one developing country diplomat called 'another Blair House' – a deliberate reference to an EU–US deal on agriculture in the latter stages of the Uruguay Round (Narlikar and Tussie 2004). The emergence of mini-ministerials may not yet work as a structural device for negotiations, but their existence speaks volumes about the undesirability of a return to the Green Room era of closed-shop negotiations in the end-game of a GATT/WTO round.

One area where the decline of the European–American axis can clearly be seen is agricultural trade. In this policy area, Brazil has become increasingly influential, as its diplomats seek to open markets in response to the growth of a powerful domestic food-processing lobby. At the same time, European policies for international trade in agriculture cannot be understood in isolation from the continuing conflicts within the EU over reform of the Common Agricultural Policy (CAP). Though the EU made some concessions on export subsidies during 2003, the CAP remained a major stumbling block to progress. The EU has always had to deal with internal disagreement among member states; in agricultural trade it also has to cope with a heterogeneous group of developing states. It simply is not the case that all developing states support free trade in agriculture; some small states that enjoy preferential access to the EU, such as Mauritius, fear that their small producers will be wiped out in open competition. It is also true that many developing states are net food importers – and free trade would result in their paying higher prices as the subsidies that currently keep many commodities below market prices would vanish.

The run up to the Hong Kong ministerial during the summer and autumn of 2005 likewise demonstrated the complex internal diplomacy of the EU. In late 2005, pressure from several developing states, notably India and Brazil, was placing Peter Mandelson (Lamy's replacement as trade commissioner) in an increasingly difficult position. For successive negotiating rounds, the EU resisted increasing pressure to radically reform the CAP. It was helped to a large extent in this by other nations with a strong commitment to subsidized agriculture, principally Norway and Japan. However, the United States helped keep the pressure off the CAP with its own spectacularly protectionist Farm Bill.

At the Hong Kong meeting, the EU again came under pressure to do more to liberalize its agriculture markets. The US likewise saw its cotton subsidies targeted by West African countries. The long-standing and extensive support of US cotton farmers offered the EU a chance to reduce the pressure on its own policies. Mandelson took the opportunity when, in a Hong Kong press conference, he drew attention to the particularly egregious support of cotton farming in the United States. Mandelson again drew attention to US agricultural support at the collapse of the Doha talks in July 2006. The omens surrounding the negotiations had not been good since Robert Portman moved from USTR to commerce secretary earlier in 2006. Given the inevitable disruption it would cause in the negotiating process, Portman's removal was viewed as a signal that the Bush administration placed much greater emphasis on domestic economic affairs. The mid-term congressional elections in November 2006 further dampened hopes that the president might be able to sell a Doha package to congress, as the Democrats succeeded in gaining control of both houses. Even if Democrats prove more accommodating than expected the politics of trade liberalization have become more difficult for pro-WTO forces. The narrowness of the Democrat victory in 2006 seemed likely to make both parties extremely sensitive to public opinion in advance of the 2008 presidential and congressional elections.

The EU, the US and disputes in the WTO

Whereas in the previous section the focus was particularly on the EU–US relationship in the overall WTO framework, here we focus on a more specific set of processes – those related to the settlement of disputes in the organization. Many commentators argued that the key development of the Uruguay Round was the creation of a robust dispute settlement mechanism that succeeds in being at once effective at settling disputes without trampling on national sovereignty (Jones 2006). From one perspective, the aim of the DSB was to tie down large trading members – particularly the United States – and make them subject to the same rules that bind other states. The system has been used regularly since its creation, with over 300 cases being heard (and many more settled by mutual agreement), though many commentators still note the resource asymmetries that affect the fair working of the system. Developing states still struggle to make truly effective use of the system. However, the high level of compliance with WTO decisions by all actors suggests that members do feel relatively obligated to respect the decisions of the panels.

How does the disputes process affect a major actor like the EU? The sugar dispute is an example of the WTO's effect on EU-level price support mechanisms. In middle 2004, a panel ruled that key elements of the EU's sugar regime were inconsistent with obligations under the Uruguay Round's Agreement on Agriculture (WTO 2004). The domestic support price, at over three times the prevailing world price, had the effect of subsidizing exports. Moreover, the EU had vastly exceeded its allowable export level of subsidized sugar, and was asked to withdraw the measure. The panel noted that developing states with preferential access to the European market could be adversely affected by this decision (ibid. p. 200) and so urged the Commission to take this into account when developing a new scheme. The Commission had, of course, anticipated this decision since the circulation of the panel report in June 2004 and one month later issued a paper outlining the key changes, all of which meant the withdrawal of key subsidies to sugar producers. In outlining its response the Commission noted:

> [I]t is clear that the objectives of the reform should be those of the of the recent overall approach to CAP reform. This, in turn, must be based on improved competitiveness, greater market orientation and a sustainable market balance consistent with the EU's commitments, with respect to third countries and international trade rules. (European Commission 2004b)

The EU none the less appealed against the decision, but in April 2005 lost again on most issues. Agriculture Commissioner Boel announced that the Commission would press for a greater liberalization of the market, though several developing states with preferential access to the EU sugar market were deeply disappointed with the decision. The importance of this case goes well beyond sugar, and reaches a key aspect of agricultural trade. Both the United

States and the European Union have seen agriculture becoming a 'normal' trade sector, where rules that have long applied to manufactured goods are applied to agricultural produce as well. The original disputes panel stressed that the main subsidies code applied in agriculture as well as any other sector, and press coverage of the appellate decision noted that the panel's reasoning followed previous subsidies cases.

In the United States too, various WTO decisions have reinforced the traditional scepticism of American policymakers towards multilateral institutions such as the WTO. Controversial issues like the Foreign Sales Corporation case illustrate these tensions: here, the EU referred a complaint about the workings of US domestic legislation, which gave privileges to multinational companies operating abroad, to the WTO, and the organization found in favour of the EU, allowing them in principle to impose up to $4 billion a year of penalties on US firms. Few American legislators would have imagined that the WTO might have the ability to pass judgement on US tax law. A key element of selling the Uruguay Round agreement to US legislators in the early 1990s was that the new organization represented no threat to American sovereignty (Pigman 2004). Likewise, US anti-dumping (AD) laws have been a favourite target of other WTO members. US legislators were concerned enough at the trajectory of early WTO cases for Congress to note in the preamble to the 2002 Trade Promotion Authority Act that:,

> Support for continued trade expansion requires that dispute settlement procedures under international trade agreements not add to or diminish the rights and obligations provided in such [WTO] agreements ... The recent pattern of decisions by dispute settlement panels of the WTO and the Appellate Body to impose obligations and restrictions on the use of antidumping, countervailing and safeguard measures by WTO members under the Antidumping Agreement the Agreement on Subsidies and Countervailing Measures, and the Agreement on Safeguards has raised concerns. (US Congress 2002)

Though the US succeeded in keeping anti-dumping off the Doha Development Agenda in 2001 – and likewise sought to avoid discussion during the negotiations – the disputes process has provided an avenue for placing pressure on the US to reform. The European Union, as well as Japan, Korea and other states, brought a series of cases to the WTO in respect of US anti-dumping policies (Lawton and McGuire 2005). Most of these cases related to minor methodological matters but one case related to a much more substantive issue. The Byrd Amendment allowed petitioning US firms to keep money raised by the US from successful AD investigations. The law outraged many trade partners, as it provided even greater incentives for US firms to file AD cases. In a rare case of non-compliance, the US refused to withdraw the Byrd Amendment, in spite of WTO panel rulings that it should do so; eventually, years of pressure led them grudgingly and gradually to withdraw it. However, the constant stream of AD cases has served to heighten the political salience of the issue, both within the US and among trade partners. Moreover, as other states such as China and India make greater use of the anti-dumping instruments as well as the disputes process, the efficacy of anti-dumping for major traders like the US (and the EU for that matter) has been called into question. There is considerable evidence that the overall use of AD is in gradual decline (Lawton and McGuire 2005; WTO 2006).

It is clear from this discussion that both the EU and the US have been affected by the growth of the dispute settlement process, and its increasing effectiveness. It is also clear that disputes specifically between the EU and the US have been central to the 'testing' of the process. Some of these EU–US cases, such as the foreign sales corporation (FSC) dispute, have involved potentially huge penalties for one party or the other; for the FSC case, the penalties would have fallen on the US, but in other cases, such as those involving the EU's banana regime, the Union has felt the weight of retaliation. There is a series of ongoing trade disputes between the two partners, but as noted earlier this is only to be expected in a highly interdependent and competitive relationship. What is more, none of the disputes has led to the breakdown either of EU–US relations or of the WTO process itself. As noted in Chapter 2, the idea of 'competitive cooperation', in which the parties compete as much over how to cooperate as over substantive issues, may help in understanding this situation.

Overview and conclusion

This chapter has reviewed key elements of the trade policy process in the EU and the US and has linked these to their relationship, especially in the context of the World Trade Organization. The key points in the argument have been:

- First, the EU – US trading relationship is both broad and deep; it is also underpinned by broadly similar conceptions about the role of markets and trade in promoting global economic growth and social development.
- Second, the extent of interdependence and integration between the EU and the US in trade creates inevitable frictions and disputes, but the key to understanding these lies in the ways they are managed and 'contained'.
- Third, the Doha Round may signal the end of the time when WTO rounds – and thus the development of the trade negotiating framework – hinged on the ability of Brussels and Washington to hammer out a deal. Both the EU and the US now operate as key actors, but the stage is more crowded as China, Brazil and India (to take a few examples) exercise more influence at the multilateral level.
- Fourth, the EU and the US are key participants in the management of trade disputes through the WTO, and their disputes often have major implications for the wider global trading system.
- Finally, both the EU and the US, to varying degrees, are ambivalent about the future development of the global trading system. The US has been most tempted to engage in bilateral or interregional trade agreements, but the EU has not been far behind.

This set of judgements has considerable bearing on the key themes in this book, since it seems to demonstrate in a sharp form the coexistence of competition and convergence between the EU and the US. It also demonstrates that the background against which the EU and the US conduct their relations is not static; rather, it is dynamic and often challenging, both to the partners individually and to the continuing dominance of their relationship.

Chapter 4

Money and the Macroeconomy

Although, as we have seen in Chapter 3, trade has formed the longest-standing and deepest area of interdependence between the EC/EU and the US, it has come to be rivalled by the transatlantic relationship in money and finance. For political economists, international finance is a key, perhaps *the* key, driver of the international economy. The liberalization of financial markets, combined with technologies that enable the virtually instantaneous trading, has allowed financial institutions to act globally. The power of investment banks, hedge funds and other investors to influence, indeed in some respects reorder, national economies seems almost limitless. Yet, this view can understate the importance of political management of the sector. The chairman of the Federal Reserve may earn vastly less than the managing partner of Goldman Sachs, but the former remains a powerful and influential figure in international finance, not least as he has access to the range of political actors and processes in the most important economy in the world. Moreover, as actors like China attain greater prominence in the international economy, their relative imperviousness to corporate interests underpins the importance of state-to-state relations for managing the world's money. Thus, while financial markets are indeed highly privatized, there remains an enduring management function at the political level, particularly among the big international economies: China, the US and the EU. In this regard, the European Union has used its experience with the Single Market Programme, and the resultant leverage as one of the world's largest economies, to become increasingly activist in the area of financial services regulation.

For most of the past fifty years, the US dollar was effectively a global currency: it remains the world's most popular reserve currency and important goods and commodities, from oil to aircraft, are denominated in dollars. US dollars remain the principal reserve currency for the world's central banks, though the euro is gaining ground rapidly. Whatever other risks US firms might run when operating internationally, they are far less exposed to one risk that other firms take for granted: currency risk. Prior to the euro, other European currencies were important international currencies, most notably the German mark. As such, this chapter will provide an overview of the important 'management' functions performed by monetary authorities across the Atlantic. Aside from day-to-day contact, more formal and important efforts occur from time to time. For example, in the 1980s, major European central banks joined Japan and US in managed intervention to realign the value of the US dollar. A similar effort was seen in September 2000, when central banks in Europe, Canada, Japan and the US intervened to prop up the euro, which had steadily lost value against the dollar throughout 2000. The euro had eroded in value against the US dollar because America's excellent economic performance at the time caused international investors to shift money out of Europe and into the United States, seeking better returns.

A key theme in this chapter is that the internal performance of the American and European economies has important implications for the international economy. As such, both actors are under immense international pressure to pursue responsible economic policies. However, what is good internationally may *not* be economically or politically wise internally. Moreover, this management function is made more complicated by the activities of Asian central banks and their economies. Years ago, it was possible for international monetary affairs to be governed by the Group of Three (G-3) of Germany, Japan and the United States. Now several Asian states, most notably China but also Korea and Taiwan, have accumulated significant international reserves as part of their economic strategy and so their policy choices must be factored in. As with other economic issue areas, the Euro-American dominance of the system is eroding, though not yet collapsed. International finance is entering an age of multipolarity, similar to that seen in the trade arena. The removal of national controls on the flow of international capital has been a key catalyst for the growth of a truly borderless international financial system. Global finance has in turn provided the means by which new economic powers such as China and Brazil facilitate economic development. These states now seek a place in the international governance structures commensurate with their new status (Ahearne and Eichengreen 2007).

The Evolving role of the Euro

In the relatively brief life of the euro – it has existed as a currency since 1 January 1999 with notes and coins circulating since 2002 – it has gone up and down wildly in terms of public and policymaker expectations as to its role in the European and international economies. Early views that it would rapidly challenge the dollar as the world's major reserve currency seemed well off the mark as it depreciated against the dollar in the first years of its existence. Attitudes have changed, however, as the Euro has both recovered its value against the dollar and is rapidly becoming the reserve currency of choice for central banks. By December 2006, less than eight years after its launch as a circulating currency, the Euro had eclipsed the dollar in terms of notes in circulation (Figure 4.1). The euro, as Becker notes, seems on the brink of doing what the neither the yen nor the deutschmark were able to do: challenge the dollar for the title of the world's currency (Becker 2007).

It is important in this context to remind ourselves of some of the background outlined in Chapter 1. Though monetary integration was considered as part of the negotiations for the Treaty of Rome, it was not at the forefront of states' collective vision of the Community. Rather, though it was appreciated that a common

Figure 4.1   Banknotes in circulation (in billions)

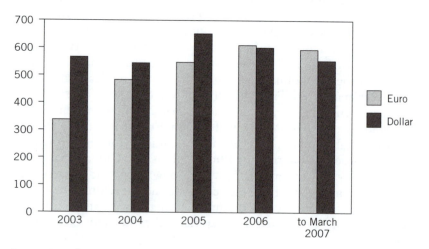

Source: Data from Becker (2007).

European currency would help in some respects, the Bretton Woods system rather seemed to obviate the need for greater European efforts in the area, since it established a broad framework for monetary discipline and stability. Moreover, with extensive welfare states to protect and nurture, EC members were reluctant to accept the loss of fiscal and monetary control that would clearly flow from a common currency (Tsoukalis 2000: 151). This thinking changed by the 1970s, as the Bretton Woods system crumbled. The realisation that the United States was content to see a world of managed but floating major currencies sharpened the debate about how European states could best cope with currency movements and their attendant consequences. Although the preference for a single currency was a strong one, and the decline and collapse of Bretton Woods seemed to offer every incentive, robust plans for the currency did not survive either internal EC wrangling or the economic storms of the early 1970s, including the first OPEC oil crisis in 1973.

As the German economy grew to become by some measure Europe's largest, the process of monetary integration became essentially a system where some (but not all) member state currencies were linked to the deutschmark in what was known as the 'snake'. The snake was essentially a pegged currency system where members agreed to assist each other in maintaining a given parity with the mark. The system was a rather 'mutilated snake' as countries dropped out altogether or merely opted for a looser peg (Tsoukalis 2000: 152). European countries, like other major economies, spent much of the 1970s coping with 'stagflation', the toxic mix of inflationary growth and rising unemployment. These were hardly the best of circumstances for states to make the leap of faith required of deeper monetary union. Gradually, however, economic problems produced dissatisfaction with Keynesian solutions; what was needed, it was increasingly argued, was tight monetary and fiscal discipline to defeat inflation and keep public sector spending from 'crowding out' private investment. These policies owed much to Germany's economic success, particularly its well-earned reputation for anti-inflationary monetary policy. Paradoxically however, these policies, which are central to the construction of the EMU project, owed something to the success of UK Prime Minister Margaret Thatcher. Thatcher was no friend of monetary union, yet it was her apparent success in changing the terms of economic debate during the early 1990s that helped pave the way – years later – for a new neo-liberal consensus necessary for the euro. Though British citizens and policymakers would not always agree, in monetary policy as in other areas, the EC would gradually adopt neoliberal economics (based on deregulation, a reduction of the state's role in the economy, and the control of monetary policy) and not corporatist welfare state policies as the basis for further integration (McNamara 2006).

Momentum for monetary union built during the 1980s by building on the Franco-German discussions catalysed by West German Chancellor Willy Brandt a few years earlier (Tsoukalis 2000: 153). The European Monetary System (EMS) maintained many of the features of previous managed currency systems, particularly the use of fixed, but adjustable, parity rates manifest in the Exchange Rate Mechanism (ERM). Throughout the 1980s, EC member states gradually joined in and by 1992 all the major European economies were in the managed exchange rate regime. The ERM, however, did not survive further international exchange rate turmoil in the early 1990s. Though technical aspects of the system were an improvement on the 1970s 'snake', the system still hinged on the willingness of Germany to take on the bulk of the adjustment costs of periodic intervention to defend a given parity. The system remained essentially a deutschmark peg. This would have been less of a problem had the EMS member states' economies continued their convergence; in the late 1980s and early 1990s there were indications of greater convergence in inflation rates, thus reducing the need for periodic interventions. However, countries lacking the highly competitive productivity of Germany struggled to maintain their performance, and market expectations of greater divergence in economic performance became self-fulfilling. German monetary authorities increasingly found themselves drawn into currency markets to defend the parities. By the mid-1990s, with Germany grappling with the economic and social effects of unification, the EMS passed quietly into history. Its successor was, however, already well advanced – and on this occasion the integration of the European monetary order would be irrevocable.

Problems with the operation of a *de facto* deutschmark standard in the EMS, as well as the strains and opportunities afforded by German unification, prompted another but more ambitious attempt to use monetary affairs to both macroeconomic management and political integration. The development of the Single Market Programme was the catalyst, for once the notion of an integrated European market was conceded it became easier to press the political case for harmonized monetary relations through a common currency. French desires to keep a united Germany securely within the European community dovetailed with an increasing German reluctance to keep shouldering the bulk of the costs of the managed EMS system. The 1989 Delors Report had provided the roadmap for Economic and Monetary Union, and the changed political circumstances of the 1990s, combined with widespread acceptance of greater economic liberalism, provided favourable circumstances. The currency, the euro, would be launched in two stages. In Stage One, the currency remained merely a unit of account, but was underpinned by greater capital movement liberalisation among member states and the irrevocable fixing of exchange rates. In Stage Two the new currency would circulate in member states and would be overseen by the European Central Bank (the ECB).

The last obstacle to Stage Two EMU was the vulnerability of Stage One to the same market speculations that had so damaged both the 'snake' and the EMS. Germany policymakers in particular wanted Stage One to be as tight as possible – and indeed any monetary discipline needed to be maintained if the currency was to have any chance of success. Hence the development of the Stability and Growth Pact (SGP), perhaps the most controversial of all EMU-related provisions as a necessary precondition for German acceptance of the mark's demise.

It can thus be seen that European monetary union had been a point of discussion for decades prior to the eventual appearance of the Euro in 1999. Equally, European monetary integration cannot be understood separately from the collapse of the Bretton Woods system. The economist Robert Mundell is often credited with the earliest articulation of the logic of a single currency as a desirable – indeed necessary – adjunct to the development of the single market. That said, single currencies require single monetary policies and imply uniform fiscal policies or at least closely coordinated ones. In the context of the late 1990s this raised the question of what European countries ought to participate. The theory behind optimum currency areas (OCAs) is that national economies, once they enter a single currency, give up domestic abilities to respond to external shocks via interest rates or budgetary policy (McNamara 2006). Thus, the 'optimum' currency area is one where national economies are not so divergent in their proclivity to experience external shocks. Many economists did not regard the Eurozone as an optimal currency area, as national economies remained sufficiently distinct so as to be asymmetrically vulnerable to external shocks (MacKinnon 2004).

Perhaps in tacit recognition that the Eurozone was not a natural currency area, considerable energy went into devising a mechanism for imparting monetary and fiscal discipline among Euro member countries. The development of this discipline resulted in the Stability and Growth Pact (SGP), agreed as a necessary condition for a successful single currency. Though the SGP was designed to buy credibility for the single currency in the international market, its existence has always proven controversial, with some critics regarding it as unnecessary and some more trenchant observers arguing that it does actual damage to European economies. A key issue internationally is whether the SGP was in fact impairing the ability of the EU to take on a leadership and managerial role in the international economy. The overly tight economic policies it seemed to require (based on the strict control of inflation via both the ECB's interest rate policies and national budgetary discipline) made it difficult for European economies to become consumers of last resort in the same manner as Americans – put simply, national governments have given up some of their ability to expand their economies through fiscal and monetary policies. Criticisms of the SGP's structure appeared frequently in the early 2000s, and clustered around the deflationary bias the various rules impart into member states' fiscal policies. The SGP makes it difficult to implement countercyclical fiscal policy (that is, increased government spending) in response to economic slowdowns. The pact doesn't simply impede deliberate countercyclical policies, but also automatic responses; government spending tends to rise automatically in a slow-growth environment as, for example, laid-off workers claim unemployment benefit (Baily and Kirkegaard 2004: 257).

Germany was the strongest advocate of the pact when the issue was first raised in the 1990s, and succeeded in getting its preferences for the monetary regime approved at the European Council meeting in 1997 (Baily and Kirkegaard 2005: 249). The Exchange Rate Mechanism (ERM) that had governed European monetary affairs since the 1980s placed particular responsibilities on Germany as the 'anchor' economy of the European Community. This was because the ERM was essentially a flexible, fixed-exchange-rate regime with the deutschmark as the key currency.

Thus, while other members were obliged to defend their currency's parity vis-à-vis the mark, it was the case that Germany – like the US in the Bretton Woods system – was required to behave in such a way as not to imperil the parity rate. Moreover the Bundesbank itself would be expected to intervene to assist other currencies against speculative attacks. German monetary leadership was an immense source of pride and was 'cherished as a common good of paramount significance' (Muller 2005: 142).

None the less, German monetary policy was subject to a variety of criticisms, even during the years of the German economic miracle. Germany was accused of not appreciating the role it had in helping govern the international political economy and in 'free-riding' on American economic policy. Germany pegged its currency at an undervalued rate against the US dollar until the mid-1970s, helping maintain the export competitiveness of its firms (Eichengreen 2004: 10). The Bundesbank enjoyed a fabled reputation for independence from government interference, though this related mainly to the operational aspects of monetary policy, not the policy direction. For the latter, the German government was more influential than often appreciated (Duckenfield 1999).

Perception of the euro has been transformed in the years since it was launched. When it was first launched in 1999, there were high expectations that the euro would quickly rival the US dollar as the preferred instrument for international financial transactions (Bergsten 2005) However, the first two years of the euro's existence looked to make a mockery of such claims, as the currency steadily depreciated against the dollar (Cohen 2003). The proximate cause of this was the massive inflows of money attracted to the US in the earliest years of the new millennium, as investors rushed to get a piece of the American productivity miracle. By contrast, the Eurozone's productivity growth remained sluggish and investors were unimpressed by the region's prospects. In 2001, the euro had fallen so much that central bank intervention was used to stabilize its rate against the dollar and other major currencies. The decision in 2003 to suspend a key element of the Stability and Growth Pact, so as to spare France and Germany the political costs of reigning in excessive deficits, added to the pessimism about the euro (LeBlond 2006). The euro's performance appeared to affirm the views of numerous sceptics of the project, who had argued against it as a flawed vision grounded more in politics than in economic sense. At least in the US this led to something of a neglect of the implications of the euro for the dollar. As Posen observed, 'Why think about the implications of a currency that is deemed at best doomed to second-tier status and at worst a cause of economic weakness in the issuing area?' (2005: 2).

Move forward to today, and the perception has been transformed. The euro has appreciated steadily against the dollar, and has become much more widely used in international reserves. Both factors reflect the onset of the long-awaited depreciation of the US dollar in response to chronic current account deficits. However, the upturn in the Eurozone economies, particularly Germany, had also convinced international investors that the EU was again a place to put capital. In mid-2005 there seemed a real possibility that the Euro could collapse; the SGP was coming in for intense criticism in both media and academic circles. The backdrop for this crisis was the French and Dutch referenda on the proposed European constitution. Though the French result was more dramatic, in both countries some of the blame for the loss of the vote was laid at the euro's door. Dutch voters bitterly criticized the price rises associated with the replacement of the guilder with the euro three years before while French voters feared the fiscal austerity measures implied by the pact's limits on government debt and borrowing. Yet, though the pact had been watered down by both France and Germany in 2004, the main outline of the agreement was known when the single-currency project was agreed. What had gone wrong?

The ECB's central objective was price stability – not the promotion of economic growth (though in theory the two are complementary). The bank is required to keep Eurozone inflation below 1.5 per cent: it has no other formal policy objective. The concern for price stability made sense from a historical perspective; German policymakers are famously fearful of a repeat of the hyperinflation of the 1920s. Moreover, a tight inflation target was felt necessary as an insurance policy against the admission of member states such as Greece with reputations for fiscal laxity. Yet the concern with price stability did have something of 'fighting the last war' about it. As early as the mid-1990s, some economists were pronouncing the death of inflation as the main economic enemy facing developed states. The explanation was that in an increasingly globalized and liberalized world, fierce competition from low-cost developing states would keep wages down. In respect of raw materials, the 'death of distance' heralded by the internet made prices for intermediate goods much more transparent, with the happy result again of holding these prices down. As European economies continued to stagnate in the years after the euro's introduction, criticism grew that the ECB simply did not appreciate the deflationary effect of its high-interest-rate policy.

A clear riposte to this criticism is that the ECB's target was designed to force structural change in European economies. In the absence of an ability to devalue the currency to maintain competitiveness, countries would be forced to make changes in the structure of the economy. Social safety nets that did not encourage the unemployed to seek work, but rather to remain long-term unemployed, had to be changed. Productivity would have to improve once the monetary instrument was taken out of national hands.

By 2005, three economies in particular were causing concern: France, Germany and Italy. The Italian government complained loudly about the euro's impact in the aftermath of the failed constitutional summit in June 2005. One minister called for Italy to withdraw from the euro, a call that Prime Minister Berlusconi appeared to sympathize with. Italian economic performance had indeed been shocking since the advent of the euro. Though most of Europe's economies were growing slowly, they were at least expanding. Not so Italy, which saw economic growth fall in 2004. Italian industrial sectors, such as textiles and footwear, saw their competitive position within the European Union eroded dramatically, thanks mainly to increased competition from Chinese producers. Italian producers, along with those in Iberia, were key to the imposition of textile safeguards in 2005, though the high-end Italian fashion producers, aware of the massive emerging middle class in China, were less supportive (Lawton and McGuire 2005). Italian industry had long been based on two pillars: large firms with close ties to the state, and smaller, family-run or specialist firms lacking in production scale and product scope.

Concern about the growth of the Eurozone countries had subsided somewhat in late 2006, as a series of upbeat economic forecasts suggested that the worst was behind the continental economies. Part of the explanation for these more optimistic forecasts was economic growth elsewhere in the world, most notably Asia but also in the Middle East. Germany's exports to China soared, as the booming Chinese market offered ever greater opportunities for high-quality German goods, including cars, consumer goods, machinery and other intermediate manufactured goods.

Though export markets undoubtedly helped, in the case of Germany, painful structural reforms – including relocation of plants to central Europe and the negotiation of wage concessions from German unions – were also responsible for the revival. The growth of the Middle East on the back of a rising oil price also benefited European producers. Middle-Eastern states began to shift reserve assets out of US dollars and into euros, reflecting the growing economic ties between the regions: there was even specu-lation that several Middle-Eastern states would abandon their longstanding practice of linking regional currencies to the dollar in favour of a trade weighted peg in which the Euro would be a sig-nificant component (ECB 2005).

The US economy: living on borrowed money?

As outlined in Chapter 1, during the formative years of the European Communities, the US dollar had provided a dominant currency against which others might be fixed. From an early stage, though, the dollar had begun to show signs of weakness, culmi-nating in the 'Nixon Shock' of August 1971, through which the US authorities effectively rewrote the rules of the Bretton Woods system. From the mid-1970s onwards, the system of fixed exchange rates gave way to floating or 'managed' exchange rates, and the dollar was notable for its relative instability. This meant that US interest rates also had to fluctuate in order to finance US investment and government expenditure, with consequent effects for the international monetary system. By the late 1980s, as EC member states began to plan for the euro, a certain amount of management had returned to the international arena, but the end of the cold war and associated economic changes meant that once again there was pressure on both exchange rates and national eco-nomic policy management.

Beginning in the early 1990s, the US economy began to expand at a spectacular rate, well above the accepted trend rate for a mature economy of about 2 to 2.5 per cent. Millions of jobs were created and US firms enjoyed remarkable gains in productivity. The productivity performance was one of the signal characteristics of the decade following the 1992 recession. There is a vibrant debate in both academic and policymaking circles over the exact extent of this above-trend growth in productivity. For some the IT revolution has indeed lifted productivity throughout the economy, not least by increasing price transparency via auctions and allowing much tighter control of supply chains. Other analysts doubt this, and point out that most of the observable productivity growth is contained within the IT sector (Gordon 2003).

The growth of the US economy in the 1990s had important implications for the transatlantic relationship. First, the explosion of consumer spending in the US, buoyed by sky-high stock markets, saw an appreciation of the dollar as foreign direct investment poured into America as firms sought returns that could not be gained in the 'sclerotic' Eurozone. The resulting slump in the value of the euro was not merely a symbolic blow to European pride: it also resulted in higher real interest rates in the Eurozone as the ECB sought to attract money into the continental European economies. The concern was not merely perception; if Europe was not an attractive place to invest, it was only a matter of time before European multinationals began to desert to locations with better prospects. This concern about Europe's economic attractiveness was a key driver for the Lisbon Agenda discussed in Chapter 5.

George W. Bush came to the presidency just as this economic miracle was running out. Though the expansion was coming to an end of its own accord, the catastrophe of 11 September 2001 also played its part. In the weeks after that event, US airlines went bankrupt and manufacturers ran up huge losses as the enhanced security arrangements delayed shipments and added costs. Aside from terrorism, economic factors also played a role. The internet bubble burst amid concerns that these 'new economy' companies were hopelessly overvalued. Enron was merely the most prominent of a string of episodes of corporate fraud and misbehaviour. Buffeted by adverse economic and political conditions, the Federal Reserve cut interest rates aggressively, seeking to restart economic activity. Now that US interest rates were so low, international investors began to rethink their exposure to the US market. By early 2003 the US dollar was in decline against the currencies of two of its major trading partners, Canada and the Eurozone.

President Bush provided his own solution to the recession of the mid-2000s: tax cuts. Politically controversial, Bush's tax cut package sought to reassure frightened investors with generous treatment of investment income. Economists argued that if an economic stimulus was needed, it ought to appear in the form of more broadly applicable tax cuts or even rebates, which are more likely to be spent. President Bush and the Republican-controlled Congress passed tax cuts with an estimated cumulative value of $2 trillion over the ten years from 2001–10 (Leiserson and Rohaly 2006). The US budget deficit, which had disappeared under President Clinton, re-emerged and was heading towards $300 billion as the tax cuts, slower economic growth and increased US military commitments all took their toll on the fiscal health (Figure 4.2).

American economic growth during the recovery from the dotcom bubble displayed an element of continuity and other discontinuities from earlier periods. The continuity was seen in the persistent US deficit in merchandise trade, which resulted in a significantly deteriorating US current account (Figure 4.3). By late 2006, the current account was in deficit by an unprecedented $800 billion – or about 8 per cent of GDP. Current account deficits are financed by the willingness of foreign sources of capital to 'lend' the US money in the form of the purchase of US debt securities (bonds) or assets. The US had long confounded expectations about a correction in its current account: the widely expected depreciation did not seem to be happening. As long as the US economy performed well enough to attract capital, the deficit could be financed. Moreover, exporting countries like China helped with this process though the purchase of US treasury bonds, thus keeping US interest rates lower than they otherwise would have been.

However, by 2006 the US economy began to show sufficient weakness for the depreciation in the dollar, which had begun in 2003, to gather pace. Several factors contributed to economic

Figure 4.2   US budget deficit

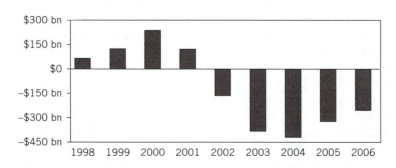

Source: Congressional Budget Office, *The Budget and Economic Outlook: An Update*, August 2007, www.cbo.gov, accessed 15 September 2007.

Figure 4.3   US balance of trade as a percentage of GDP

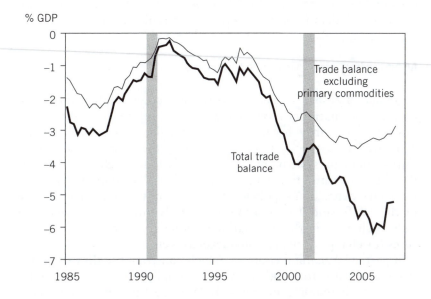

Source: Congressional Budget Office, *The Budget and Economic Outlook: An Update*, August 2007, p. 28, www.cbo.gov, accessed 15 September 2007.

weakness. A major factor was the rise of inflation, due largely to higher energy prices (Federal Reserve 2006). Higher oil prices damaged consumer confidence and added to manufacturing costs. Another factor was the stalling of the US housing market; rising house prices had underpinned consumer confidence and this willingness to spend was shaken with the realization that house equity growth was slowing. Finally, the US is in competition for capital, and in 2006 more and more speculative money was flowing elsewhere, including South-East Asia, where the sheer volume of flows unnerved the Thai central bank enough to (briefly) impose capital controls. More important, however, was the clear indication that international investors were increasingly reluctant to hold the overwhelming bulk of their cash in dollars. As we noted above, demand for euros increased on the back of this trend.

In sum, by early 2007 the Eurozone was undergoing a tentative recovery, led most notably by Germany. The US had slowed dramatically under the weight of debt – both government and consumer. Both Europe and America were more reliant on Asia than ever; Asian consumers helped European exports, while Asian purchases of US debt underpinned the US current account.

Managing the global economy

In an age of global finance, it has become commonplace for people to view international monetary affairs as an area of light regulation. This is partly because, indeed, regulation has been relaxed compared with twenty years ago. During the early decades of the Euro-American system, monetary regulation sought to constrain the ability of states to engage in competitive devaluation or reckless monetary expansion – policies implicated in the economic collapse of the 1920s and 1930s. From the 1970s onwards, however, the radical changes in the international monetary system created pressures for change at the national level as well.

In particular, capital controls, which constrain the flow of money from one state to another, were gradually removed during the 1970s in all major economies. Related to this, major currencies moved away from rigid fixed currencies toward managed float systems of economic governance. Technology also played a role: the explosion of private financial flows was made possible not merely by capital control removal but also by the development of computerized trading systems and telecommunications infrastructures that facilitated this growth. New products were also developed. Private finance has proved very adept at developing new financial products in response to regulatory constraints – with the eurodollar market being an excellent example (Walter 1993). Deregulation, if anything, accelerated this trend for the development of financial products – such as derivatives – that can be customised to client requirements. In the City of London, Europe's financial centre, daily currency trading is worth billions of dollars: far larger in money terms than central bank deposits. Private investors, not merely investment bank traders but also pension and hedge fund managers – who operate in foreign exchange markets as well as international debt and equity markets – are increasingly influential in determining medium-term exchange rates (Gehrig and Menhkoff 2005).

But any notion of international finance as a regulation-free zone is entirely illusory: private actors have an interest in a robust (that is not the same thing as heavy-handed) regime of cooperation. Both the United States and the European Union thus play a key role in the governance of the international financial system. This management function is usually conceived of as the management of exchange rates as a policy tool to react to economic shocks and government policies. In August 2007, both European and American central banks played the role of 'banker of last resort', pouring money into volatile markets that threatened to seize up as the crisis in the American housing market scared investors off all kinds of debt instruments. While it is true that this emergency market making is an important function, international finance is subject to a wide range of private as well as government structures and institutions (Scholte 2002). For example, the International Organization of Securities Commissions (IOSCO), which has an important role to play in the development of international securities regulations, draws it members from both government regulatory bodies and banks and other financial institutions (IOSCO 2007).

The EU–US relationship here, as in other spheres, cannot be grasped by merely examining the interactions of top policymakers conducting economic summitry. Rather, high politics intersects regularly with daily meetings among private and public sector technical experts across a range of financial issues. However, a clear evolution in the relationship is the relative decline of political considerations as important variables in monetary relations. The relationship remains extremely important, yet is now more characterized by 'technical' interactions on exchange rates in support of macroeconomic stability. Arguably, the most 'politicized' monetary relationship the United States now has is with China, not the European Union. The export-led growth strategy China is employing is underpinned by a dollar peg system created in 1994, with the yuan trading at 8.3 to the dollar (Funke and Rahn 2005: 466). China's dollar peg has attracted enormous criticism, particularly in Washington. Indeed, EU–US trade disputes pale in terms of the opprobrium generated. Keeping the yuan artificially low allows Chinese firms to undercut American firms in sectors like textiles and apparel, furniture and intermediate manufacturing. The US imposed quotas on Chinese textile imports in early 2005 and threatened more action unless China moved to curb exports that had increased the Chinese share of US clothing sales by 500 per cent. In May 2005 China imposed a new export tax on its firms in an effort to head off more controversy. That did not stem the flow of protectionist rhetoric from Congress, however, which continued to generate a series of legislative proposals designed to counteract allegedly unfair Chinese trade practices (Scheve and Slaughter 2007)

There are of course other reasons for worrying about the Chinese peg. China recycles its export earnings to buy US treasury bonds, and increasingly equities. In doing so, it accumulates US dollar balances that help keep the yuan peg, but the policy has two consequences, one domestic and the other foreign. When the Chinese government chooses to recycle export earnings, it penalizes the domestic economy. Firms have less money to invest in new plant and employees, while consumers have less money to spend on themselves. It is not clear whether Chinese consumers will tire of waiting for export success to manifest itself in higher purchasing power for the mass, not just a lucky few. US and European firms with investments in China are, to a much greater degree than Asian investors, concentrated in domestic sectors such as automobiles (Lardy 2005). These investors too are adversely affected by a policy that depresses domestic demand. Export-led growth also starves government of funds to investment in infrastructure. The other consequence is foreign. China's willingness to buy US bonds and assets allows the US to continue to live beyond its means. By 2005, there was immense concern that this imbalance was not sustainable. By the middle of 2006, the dollar was sliding on international markets amid concerns that China was working to slow its overheated economy, with consequences for the ability of the US to finance its current account deficit via Chinese purchases of US debt.

These events happen against the backdrop of the declining influence of the United States in international finance. London is rapidly becoming the financial centre of the world, with New York remaining dominant – for now – in the issuing of initial public offerings. The decline of New York was blamed on various factors, both international and domestic. As noted above, it was inevitable that the dominance of the US would erode as the centre of global economic growth shifted to Asia. Hong Kong and Shanghai have emerged (or re-emerged in the former's case) as key financial centres. The two Chinese exchanges were, unsurprisingly, the place where large Chinese firms floated their shares. By the end of 2006 Hong Kong was emerging as one of the three main exchanges for flotations, thanks largely to the initial public offerings of 'red-chip companies': major mainland Chinese firms such as the Industrial and Commercial Bank of China (ICBC)(Hong Kong Stock Exchange 2007). Domestically, new audit regulations embodied in the Sarbanes–Oxley Act of 2002, introduced in the wake of several corporate scandals, were to blame for the decline of American dominance. This is because of the allegedly onerous compliance and governance procedures imposed by Sarbanes–Oxley. Faced with these costs, it is suggested that firms simply looked elsewhere for their capital.

Competition and convergence in financial regulation

In much the same way that the dollar was the world's currency for most of the past 50 years, so too American financial regulation was regarded as the *de facto* standard for a swathe of banking, insurance and related sectors. Even though many other states did not formally adopt, for example, American rules on accounting or corporate governance, firms with any stake in the US market would have to adopt those standards if they wished to tap the world's deepest, most liquid and most innovative capital market. America's dominance of the world economy was reflected in its dominance of the regulatory agenda. This is changing, with European standards gaining international acceptance.

The European Union is using the convergence dynamic of its Single Market Programme to set the regulatory agenda for a variety of operations in the financial services industry. Internal Market Commissioner Charlie McCreevy noted when speaking about a European reform package for the insurance industry that, 'Our aim is to establish a modern, innovative and liberalizing regime, based on sound economic principles. I believe that Europe now has a real chance to set the global standard' (McCreevy 2007). The EU's efforts in financial services reflect a complex mix of internal politics and external events. The Lisbon Agenda has provided a rationale for the pursuit of wide-ranging harmonization and liberalization of financial services regulation within Europe. Experience of the single market for goods helps this process. Equally, however, American concerns about corporate governance in the wake of scandals manifested themselves as increased regulatory burdens and political risk for firms operating in the US. This mix produced a situation where Europe appeared a more conducive environment for financial services.

As with insurance, so too with accountancy. In the area of accounting standards in 2005 the EU adopted a version of International Accounting Standards (IASs) from the London-based International Accounting Standards Board (IASB) for application to all member states. This use of the International Financial Reporting Standards (IFRS) obviated the need for firms to comply with two sets of accounting standards: their national system and the EU-level regime. The reverberations of this policy were seen around the world as other nations came to the view that, given the significance of the EU for their firms' operations, the *de facto* adoption of IASB regulations would simplify matters by reducing the need to prepare sets of accounts to two standards (Ashbaugh 2001). The US operates its own accounting system, the Generally Agreed Accounting Principles (GAAP), but, with more and more international firms (and their states) adopting the IFRS, American policymakers and accounting experts opened discussions about how to harmonize IFRS and GAAP. In April 2007 the US Securities and Exchange Commission allowed companies filing accounts in the US to choose which standard they adopted (GAAP 2007). The cumulative effect of these developments has been to galvanize international acceptance of IAS (Ding et.al, 2007).

From Bretton Woods to Plaza and beyond

Co-ordination of monetary policies has been a feature of the Euro-Atlantic system for decades, indeed longer if one counts the gold standard period. European and American monetary policies locked themselves tightly together in the Bretton Woods system, where the US dollar linked directly to gold while sterling, the franc and the deutschemark maintained their respective parities to the US dollar.

The demise of the Bretton Woods system did not mean the end of Euro-American cooperation and coordination on monetary policy; it meant the end of a formal, pegged currency system. Continued cooperation was necessary, as serious currency misalignments had such considerable consequences for national economies that the neglect of currency levels was neither economically nor politically responsible. What evolved was a system of constant consultation among central bankers and finance ministers, augmented at times by formal intervention in the foreign exchange markets to correct imbalances. Posen (2005) notes that formal intervention in the foreign exchange markets wasn't always necessary: sometimes a statement of intent by key policymakers was enough. He argues that one important example of this was the managed decline in the value of the dollar in the late 1980s. The 1985 Plaza Accord helped catalyse a continued decline of the dollar and appreciation of, most notably, the Japanese yen and in so doing eased protectionist pressures that had been building in the US congress. Yet, as Posen notes, this achievement did not rest on aggressive or even substantial exchange market intervention by central banks, but rather a credible commitment among policymakers. When the dollar's decline continued, however, the Louvre Accord of 1987 to stem this decline did rely on formal intervention (Posen 2005: 57). Formal exchange rate intervention was used again in 2001, with the euro's dramatic decline against the dollar again raising the possibility of severe economic disruption. However, in a world where billions of dollars are traded every day in the London money market, formal central bank intervention cannot be the main policy tool for addressing economic problems or coordinating policies. To the extent that currency misalignments reflect judgements about the policies governments pursue, the most viable way to maintain currency stability is to follow viable macroeconomic policies at home. That said, were the situation to call for it the EU and the US would likely be required to intervene in a coordinated manner, just as with the Plaza and Louvre Accords. The growth of China – particularly the explosive growth of its currency reserves – kept this matter in the public policy spotlight.

The growing influence of China

For most of the post-World-War II period, the dollar reigned supreme in international currency markets. It was the most widely circulated currency and by far the most widely held by foreign central banks. The emergence of the euro was thought by many to presage a move toward a twin set of major currencies with both the dollar and the euro becoming truly global currencies (Bergsten 2005). Such thoughts gained weight in the early 2000s, as more and more central banks increased their reserve holdings of euros, partly in response to fears that US indebtedness was at unsustainable levels. An ECB report noted that something over 30 central banks had increased the Euro component of their reserves, while only a fraction had increased their dollar exposure (Papaioannou *et al.* 2006). As already noted, China's emergence as an economic power has been met with a mixture of excitement and trepidation in Washington and the EU. Major multinational companies such as Boeing had long pressed for normalized trade relations between Washington and Beijing and years of lobbying finally paid dividends in 2000 when the US Congress granted China permanent, normal trade relations. This unilateral concession paved the way for a much more ambitious but equally long-cherished Chinese goal: membership of the World Trade Organization (WTO). American business was strongly supportive of Chinese accession to the World Trade Organization in 2001, seeing China as a truly gigantic market of 1.2 billion consumers. Not surprisingly, the EU was also strongly in support of it, stressing not only the market opportunities but also the disciplines that would be exerted on China as a result.

In early 2006, the US trade deficit grew to 6.5 per cent of GNP (Bergsten 2007). This deficit was financed by the willingness of foreigners to hold US assets – mainly treasury bonds – but also equities. The purchase of US corporate assets is of course manifest in the FDI figures, which held up well in the early part of the new millennium. In the first decade of the new millennium, the dollar – yuan relationship had eclipsed the euro–dollar relationship as the key political macroeconomic issue, though the euro remained important as an international reserve currency.

China has rapidly emerged as the 'Japan' of the new millennium as far as the United States is concerned, in that it has become the key target of accusations of unfair trade practice. Much of the criticism revolves around China's managed currency peg, which kept the Chinese currency stable at about 8:1 against the dollar. In 2005, there was a slight revaluation but it was widely regarded as a political ploy to buy off American politicians. In 2005, China's international reserves stood at $1 trillion – an amount far in excess of any requirement for maintaining the currency's value in international markets. Moreover, the Chinese central bank intervened regularly to keep the yuan at its parity with the American dollar. One estimate offered to US policymakers was that China was spending $45 billion per quarter in 2007 to keep its currency from appreciating against the dollar (Bergsten 2007).

Throughout 2004–6 Congressional scrutiny of China's growing economic strength grew. In somewhat parallel fashion, the EU pursued a much more active 'China strategy' after 2000, seeing China as a 'strategic partner' and making persistent attempts to develop new forms of economic as well as political dialogue with Beijing. But it appeared that the euro did not give the EU as much clout in pursuing currency readjustment as the dollar did the Americans; although the Chinese held increasing amounts of their currency reserves in the euro, this did not make them susceptible to pressure from Brussels or Frankfurt. Europe's trade deficit with China was about 60 per cent the size of the United States deficit in 2006 (Wan 2007). Moreover, exports of European luxury goods, from German cars to French and Italian designer goods, meant that Europe's trade deficit with China was not as large, nor as political contentious, as America's.

That said, the sheer weight of the euro in the international economy by 2006 suggested that Europe would play a key role in any new efforts to manage currencies and monetary policies. Fred Bergsten has suggested that a G-2 comprised of the European Union and the US would have to be created to take responsibility for managing potentially volatile currency markets (2005). However, he acknowledged that the institutional arrangements for monetary policy in the EU remain incomplete. These arrangements, where national governments, the Commission and other stake-holders interact with the ECB, are indeed complex, not least because membership of the euro is not coterminus with EU membership. That said, there is an argument that the *modus operandi* of the Eurozone has been to adopt the German practice of intervention: operational independence for the ECB within a negotiated political framework (Henning 2006). Whether this arrangement would survive if the Eurozone was asked to make significant currency interventions as part of a global management role is open to question.

Overview and conclusion

International finance is at once one of the least-regulated economic sectors, and one of the most politicized. The US and the EU have both benefited from the dramatic explosion of international capital mobility that has developed in the past forty years. However, both actors have a significant management function to play, not least because both the dollar and the euro are key international currencies for a range of financial activities. Moreover, American and, latterly, European regulations for international finance have a profound effect on other states. European efforts to globalize EU standards in the financial world do present a challenge to the United States, yet EU efforts are liberalising and as such very much reflect the Euro-American preference for open markets. The challenge, in other words, is one of process, not underlying philosophy. As with other policy areas, EU–US influence in shaping the structure of international system is strong, yet both actors now confront increasingly influential players. China is the most obvious candidate here, as its dramatic economic growth and exchange rate policy have created both opportunities and tensions for Europe and America. In this chapter, we have outlined the key developments in monetary and macroeconomic relations between the EU and the US. The following central points have emerged:

- First, because of their dominant positions in the international economy, the domestic monetary and fiscal policies of these actors assume international importance. Developments in the euro and the dollar since the end of the cold war have given added weight to this point.
- Second, the bilateral relationship cannot be understood as comprising only the interactions of top economic policymakers. In this sphere, the private sector has a key role to play in broader issues of economic governance. For example, the accounting standards adopted by the European Union, the IFRS, were developed by an international organization of accountancy professionals, the International Accounting Standards Board.
- Third, there has been a tension in the relationship between the demands of domestic economic management and those of international currency stability. In the case of the Euro, this has a 'two-level' aspect, reflecting tensions between Eurozone member state priorities and those of the ECB; in the case of the US, there has been a continuing tension between the need for the US to maintain a high level of domestic consumption and the resulting need to borrow large amounts of other people's money.
- Fourth, both the EU and the US have been affected by the rise of China, which has placed demands on their trade and investment policies, and which has demanded adjustment. The EU–US relationship is no longer as central as it was to the global economy, although it would be wise not to understate its continuing significance.

Chapter 5

Investment and Competition policy

Chapters 3 and 4 have dealt with two of the 'classic' issues of inter-national political economy – trade and money. In each case, we have seen that the development of policy and institutions in the EU has come into contact – or collision – with policies and institutions in the US. Thanks to the development both of trade and of the euro, the EU constitutes the US's largest partner and/or rival in the world arena, and not unexpectedly this has given rise to disputes and sometimes confrontations. What we have also seen, though, is that there have arisen practices of cooperation and areas of common interest, both within EU–US relations and between the two and the rest of the world. With this chapter we move into a different area, one now especially prominent with the development of increased economic interpenetration and which involves the domestic regulatory structures of both the EU and the US. The impact of processes of globalization, leading to the intensification of interconnectedness between societies, especially in the industrial world, creates new issues of management and of institutional development, and this is one of our key concerns here.

As we saw in Chapter 3, the trade liberalization of the past several decades has allowed American and European firms consid-erable access to each other's markets and to those in third coun-tries. The lowering of trade barriers, however, cannot necessarily achieve effective market contestability; it can still be the case that a market free of 'at the border' barriers can severely handicap foreign firms thanks to domestic regulations and practices. Dealing with these problems requires effective competition policy. An addi-tional layer of complexity has arisen thanks to the vast increase in international investment flows, manifest among other ways in the increase in international mergers and acquisitions. This process has now made the international coordination of competition policies – and investment regulations where they exist – an object of European and American interest. However, unlike traditional trade barriers, investment and competition policies are deeply rooted in domestic political economy and national institutions which themselves embody decades – centuries even – of norms, traditions and practices. In many countries, investment and competition policy regulation is weak, and neither is it a priority for poorer countries.

Europe and America are the world's most important investors and bankers and as such occupy a key place in the international political economy. In 2006, the EU's twenty-five member states attracted almost half of the world's inflows of foreign direct investment, worth $422 billion (UNCTAD 2006). The United States, along with the UK, has been the leading outward investor in recent years; the United States is also a key recipient of inward foreign direct investment (FDI), vying with China as the world's favourite place to invest. The dramatic growth of FDI reflects the continuing importance of location as an economic driver (UNCTAD 2006). FDI used to be thought of as an alternative to trade: where trade barriers were high, firms would invest directly. Though this is historically true, in recent years trade liberalization has been accompanied by an explosion in foreign investment. This is because trade liberalization has been about not just removal of tariffs but also the reduction of non-tariff barriers such as discriminatory government procurement policies. Trade liberalization thus makes foreign markets more open and, other things being equal, contestable. Investing in preference to trade shows the enduring importance of location for firms; having a presence on the ground helps facilitate business in ways that arm's-length trade cannot.

The European Union and the United States have long been significant, perhaps the most important, investors in each other's economy. As can be seen from Figure 5.1, North America (essentially the US, as Canadian investment is minor) accounts for the largest share of inward investment to the EU. FDI data can be 'lumpy' owing to the influence of a small number of large investments, so year-to-year activity is not as useful as data over a five-to-ten-year span. Using this approach, it becomes clear that while Europe and America each remain the major investor for the other's economy, the geographic spread of investment is increasingly taking account of the growth of India, China and South America.There is some evidence that Europe and America are gradually becoming less important to each other as locations for investment (see Figures 5.2 and 5.3) [I]n 2004 the EU had a net disinvestment in the US, and a clear shift in European FDI patterns

Figure 5.1 European outward investment: EU-25 FDI outward stocks by main destination (end-2003)

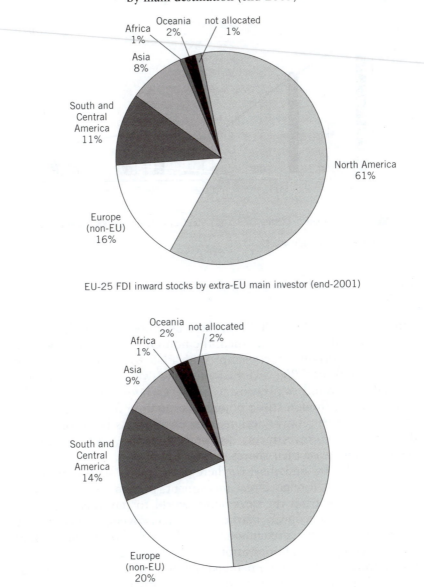

EU-25 FDI inward stocks by extra-EU main investor (end-2001)

EU-25 FDI inward stocks by extra-EU main investor (end-2004)

Source: Eurostat, *European Union Foreign Direct Investment Yearbooks, 2001–2005*, p. 13.

Figure 5.2   Patterns of European investment: outward FDI by main partner, 2000–4 (EU-25 for 2001–4, EU-15 for 2000)

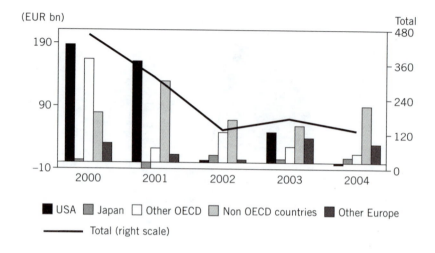

Source: *Eurostat FDI Yearbook 2006.*

could be discerned. 'Until 2001, the most important destination of EU FDI was the USA. Since then, the non-OECD countries became the most important target group. With EUR 87 billion, more than three-quarters of 2004 EU FDI outflows were directed towards non-OECD countries' (Eurostat FDI Yearbook 2006: 24). The United States, though still a popular destination for foreign investment, has seen a relative decline in its positions as both source and destination for investment, as both the EU and developing economies increase their shares (UNCTAD 2006).

In both the US and the EU, there is increased sensitivity about certain types of foreign direct investment, principally the growing ability of firms from the developing world to buy their way into American and European markets. The controversies surrounding the purchase of the Luxembourg-based Arcelor by India's Mittal Steel, or congressional opposition to the Chinese National Offshore Oil Company's (CNOOC) planned purchase of Unocal are illustrative. China's rapid economic expansion is now manifesting itself as outward foreign direct investment, some of which has touched national sensitivities. Much of this investment has been concentrated in commodities and natural resources, as China seeks raw

Figure 5.3   Patterns of European investment in the European Union: inward FDI by main partner, 2000–4 (EU-25 for 2001–4, EU-15 for 2000)

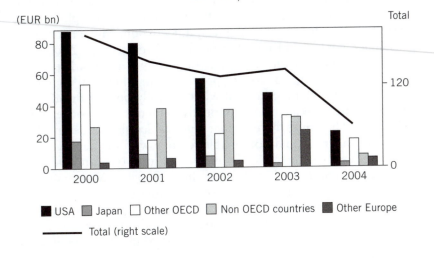

USA   Japan   Other OECD   Non OECD countries   Other Europe

Total (right scale)

Source: Eurostat FDI Yearbook 2006.

materials to feed dramatic economic growth. In the United States, a lively debate has broken out in Congress about whether legislative oversight of foreign acquisitions ought to be enhanced.

As trade barriers come down and FDI increases, competition policy enforcement becomes important in shaping the domestic economy. Foreign rivals enter the market and erode the market power of incumbent domestic firms – assuming these foreign firms are able to effectively contest the market. This is the first area where competition policy enforcement becomes important under liberalized trade. Fred Bergsten highlighted that several 'trade' disputes between the US and Japan during the 1980s and 1990s, such as those concerning auto parts, photographic film and semiconductors, were really about alleged anticompetitive activity by firms and not trade regulations *per se* (Bergsten 1998). Foreign firms must be able to compete effectively; evidence suggests that once firms are established in a jurisdiction they tend to stay (Evenett *et al.* 2000: (12). Thus, effective competition policy has the long-term benefit of making markets more contestable. If foreign firms are significantly larger than domestic firms, a second threat is that they may gain too much of the market; antitrust law is thus important in maintaining a competitive market. The rise of network industries, such as software and telecommunications, also pose problems for the international coordination of competition policy. In industries where the utility of a product is a function of how many other people have it, a firm that establishes leadership can quickly dominate a market, as consumers 'coalesce' around the product (Evenett *et al.* 2000: 15). In software there is an additional opportunity for market dominance since the marginal cost of producing an additional copy is so low (and indeed can be transmitted at virtually no cost through the internet), thus making it exceptionally difficult to dislodge dominant firms. Though early fears that antitrust legislation designed for the industrial era would not be able to cope with the new economy have appeared exaggerated, the increasing level of economic interdependence epitomized by firms like Google, Microsoft and Netscape offers increased chances of regulatory conflict.

Finally, the expansion of foreign direct investment across the globe to developing states provides an additional rationale for further development of competition policy. Many developing states have few if any antitrust rules and the further development of these economies – and the firms that invest there – may hinge on the creation of robust competition policies. Though the European Union dropped competition policy from its list of Doha Round negotiating objectives after the Cancún ministerial (see Chapter 3), it was instructive that Brussels warmed to the idea of a multilateral competition policy as European firms began to invest more in developing economies.

Competition policy enforcement has become more important because of increased foreign direct investment. However, as a policy area it is distinct from investor protection agreements, which are enshrined internationally in bilateral investment treaties (BITs). Competition policy sets out the parameters of how private parties interact with one another: it is about regulation of the marketplace. Investment protection, by contrast, is concerned with the relationship foreign investors have with the host government. Host governments will often, in an attempt to gain further from an initial investment by a firm, make continued operations contingent on compliance with regulations relating to sourcing of parts, employment of the local population and other performance requirements. The ultimate sanction for a non-complying firm is expropriation. BITs seek to constrain the ability of host governments to impose and enforce performance requirements (Bora 2004). BITs have become an important element of US regional trade agreements; EU does use them, but has paid more attention to the international dimensions of antitrust (Gagne and Morin 2006).

The salience of international antitrust measures – whether pursued through multilateral or bilateral means – has declined in recent years. Interest in the topic reached its height in the 1995–2002 when a global mergers boom seemed to signal the need for international coordination of policies, if only to reduce transaction costs. However, a couple of high-profile EU–US disputes, discussed below, seemed to signal a greater need for international cooperation beyond that of saving firms money on compliance costs. In 2006, the world saw a merger boom that eclipsed the technology-related frenzy of ten years earlier. The European Commission received notification of 360 mergers in 2006 and the first six months of 2007, a figure Commissioner Neelie Kroes described as a 'tsunami' of merger activity (2007b: 5). Yet competition policy has not resumed its place on the international policy agenda as an area of controversy – despite the dramatic increase in foreign direct investment flowing to developing states where the risk of anti-competitive practice ought to be greatest.

Evolution of EU competition policy

It is important to understand at the outset that many of the roots of competition policy in the EU owe much to existing US antitrust measures (see below). American influence on European competition policy began immediately after World War II, when the United States insisted that West Germany adopt strict anti-cartel legislation to prevent the re-emergence of the Nazi-era industrial combines such as Farben (Devuyst 2001). However, in marked contrast to their American counterparts, it took many decades for European-level competition authorities to make a significant policymaking impact, the key catalyst being the Single Market Programme of the late 1980s and early 1990s. The early and mid-1990s saw something of a boom in EU competition policy development, but this has not necessarily been sustained. Indeed, there are indications that recent years have seen something of a retreat for the Commission on the issue of antitrust measures, after a series of high-profile cases in the late 1990s and early 2000s fuelled the impression that the Commission was overextending itself.

Box 5.1　The Microsoft case in Europe

As in the United States, the dominance of the Microsoft Corporation in key areas of the software business attracted the interest of European Union regulators. Litigation in Europe continued long after the case in the United States had been settled. The European proceedings highlight the extent to which many competition policy cases are in fact complex negotiations between the regulator and the company. The Commission began its investigation of the company in 1998, after a complaint was made by Sun Microsystems about Microsoft's refusal to share information that would allow Sun's products interoperability with Microsoft's. Sun alleged that, given Microsoft's dominant share of the PC market, the failure to offer this information was intended to prevent Sun from offering products that might compete with Microsoft's operating system. The Commission also expanded its investigation into Microsoft in 2000, when it considered whether the company, by bundling the Media Player into the Windows operating system, effectively froze out competing products. After a three-year investigation, the Commission found Microsoft guilty of damaging competition and ordered the company to: first, allow competitors information such that they might offer competing products that were interoperable with the Windows system; and, second, offer a version of the Windows system without Media Player, thus allowing the consumer a choice of version to purchase.

Microsoft appealed the decision and two more years of negotiations continued. The EU's court for competition policy cases is the Court of First Instance (CFI) and in late 2004 Microsoft lost the appeal. By November 2005 the Commission imposed fines of €280 million on the company, arguing that Microsoft's efforts to comply with the ruling were unsatisfactory. In 2007 Microsoft made a new offer to end the dispute, by unbundling Media Player and by creating a new mechanism for competitors to develop interoperable products. The Commission was not satisfied by this offer and held out the option of imposing further penalties on the Company.

Source:
http://ec.europa.eu/comm/competition/antitrust/cases/microsoft/, accessed 4 June 2007
http://www.microsoft.com/about/legal/eudecision/default.mspx, accessed 4 June 2007
http://europa.eu/rapid/pressReleasesAction.do?reference=IP/07/269&format=HTML&aged=0&language=EN&guiLanguage=en, accessed 4 June 2007

Like the trade directorate, competition authorities in the EU enjoy relatively high levels of authority and autonomy *vis-à-vis* national governments. Though trade policy authority owes much to the enhanced leverage gained by pooling sovereignty for trade negotiations, the nature of the Commission's dominance in competition policy owes more to internal European factors. From the outset, developing a common economic area was bound to require the development of a competition authority:

> The Treaty of Rome's aspirations to prevent any such distortions to trade and to create and complete a genuine common (and later single) market were inconceivable without the application and enforcement of rigorous competition rules. (McGowan and Cini 1999: 176–7; see also Todorov and Valke 2006; Wilks 2005)

The Commission enjoys clear primacy in the development and implementation of competition policy, with the Council of Ministers and the European Parliament finding themselves 'on the sidelines' (McGowan and Cini 1999: 177). That said, the Commission's competition enforcement activity was not particularly prominent in the early years of the Communities. This was partly because national-level policy frameworks seemed adequate for the task and because some Member States were adamantly opposed to further extensions of Commission power. It was also due to the fact that the Commission's authority resided largely in the domain of price collusion and abuse of dominant position. Mergers and acquisitions – two key methods firms use for entering new markets – were not included in the list of powers. Mergers were not under Commission remit until the Merger Control Regulation of 1989, though various European Court of Justice (ECJ) decisions had helped enhance the Commission's powers in this area. The 1973 Continental Can judgement reinforced the Commission's assertion that it could use its existing – albeit limited – powers to regulate the competitive effects of mergers (McGowan and Cini 1999: 179).

The adoption of the Merger Control Regulation finally affirmed the Commission's primacy where mergers were concerned and coincided with a clear neo-liberal shift in European politics towards more competitive markets and in turn the need for a robust competition policy. The Single Market Programme would not work if local collusive practices were tolerated. Successive competition commissioners used the bureaucracy's powers with considerable zeal, making the directorate among the Commission's most activist and internationally well-known bureaucracies (McGowan and Cini 1999; Damro 2003). By taking authority over mergers and acquisitions, the Commission was now the key regulator for the prime method of entering new markets – and not just in Europe. Throughout the 1990s mergers and acquisitions boomed, reaching a peak in the early part of the new millennium, when mergers worth over $3 trillion were completed. Business demands for a single regulator to oversee all this merger activity were also key to the success of Brussels in extending its powers in this area. Indeed, the European-level process of developing a single regulatory body – with its attendant reduction in transaction costs for firms – has rather prefigured and informed current debate about the wisdom of an international competition policy (see below). The Merger Task Force (MTF) was set up within DG Competition to attend to the expanding case-load falling under the MCR.

Though the Commission is now recognized and praised as one of the world's leading antitrust authorities, its activities have not been uncontroversial. As the merger boom of the late 1990s and early 2000s pressed on the Commission's resources, a series of questionable decisions began to undermine business confidence in the process. A small set of these decisions involved the United States (see below) but most referred to mergers among European firms. In a series of decisions, including Lafarge and Airtours, outside experts and business people began to question some of the underlying practices of the MTF. They noted that in contrast to American practice there is no separation of powers among bureaucracies; DGCompetition was the investigator, judge and jury for merger cases. From a practical standpoint, critics wondered how a relatively small staff – operating without a chief economist – could cope with the number and complexity of merger cases coming before them. By contrast, American antitrust authorities operate with much greater resources (see below). Further damage on the MTF's credibility was inflicted in 2002 at the Court of First Instance (the EU's court of appeal for mergers) when the judges overturned the MTF's decision to block the merger of two UK travel firms, First Choice and Airtours. It was the first time a Commission decision in the area of mergers had been overturned and was described as a 'hammer blow' to the Commission's standing (Veljanovski 2004: 154). Two further cases were lost and more appeals filed – crucially including the controversial General Electric/Honeywell case (see below).

In response to these criticisms, and adverse judgements at the ECJ at the appeals stage, the Commission launched an extensive review of merger regulations. The Commission had in fact developed and implemented some reform proposals as early as 2002, but more change was needed (Wilks 2005). The MTF was disbanded and its functions spread across other units in the Competition Commission. There is now much bolstered economic analysis thanks to increased resources, including the creation of the post of chief economist. A key reform in the substance of merger policy was the greater acceptance that mergers can generate considerable economic efficiencies – even if the combined group has a significant market share. This reform, which owes much to the General Electric/Honeywell case, moves the EU merger rules away from a central concern about market structure towards a more American-style interest in market operations (European Commission 2004a; Todorov and Valke 2006).

Upon taking office in 2004 Commissioner Neelie Kroes signalled changes in the policy trajectory (2007b). These included a greater emphasis on consumer welfare in relation to competition, thus signalling a slight shift away from the producer orientation taken by EU authorities over many decades. Among the key shifts was the desire to pay more attention to the anti-competitive consequences of state aids, amid continuing evidence that member states were reluctant to let market forces work where politically sensitive (automobiles) or prestigious (airlines) sectors were concerned. Whereas competition policy in the EU in the 1980s was concerned with creating a competitive marketplace, attention now is focused on the EU's lagging productivity and poor record on innovation. The Competition Directorate, no less than other Brussels bureaucracies, has been keen to develop its own policy role in respect of the Lisbon Agenda. 'Strong competition, encouraged and protected by EU competition policy, is rightly regarded as instrumental for achieving the competitiveness objective of the European Union and the Lisbon Strategy' (European Commission, 2004a). In this respect EU policies do reflect traditional American beliefs and policy that innovation is best secured through fiercely contested markets.

Evolution of US antitrust law

The American preference for fierce competition in the marketplace has a long lineage, though it was not present at the creation of the US, as some of the mythology would have us believe. As Peter Gourevitch noted, American economic policy took a pro-market turn in the late nineteenth century that fundamentally altered the relationship between market and state (Gourevitch 1996). Until this turn, America shared more than is commonly believed with continental European economies with their more corporatist, social market orientation. This mercantilist economic tradition, championed by Secretary of the Treasury Alexander Hamilton, has tended to be forgotten in commentaries on American economic policy until recently, when increasing foreign competition led some policymakers to call for a renewal of the Hamiltonian tradition of state involvement in the economy.

America's turn toward the open, competitive market we see today took place in the late 1800s amid increasing public disquiet – anger even – over the anti-competitive activities of large firms such as the Standard Oil Trust. The Sherman Act of 1890 is one of the best-known pieces of American legislation, and was passed in response to public concern about the activities of 'large industrial conglomerates' in rigging markets (Devuyst 2001). That said, it was immediately obvious that the act would work to encourage fair, market-based competition. This was because one immediate consequence of the Sherman Act – and its active interpretation by the courts – was to spark a merger boom between 1895 and 1904. As Mowery and Rosenberg point out, since the Sherman Act prohibited rigging markets via cartels and informal arrangements, firms simply internalized the market via mergers. The Supreme Court's subsequent decisions reduced the attractiveness of mergers and indeed created incentives to diversify product portfolios so as to avoid legal scrutiny that came with dominance of one industry (Mowery and Rosenberg 1998: 14–15). The Clayton Act passed in 1914 is less known to many but is arguably the more important element of US competition policy legislation. This is because it deals with the forms of collusion and sharp practice and does so by forbidding price collusion, supplier agreements and other restraints on trade. As such, it sought to protect small businesses by ensuring that no company could through its activities substantially reduce competition in the marketplace. The Clayton Act is the foundation of US merger law to this day (Devuyst 2001: 128).

More merger legislation was passed in subsequent years, often with the intention of preserving small businesses in the face of larger competitors. Though it will strike many as odd given the numerous large multinationals domiciled in the US, competition policy in the US has long been shaped by a fear of large business units. US antitrust policy is generally more active than comparable bodies of merger and competition control. None the less the aggressive promotion of competition by American authorities in the early part of the twentieth century may have had one paradoxical effect: it allowed some US firms to become very large. By forcing firms away from collusion, legislation induced a form of natural selection into the market; those firms able to manage a portfolio of activities thrived, as did those able to harness gains from in-house innovations. Firms that did not develop excellent in-house management failed. Antitrust policy was central to the growth of the modern – large – American firm that dominated twentieth-century business around the world (Mowery and Rosenberg 1998: 16).

The US was one of the first nations to create and implement competition policies; indeed, it was decades ahead of other states. Until a few years ago relatively few states had antitrust policies in place, reflecting perhaps different views on the nature and desirability of competitive marketplaces. US antitrust policy was also notable for its early acceptance of extra-territorial application competition law. In 1945, the US Supreme Court ruled that existing provisions outlawing anti-competitive behaviour, though intended for domestic application, could be applied irrespective of the location of the firms involved, provided their activities had an effect on the American market. This was an extremely controversial aspect of American law, and one fiercely resisted by other states. The European Union adopted the effects doctrine in its Dyestuffs case, where it sought to fine several international firms for price collusion in the industrial dye market even though those firms were domiciled outside the EU, and this also became an issue in the cases centring on Boeing–McDonnell Douglas and General Electric/Honeywell during the early 2000s.

Like any other body of law, American antitrust law has evolved in response to changes in the political and economic environment. In the 1980s, for example, concerns about the competitiveness of American semiconductor firms in the face of Japanese competition resulted in antitrust waivers for several government-brokered research consortia, via the National Cooperative Research Act

(1984) (Fox *et al.* 2004). Likewise authorities' views on agglomeration have altered in the face of evidence that efficiency gains can be extracted even from mergers that result in a more concentrated industry. However, some features have stood the test of time. Compared with European conceptions of antitrust policy, US enforcement traditionally gave primacy to consumer – as opposed to producer – welfare and has been more concerned with market efficiency than industry structure *per se* (Fox *et al.* 2004).

Coordination and conflict

Transatlantic relations in competition policy are very harmonious and illustrative of the kind of policymaking characterized by expert dominance of a technical process, shared understandings among these experts, and the relative lack of political salience and visibility of the competition policy area. This has produced a policy area characterized by relatively high degrees of cooperation among American and European authorities in relation to procedures and, to some extent, the substance of competition policy. This is partly a concession to the realities of enforcement. Devuyst notes that very often information crucial to the prosecution of an antitrust case lies in another jurisdiction. Thus, effective enforcement requires healthy degrees of inter-agency cooperation (Devuyst 2001: 132). Competition policy, in common with a number of other regulatory policy areas, has thus been central to the development of what we described in Chapter 2 as 'transatlantic governance'.

Competition policy relations are a stark contrast to trade:

> In comparison with the 'conflict management' focus of trade negotiators trying to protect their own domestic producers' interests, the EU–US competition relationship is characterized by a culture of genuine 'regulatory cooperation' with antitrust agencies trying to increase the effectiveness of their common enforcement task. (Devuyst 2001: 127)

Eleanor Fox, in testimony to the US Congress, highlighted the successful nature of most EU–US competition enforcement when faced with the merger of WorldCom and MCI in the late 1990s: 'Enabled by confidentiality waivers, the agencies [DoJ and the Commission] coordinated requests for information, jointly met with the parties, and concluded settlements that met the concerns on both sides. (Fox 2006b: 3). Her comments draw attention to the centrality of procedure and day-to-day management in the smooth running of transatlantic competition policy relations.

This propensity to collaborate is also bolstered by the strong business links across the Atlantic, including the significant amounts of FDI that flow between the partners. Foreign investment can take the form of portfolio investment, but the purchase of assets in the other economy is a major route to market for American and European firms. As such, competition policy compliance can be an important issue and a transaction cost for firms. Thus firms have an interest, if not in convergence of regimes, at least in the development of transparent and predictable policy systems. That said, business interest tends to be confined to input on an ad hoc basis. Devuyst explains this by pointing out that antitrust regulators are supposed to supervise businesses in the marketplace and as such are careful about the form and amount of firm-level influence allowed in to the process (Devuyst 2001: 138).

Some political issues, because of their very technical nature and their distance from the consumer, remain the preserve of a relatively small group of technical experts and are rather immune from the populist pressure politics seen in areas like consumer health and agriculture. A similar argument can be made about competition policy: officials on both sides of the Atlantic have succeeded in keeping this considerably depoliticized. In part, this reflects the arcane and specialist nature of the policy area. Moreover, notwithstanding its interest in consumer welfare, most consumers are blissfully unaware of the effect of competition policy enforcement on their lives. However, Damro notes that regulators in Washington and Brussels have been keen to preserve their power and autonomy *vis-à-vis* political authority. Thus they have exhibited a strong preference for bilateral linkages at the official level, partly in an effort to head off more onerous, formal political agreements that might impinge on their autonomy. By taking it upon themselves to promote cooperation, regulators 'reduce the likelihood of politicians becoming involved in competition cases and linking outcomes to trade policy' (Damro 2006: 872).

The basis for European–American cooperation on competition policy is the 1991 agreement which set out a framework for transatlantic cooperation (and which reflected the bargaining power acquired by the EC through the development of the Single

Market Programme at that time). The agreement is illustrative of the deep and rich set of relationships that characterize transatlantic economic relations. It commits each party to consider the interests of the other in pursuing enforcement activities ands formalizes this with comity provisions. Exchanges of information and the cultivation of a culture of cooperation were embodied in commitments among officials to regular, bilateral meetings. Finally, the accord called on each party to cooperate and coordinate with the other to greatest extent possible without prejudicing or impairing domestic enforcement of competition laws (Janow 2000: 32). The agreement was an important milestone in the development of international efforts to coordinate antitrust enforcement. Nonetheless, the agreement had significant limitations; it was designed mainly to avoid jurisdictional conflict via the timely exchange of information; it is not equipped to resolve conflicts once they arise. The agreement lacks a dispute settlement mechanism and does not impose limitations on the ability of one party to exercise its rights to investigate a particular merger if it feels it is in the national interest to do so. There is nothing unusual *per se* about these arrangements; they reflect the reality of the 1991 agreement as an international agreement between sovereign nation states (with the EU acting on behalf of members) rather than a supranational treaty (Damro 2004)

In addition to the direct, bilateral relationships between Washington and Brussels, both participate in an array of multilateral forums, which aim to foster closer ties and more effective cooperation among numerous competition agencies. This network of organizations is not particularly new, reflecting the realization some years ago that extraterritorial application of competition laws was fraught with controversy. In the wake of the 1945 Alcoa decision, the United States began a period of 'aggressive extraterritorial enforcement' in areas such as international shipping, the petroleum industry and watchmaking (Guzman 1998: 1507). As early as the 1940s, consideration was given to an international competition policy, packaged as part of the Havana Charter that was to have given birth to the International Trade Organization. As with the rest of the Havana process, the competition policy proposals were shelved in the face of American uncertainty over the implications for US sovereignty.

As it did in other spheres of policymaking, the OECD assumed a role as key facilitator of cooperation on antitrust measures. In 1967 the organization's members agreed a series of recommendations on antitrust policy in the context of increasing international trade (Damro 2004: 271). Gradually, through the successive issuing of recommendations, the level of cooperation among OECD member countries in respect of competition policy has increased. Originally designed to facilitate information-sharing, later versions of the OECD agreements allow states to request investigations by another member and makes greater calls on members to actively assist in each other's enforcement proceedings (Damro 2004: 272). The organization has developed a particular niche role in respect of cartels. The OECD Hard Core Cartel Recommendation was an effort to develop OECD-wide agreement on the identification and prosecution of cartels in member states. This particular agreement owes much to the United States, which has a tradition of fierce prosecution of cartel behaviour; indeed, the US extra-territorial application of its laws was typically in aid of anti-cartel activity. The OECD anti-cartel guidelines, agreed in 1998, were pursued by the US because the OECD was seen as an effective platform for progress – in contrast to the WTO – and because of the lack of a binding enforcement mechanism (Damro 2004: 273).

Exceptions that prove the rule

The Boeing–McDonnell-Douglas and GE–Honeywell mergers showed how, from time to time, there are significant differences of view across the Atlantic. It is no accident that these two controversial mergers arose in one sector where EU–US foreign direct investment is low: aerospace. In contrast to other sectors, where European firms have significant investments in America and vice versa, aerospace is characterized by international supply chains governed by contract, not shareholding. In the first major aerospace dispute, the Commission threatened to block Boeing's acquisition of its American-based rival, McDonnell-Douglas (MDC). The Commission was widely seen as acting on behalf of Boeing's European rival, Airbus, in opposing the merger. Though MDC ceased to be a significant player in the civil aircraft market, there was concern that the merged company would enjoy lock-in effects as airlines chose to update their fleets with the group's aircraft rather than incur switching costs by moving to Airbus. Boeing had indeed secured long-term aircraft purchase deals from two US airlines, American and Delta, that appeared to confirm these fears, though in fact the airline deals were concluded before the merger was announced. Both airlines agreed to purchase Boeing jets for twenty years into the future, in exchange for substantial discounts.

European Competition Commissioner Karel Van Miert voiced his concerns about the proposed merger by arguing that the combined group would enjoy a dominant position in the commercial aerospace market. Boeing had historically had half the market and McDonnell-Douglas, once a leading firm in the sector, has shrunk to approximately 10 per cent. Van Miert's view was that the combined market shares would, in a sense, augment Boeing's existing command to the market by adding customers. The American view could not have been more different. MDC's market share provided a rationale for the US Federal Trade Commission to approve the deal. They argued that MDC's market share was minimal, was likely to decline and indicated that the company was no longer a viable competitor in the market (Damro 2001: 214). In a market where customers are concerned about after-sales technical support – as well as residual values of airliners – having a small market share simply is not viable in the long run as airlines will not purchase from a supplier that might not be in business in a few years. This, combined with high entry barriers in the form or upfront R&D costs and long payout periods, leaves the sector with a pronounced tendency toward oligopoly. The Commission's concerns in this regard reflected a greater emphasis in EU merger regulation on market structure, rather than economic efficiency. It was a difference that would manifest itself again in the General Electric–Honeywell controversy a few years later.

The Boeing merger controversy was eventually settled via negotiations and the company agreed to two main concessions. First, Boeing agreed it would not enter into any new exclusive agreements with airlines; and second, the company agreed to publish data on US-government-funded corporate R&D. This latter concession was clearly informed by the long-running rivalry with Airbus Industrie, where both companies accused the other of receiving illegal government subsidies. Boeing settled partly because the suggested remedies by the Commission were not particularly onerous (it is not in Boeing's gift to enter into exclusive agreements; that requires a willing airline) and nor were they easily enforceable.

In the wake of the Boeing case, EU and US officials sought to clarify and enhance the comity provisions of the 1991 agreement. Traditional comity 'refers to the general principle that a country should take other countries' important interests into account in its own law-enforcement in return for their doing the same' (Janow 2000: 33). The two trading partners concluded an agreement in 1998 that enhanced the cooperative aspects of the 1991 accord. Foremost among these was a stronger commitment to positive comity, where a country can request that the other party enforce its own antitrust laws in cases where activity in that jurisdiction threatens to affect the partner. Positive comity increases the obligation on both the US and EU not only to consider the others' interests but also to actively protect them as requested.

The General Electric–Honeywell merger controversy was altogether more fraught, and not only because the CEO of GE, Jack Welch, was rather less diplomatic in his relations with Brussels than his Boeing counterpart, Phil Condit. The case also represented something of a high-water mark for the Merger Task Force, and in the aftermath of the controversy the criticism of the Commission's performance was such that significant changes were made to the merger review process. The Commission's particular complaint concerned the ability of a combined General Electric–Honeywell to 'bundle' aerospace products and services together and in so doing diminish competition across markets. General Electric made jet engines and, through its financing arm and aircraft-leasing company, the corporation also enjoyed a significant share of the global airliner-leasing business. Honeywell enjoyed a strong market presence in avionics – interestingly expanded via an earlier acquisition of Allied-Signal – as well as products in the small aircraft engine market. The Commission voiced anxiety over the ability of the merged group to offer both products and related financing packages that competitors could not beat.

The analysis that underpinned the Commission's view came in for considerable criticism, and not just from General Electric (Morgan and McGuire 2004). The MTF's economic analysis was regarded as flawed and the product of outdated economic theory and analytical tools. The Commission had used one technique that had been abandoned by American authorities years earlier (Morgan and McGuire 2004). Critics wondered how such a small staff could discharge its responsibilities properly given the immense caseload. The Commission's impartial handling of the case was called into question as it became clear how it relied on an economic analysis of the merger produced by Rolls-Royce, a GE competitor. These criticisms dealt with process and drew attention to the considerable concentration of authority in a small section of one directorate within the Commission. More general criticism was reserved for the Merger Task Force's views on the relationship of mergers to economic efficiency. In the United States it is recognized that mergers can enhance economic efficiency and consumer welfare. On this view, the fact that General Electric could bundle products and offer them at more attractive prices was an argument in favour of the merger, not a reason to oppose it.

The General Electric case joined a small number of other cases where the Court of First Instance became involved. In the Tetra case, the Court criticized the Commission's investigative procedures. After the GE controversy had subsided, the Commission announced a reorganization of the merger and antitrust bureaucracy. The Merger Task Force was disbanded and its responsibilities handed to several other bureaucracies. The Commission enhanced its much-criticized analytical capacity with the appointment of a head of economic analysis.

The General Electric and Boeing cases were important in highlighting procedural and substantive differences between the United States and the European Union. Moreover, the GE case highlighted weaknesses in the Commission's processes that have been addressed under Neelie Kroe's commissionership. It is also important to note that controversies are exceptional. Full substantive convergence between the partners seems unlikely given the different policy trajectories followed by Europe and America. Though the new merger regulations pay attention to economic efficiency, the Commission is unlikely to abandon its interest in market structure, particularly as smaller national markets remain susceptible to market distortion. European regulators also take a more sceptical view of vertical restraints, for the similar reason that creating the single market required the breaking down of nationally based practices (Melamed 1998). The US, with its well-established single market and cultural acceptance of competition, does not need the same focus on industrial structure.

Applying Euro-American policies to the world

The dramatic growth of investment as well as trade has led unsurprisingly to increasing calls for the internationalization of competition policy and the expansion of investor protection regulations. As in other policy areas, there is a perceived mismatch between the increasingly global operations of firms and heightened interdependence of economies, and the location-bound nature of most economic governance structures. International competition policy would seem to offer a way of enhancing trade policies designed to open markets. Trade policy has traditionally focused on 'at-the-border' issues, so removing or reducing these barriers opens trade. But the removal of trade barriers does not guarantee that a market is contestable – and this is where competition policy is important. In the absence of trade restrictions, incumbent firms might still collude with each other and government to hamper new competitors. For some observers, the best way to address this level problem is to create supranational governance structures which would provide common regulations for all. The attraction to firms is the reduction in transaction costs; compliance with one set of rules is cheaper – and should be easier – than compliance with multiple sets of regulations. The riposte, however, is that any international effort should focus on coordination and transparency rather than on convergence on a single set of regulations. It is not obvious that formal multilateralization would be any better than the existing practice of bilateral agreements in preventing market abuses (Fox 2006a). However, the issue is not so clear-cut and it would be wrong to frame it as a stark choice between maintaining competing national systems of enforcement and a global agreement under WTO auspices. In fact, both the US and the European Union use both the WTO and regional trade agreements to plurilateralize various policy areas not formally part of the WTO agenda. The difference is that the EU is more comfortable doing so in the field of antitrust measures; the US, by contrast, has placed more emphasis on investor protection legislation.

The European Union has been more comfortable with the multilateralization of competition policy than has the United States. As in the trade policy area, the Union's comfort with a multilateral process has its roots in the European political economy. The experience gained by the Commission the creation of the Single Market has made it comfortable with, and experienced in, the creation and implementation of supranational public policy. Deep integration of this sort can reduce transaction costs associated with multiple policy regimes, but it is invasive and can create tensions in member states, with politicians and voters alike resenting Brussels's interference in national affairs.

Arguably, however, the EU's warm regard for international competition policy is informed by norms and not just by the experience
of European integration. The European Union more than any other
member of the WTO had been keen to include 'trade-and' topics
for negotiation during the Doha Round. The Singapore issues of
government procurement, trade facilitation, competition policy and
trade and the environment owed their inclusion on the agenda to
the insistence of the European Union. It is true that from time to
time the United States has also raised these – or related – issues,
but in Washington this is more to do with placating domestic constituencies. Bill Clinton's ill-advised suggestion about linking trade
and labour standards was an example. The comments, made at the
start of the disastrous Seattle WTO ministerial in 1999, were
designed to reassure his Democrat-voting labour activists but succeeded in merely outraging swathes of the WTO delegates. Though
American politicians sometimes repeat the language, the US has
not adopted linkage politics to the same extent as the EU. Why is
Brussels so interested? For Sally, it is because the EU seeks to
recreate the EU at the multilateral level, by fostering the creation of
the WTO that emphasizes regulatory harmonization as its core
operating principle (Sally 2004). Earlier chapters suggest an additional, more-values-based explanation: that the European Union,
as a civilian superpower, demonstrates a comfort with, indeed
enthusiasm for, multilateralism as a mechanism for solving problems not shared by other actors, most notably the United States.

The Singapore issues attracted considerable criticism in advance
of the Cancun ministerial in 2003. Developing countries disliked
the linkages drawn between trade and other issues, and the issue of
competition policy was not an important item on their agendas.
For many smaller states, the resource implications of the adoption
of an international competition policy are serious, requiring
numerous trained staff (economists and lawyers) as well as a judicial system capable of handing antitrust cases. Many developing
states already find compliance with WTO agreements complex and
onerous. Poor economies are likely to have greater needs than creating a competition authority. As one American official asked
rhetorically, '[J]ust how many officials should a country with a
population of 500,000 have in its as-yet-nonexistent antitrust
agency?' (Melamed 1998: 7). In 2004, competition policy multilateralization was formally dropped as a Doha negotiating item, to
the relief of most developing states (Bhattacharjea 2006: 293).

That said, the European Union, before and since the dropping of competition as an agenda item, has demanded the inclusion of antitrust commitments in bilateral and regional preferential trade agreements (Bhattarchajea 2006: 273–4). The price of access to the EU market is to participate in and accept elements of the EU *acquis*, without the actual benefits of membership.

The United States's ambivalence toward multilateralized competition policy is, like the EU position, explained partly by an appeal to history. The United States is historically concerned about the constraints that might be imposed by an international organization and, as such, is generally drawn to bilateral initiatives in response. Among American policymakers, there was acknowledgement that international antitrust cooperation and coordination were necessary and desirable; it did not follow that the answer was a single, global competition authority. In response to EU initiatives, the United States created the the International Competition Policy Advisory Committee (ICPAC), designed to inform and advise American policymakers. For the US, it represented an effective way to maintain interest and influence in the evolving debate about international antitrust policy without actually committing to a binding agreement. The EU accepted, indeed welcomed, the creation of ICPAC, but viewed it as 'complementary, not as an alternative to the WTO proposal' (Devuyst 2001: 133). ICPAC was wound up in 2000, but American interest in the international dimension of antitrust regulations was maintained by the International Competition Network (ICN), an organization comprising over 100 competition policy authorities that grew directly out of the recommendations of ICPAC's final report (ICN 2007a). Membership of ICN is voluntary and the organization does not make rules, but it does foster knowledge-sharing and 'best practice'. Central to the ICN is the freedom it gives to members to implement ideas as they see fit (ICN 2007b).

Investor protection

Investor protection is a closely related policy area that has also been the subject of negotiation at the multilateral and regional level. Broadly, regulation in this area is designed to protect investors from what they would regard as arbitrary treatment by the host government. Examples of such treatment might be onerous local sourcing requirements, or expropriation of assets without compensation. For firms, limits on the ability of governments to interfere with their operations reduce the political risk associated with an investment, which should result in greater levels of investment in a given economy. However, from the perspective of governments, such constraints may prevent governments from acting in good faith for the benefit of their society. As such, the extension of investor protection requirements has been highly controversial. The Doha Declaration included investment protection in response to complaints from European and American business that the existing Trade-Related Investment Measures (TRIMs) were not able to offer adequate protection. To the extent this is true, it is partly down to the inability of firms – and government policy-makers – to agree on the precise scope and extent of investment provisions.

Another factor militating against strong investor protection provisions has been the operation of the disputes settlement process in the North American Free Trade Agreement (NAFTA) in respect of the rights accorded to firms to sue foreign governments in the their home jurisdiction (Bora 2004: 212–13; Gagne and Morin 2006). Critics charged that NAFTA set an unwelcome precedent for the ability of firms – as private parties – to make claims that affected the sovereignty of nation states. Bora argues that these fears contributed to the collapse of OECD-sponsored negotiations on the Multilateral Agreement on Investment (Bora 2004: 214).

However, American interest in securing a more predictable international environment for its firms to operate in meant that the issue was raised again in advance of the Doha Declaration in late 2001. The declaration acknowledged the link between trade and investment and trade, noting that 'transparent, stable and predictable conditions' assist in encouraging foreign direct investment and expanded trade (WTO 2001). The United States pressed for a broad agreement covering the widest possible forms of investment (Bora 2004). In the event, the text offered considerable scope for member states to regulate investment matters 'in the public interest', reflecting the fierce resistance the American proposals generated among other states (WTO 2001). The Doha language is sufficiently ambiguous for the US, while pursuing the Doha Round negotiations, to have sought to include investor protection provisions in its bilateral and regional trade pacts. However, even the US seems to have pulled back from far-reaching investor protection towards a model that preserves considerable scope for states to act in the national interest. American policymakers drew lessons from the unhappy experience of the operation of NAFTA's provisions, which led to the American government having to defend its investment policies in court (Gagne and Morin 2006). NAFTA's chapter 11 gives corporations the ability to demand arbitration where national law is deemed to have injured the firm: this represented a break from the legal tradition that only states had 'standing' before disputes processes (Capling and Nossal 2006). By the time the US and Australia began to negotiate a bilateral free trade agreement, the Americans had succeeded in getting NAFTA-like investor protection language in several bilateral free trade agreements. However, to the surprise of many observers, investor protection did not appear in the final text of the Australian–US Free Trade Agreement. (Capling and Nossal 2006). American policymakers themselves were surprised by the potential for NAFTA-style language to constrain their ability to implement policy for environmental and health standards (Capling and Nossal 2006). The American government has reverted to a less ambitious formula, using bilateral investment treaties (BITs) that are not part of broader free trade agreements. The model that forms the basis of all US bilateral investment treaties was created under the 2002 Bipartisan Trade Promotion Authority Act (US Department of State 2006). The US has signed 39 BITs, virtually all with developing countries (USTR 2006).

The European Union has not shown the same enthusiasm for BITs, preferring instead to use the OECD and WTO processes to achieve internationally agreed levels of investor protection. As was seen in Chapter 3, the EU placed trade and investment regulations among the Singapore issues on the Doha agenda. However, the EU used bilateral initiatives in this area while still pursuing the Doha objective. Thus, Brussels started the EU down the road followed by Washington: the inclusion of investor protection rules as part of bilateral and regional trade agreements. Both the EU–Mexico trade agreement, which entered into force in 2000, and the EU–Chile Association Agreement signed in 2002 included a range of investor protection clauses that, at least in the Chile case, are designed to go beyond 'existing WTO commitments' (European Commission 2002)

Overview and conclusion

Competition and investment policies attract virtually none of the headlines that trade and monetary policy matters do, but that is not because these areas are unimportant. Competition policy remains a cornerstone of any properly functioning market economy and it is significant that as the process of globalization has unfolded, it has been accompanied by a growing interest in, and adoption of, competition rules by policymakers around the world. However, the area is technical, and so tends not to be as politicized as other policy spheres. The transatlantic relationship is marked by considerable cooperation among regulatory agencies. European and American influences on international competition policy are considerable – and sometimes controversial.

Investment issues are somewhat more problematic. To the extent that investor protection rules appear to place the policy preferences of multinational companies above those of the local population, they become the target for protest. Moreover, concerns that the widespread adoption of investment protection could have unintended consequences for the US and Europe have also tended to dampen enthusiasm. Fear that the US federal or state governments could find themselves sued by firms for enacting environmental legislation under NAFTA led the US to move away from the inclusion of investor protection language in later bilateral free trade agreements. In this context, the main arguments made in this chapter are:

- First, in both America and Europe, competition policy has been a key element of market-friendly regulation, promoting economic growth. European conceptions of competition have differed from the American, but this gap is narrowing.
- Second, in contrast to the area of international trade, competition and investment politics are much less contested. This is due largely to the fact that policymaking – particularly in competition policy – remains very technocratic, with the key stakeholders sharing similar views about the purpose and content of policy.
- Third, the EU has shown more enthusiasm for developing an international competition policy, perhaps because the Commission has greater experience with international regulatory issues, while the US is more concerned that its own, tough

competition laws will be weakened by any international agreement. As such, though both the EU and the US are members of ICN, the organization owes its *modus operandi* to American preferences for looser forms of multilateralism.

- Fourth, in respect of investment, both America and the European Union increasingly use bilateral or regional investment treaties as mechanisms to safeguard the foreign investments of their firms. As with preferential trade agreements, there are concerns that this creates a patchwork of investment agreements that are in conflict with each other and makes it difficult for other firms to invest.

As Europe and America become more interdependent, not merely with each other but with the rest of the world, agency cooperation has become an important element of the relationship. In the case of competition policy, some substantive differences remain between Washington and Brussels that reflect differing historical traditions and the salience of different economic and political issues. That said, in this, a technical area where enforcement agencies share a common interest in minimizing political interference, cooperation has been prevalent. Both Washington and Brussels have an interest in extending this cooperation globally. As with the substance of policy, the mechanisms for achieving this are disputed. However in the absence of a viable WTO-based solution the European Union has found the American-inspired ICPAC a very useful forum.

Investment regulation has not had the profile as competition policy, but is none the less an area that features many of the same characteristics. European and American firms remain advocates of multilateralized regulatory solutions, but there is significant disagreement over the precise reach and content of such regulation. The US government has successfully implemented a bilateral and plurilateral solution in the form of renewed and updated investment agreements. Europe has not pursued bilateral investment agreements with the same vigour, but like the US has used bilateral and regional negotiations to press for enhanced protection on matters like investment. The EU–Chile Association Agreement seems certain to be a model for further developments.

To the extent that competition and investment policies tend to be packaged as part of trade negotiations, both policy areas could be affected by the diminished though still formidable ability of Europe and America to translate their preferences into outcomes in the

WTO. As we noted in Chapter 3, the dramatic rise of the developing world in the organization – and the dramatic economic growth of these economies – illustrates the growing confidence of states to resist what they regard as the imposition of inappropriate policies by the EU and the US. Some of this reflects political linkage among negotiating issues in the WTO rather than opposition to the ideas *per se*. China, for example, has seen a surge in foreign direct investment since WTO accession and is no doubt aware of the 'market credibility' signalled by membership and adherence to rules. None the less as WTO negotiations become more difficult for Washington and Brussels, it makes sense to shift the level of negotiations down the hierarchy to the bilateral level, where their economic power counts for much more.

Chapter 6

Innovation

In this chapter, we deal with an issue long established both in the EU and in the US, but which has been given considerable added impact by recent developments in the world political economy. To understand why Europe and America dominate the global economy – and why that dominance is slipping – it is important to assess the role of innovation. Europe, then America, both rose to economic dominance because these economies developed superior ways to manipulate the natural environment. They did so through a combination of serendipity, a trust in the ability of market forces to identify opportunities and an appreciation of the role of the state in the generation of knowledge.

Innovation is often envisaged as the lone inventor working in his laboratory, hoping for that crucial breakthrough. Though serendipity can be important, the key to the success of Europe and American innovation was that both actors created *systems*, comprised of firms, government and other stakeholders such as universities and research institutes. European universities – particularly German institutions – led the world in the developing institutions devoted to scientific research, and linked with German firms, who were among the first to develop in-house R&D facilities (Dosi *et al.* 2005: 21). American firms were also early adopters of a model where firms devoted money to research, rather than leave new product development to opportunistic acquisition. American universities were also well funded by a variety of sources – federal and state government, students and philanthropy – and played a crucial role in the ascent of the US to dominance of innovation in the twentieth century. Both Europe and America adopted what has been described as the 'linear' model, which presumed a relatively straightforward process of discovery, development and sales, with many held within the firm, or within its control (Chesbrough 2003). As the name suggests, the model envisaged a more or less linear relationship between basic research conducted at universities, leading to applied work at corporate research and development centres, with this leading in turn to successful commercialization.

So successful were Europe and America that follower states developed their own innovation systems, borrowing and adapting European and American practice as needed. Japan in the 1980s was the most successful follower state, but the new millennium has seen the field of top-quality innovating nations become much more crowded. China is merely the most obvious gainer, with Singapore, India and Taiwan other states that have developed top quality innovation systems. Just as production was globalized in the last century, it seems likely that the twenty-first century will see the true globalization of knowledge, as many economies develop the capabilities to innovate at the very frontier of a variety of technologies. This 'networked' technological system poses challenges to state policies oriented around keeping innovative activities confined to the home base.

In both Europe and America, this development has been met with apprehension and even hostility in some quarters. This is because the high-skill, 'knowledge' economy was supposed to be a safe haven for developed economies faced with the loss of manufacturing jobs. Public policy in both economies has focused on the need to enhance the innovative capacity of the economy, via improved education, government support for R&D and increased use of innovation by firms for competitive advantage. The unstated assumption was that emerging economies like China, though they were good at cheap manufacturing, would not be able to duplicate European and American efforts in technology-intensive sectors.

These assumptions are proving unfounded. The key distinction where jobs are concerned is not between knowledge workers and manual labour but between jobs that can be traded (even if electronically) and those that are non-tradable (Blinder 2006). To the extent that emerging economies develop talents in tradable, highly skilled goods and services, they will compete directly with European and American scientists and engineers, as well as management consultants and accountants. China is dramatically increasing its innovative capacity, with increased research and developing spending actually increasing faster than the overall rate of economic growth (OECD 2006a). Though a note of caution must always apply to Chinese statistics, China's overall effort in R&D, gross expenditure on research and development (GERD) is, at 1.31 per cent of GDP, not far off the European average (Zhou and Leydesdorff 2006: 84) (Figure 6.1). China is now the fifth-largest patenting nation on Earth, though with a

Figure 6.1 R&D spending as a percentage of GDP

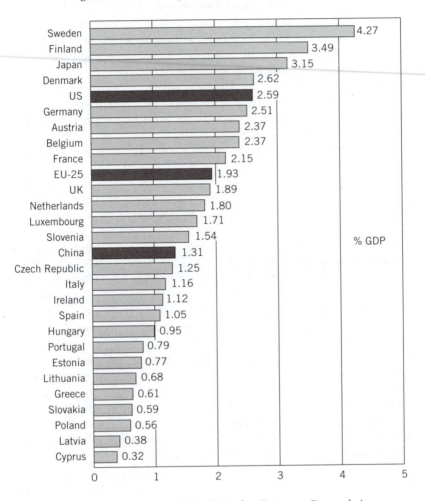

Source: European Commission (2005), *Towards a European Research Area: Science Technology and Innovation, Key Figures 2005*, p. 25, ftp://ftp.cordis, lu/pub/indicators/docs/2004_1857_en_web.pdf, accessed 10 June 2006.

share barely a quarter of Japan and America's (WTO 2006). China has put particular emphasis on nanotechnology, thus emulating several states in viewing this technology as a key driver of future innovative activity. China is now second only to the US in terms of single-country production of published scientific research on nanotechnology (Zhou and Leydesdorff 2006: 94). The overall quality of China's innovation infrastructure can however be called into question. Though money is pouring into Chinese universities, laboratory equipment and academic training remain relatively poor by European and American standards. On the other hand, the trajectory and pace of China's advance, to say nothing of renewed efforts in Singapore and Malaysia and the expansion of India, is impressive. The notion, popularized by numerous politicians, that Europe and America could find an 'economic haven' among high-skilled, high-technology sectors is proving gravely mistaken.

Though the bulk of this chapter examines the evolution of EU and US innovation systems from a comparative perspective, to some extent the trans-Atlantic area is one large innovation sector. The large flows of foreign investment between Europe and America are not entirely comprised of manufacturing plants or offices: some of the investment has gone on new R&D facilities. Pharmaceutical firms, for example, have long had R&D facilities on both sides of the Atlantic. Pfizer, the US company, has a significant laboratory in Kent, UK; GSK has significant centres in Princeton, New Jersey. Across a vast array of sectors, European and American firms conduct research in both Europe and America; in some cases the research tailors existing products to local markets, but other sites are leading facilities central to the global strategies of these firms.

This chapter traces the evolution of American and European innovation systems and places them in current context. Given that both systems have the same roots in the German political economy of the nineteenth century, both systems share many features, but important institutional differences mean that significant divergence remains even where, as in the case of economic competition from Asia, there is agreement on the challenges faced.

European innovation policy

Jean-Jacques Servan-Schreiber articulated European fears about American domination of the global economy over forty years ago, yet his work speaks to current anxieties about Europe's ability to compete. Writing in the 1960s, he observed the fantastic growth of US multinationals and feared that Europe's future was to be a mere branch plant for American multinationals, who had completely supplanted European firms across sectors (Servan-Schreiber 1968). Indeed, for pessimists, the European Union has missed not one but two major waves of innovation: the 1980s innovation of computers and related industries, and the 1990s service-based innovation that built on the earlier wave. The figures for comparative expenditure on R&D paint a depressing picture. Overall European Union expenditure on research has remained stable at just under 2 per cent of GDP for several years. Though expenditures were also stable in the US, America spends considerably more on innovation (2.6 per cent of GDP) and has done so for many years (Eurostat 2005)

Of course, a note of caution is in order: some European states are very competitive in the new technology and service economies. Sweden and Finland, for example, feature regularly among the top countries in any ranking of competitive economies. Thus, Europe's 'problem' is one of uneven performance, where lagging member states tend to create the perception that all EU members have innovation gaps. In virtually no other policy area is there as wide a dispersion in performance between the best and worst EU member state as in innovation policy (Archibugi and Coco 2005: 443). The best EU states (Sweden and other Nordic countries, for example) can hold their own with the US and Japan. The problem lies with the major economies in the EU: France, Germany, Italy, and the UK. None the less, the Commission notes that Europe's economic catch-up with the United States slipped into reverse in the 1990s, with labour productivity failing to keep pace with American improvements (European Commission 2006).

The general situation for large EU states (which comprise the bulk of the EU's economic output as well as dominating its policy-making) can be described easily enough. The EU lags both in total economic resources devoted to innovation and in business-level research and development expenditure. Its share of world patenting is in decline. European firms show a lower propensity to use IT to increase productivity than American firms. European universities are poorly funded by American standards. A National Science Foundation study of immigrant scientists and engineers noted at strong belief among European emigrants that the US offered better research infrastructure and job opportunities (NSF 2007a). As a study for the European Commission noted, the problem is 'that

Europe has *structural* lags in top level science and innovative performance *vis-à-vis* the US' (Dosi *et al.* 2005: 1; emphasis added). The problem is not simply one of commercialization – where excellent science work is left underexploited by firms – but rather one of weakness in both basic research and its application to the creation of goods and services (Dosi *et al.* 2005). Though European universities account for a significant percentage (about 22 per cent) of all research and development expenditures – and produce significant numbers of technicians and engineers – this does not translate into innovative success for firms (OECD 2006b: 209).

Europe has been here before, with the superior performance of other economies provoking concern about European competitiveness. European policymakers fastened on the scale advantages offered by the large American market, and the role of an interventionist state in Japan, to argue for the creation of national champions in various sectors. These firms, usually created by the government-sponsored merger of smaller companies, would enjoy a dominant position in a given national market and thus reap economies of scale benefits. However, the protection afforded these firms gave the wrong series of incentives; the policy produced inefficient, non-innovative firms which were unable to cope with the dynamism of Japanese or American competitors. Outside the aerospace sector, the government-led national champion policies were notable for failure rather than success. Policy failure highlighted the need to expose European firms to greater competition; this could be achieved in the first instance by creating a proper European market. The Single Market Programme was the liberal response to the poor competitiveness of European firms. Creation of the unified market would allow European firms to reap the same scale economies that the American market provided to US firms decades earlier. For reasons as yet unclear, Europe's innovative capacity did not accelerate after the SMP: indeed as indicated above it deteriorated.

The Lisbon strategy

The Lisbon summit in 2000 committed EU member states and the Commission to making Europe 'the most competitive and dynamic knowledge-based economy in the world by 2010'. The declaration was essentially an admission that efforts in the 1990s had either failed or needed to be intensified and refocused. Two measures of economic performance were cited by European poli-cymakers in defence of new strategies: the deterioration of per capita GDP growth relative to the US, and the stagnation of European productivity. European per capita GDP relative to the United States climbed steadily in the years following World War II, peaking in the 1970s at about three-quarters of US levels. The trend, if anything, has been downward and in 2006 the gap was a worrying large 32 per cent (Fassbender 2007). The second problem, in a sense, gave rise to the first. EU labour productivity growth hardly moved during the 1990s, while in the same period the US was undergoing a so-called productivity miracle (Daveri 2002). Exactly why Europe lagged behind has not been adequately answered, though various attempts had been made. One sugges-tion was that the still incomplete Single Market process was to blame; as long as firms could exist in relatively uncompetitive national markets, they lacked the incentive to increase their invest-ment in productivity-enhancing processes and assets (McGuire 2006). Another explanation drew on social and cultural attributes, with the observation that Europeans produce less than Americans because of a rational decision to devote more time to leisure (Fassbender 2007)

There is a view that the demands of innovation policy in the twenty-first century are increasingly in conflict with entrenched political and social practices in the European Union. Throughout the world, innovation policies emphasize the process of 'creative destruction' where older firms and industries are swept away and labour and capital reallocated to new activity (Schumpeter 1942). Advocates of the Schumpeterian perspective see globalization as the very essence of creative destruction. Competitiveness policies ought to assist in the process by encouraging new industries and allowing other sectors to wither away. In contrast, some Europeans see in the competitiveness agenda an effort to unpick the social market protections that citizens have enjoyed for decades. It does not follow that the need for creative destruction requires a small state and low taxes; indeed, government activity and public expen-diture might be necessary for innovation in many fields. There is thus dispute over the orientation of innovation policy. Japan and the United States are both highly innovative and successful economies with considerable numbers of competitive firms. Yet, both operate very different mechanisms for generating this innova-tion. Even within Europe, Nordic countries are reasonably successful at reconciling high taxation with appropriate incentives for firms to invest and innovate. Some European states, including the UK, Ireland and Hungary, are very reliant on foreign firms for R&D expenditures, while others such as Germany retain significant national capabilities (OECD 2006b). In short, very real and important elements of variation of technology policies exist, and European policymakers have found it difficult to articulate a clear and cohesive strategy for Europe in the face of conflicting evidence and societal pressures.

One difficulty the EU has is the multilayered nature of governance, which makes the development and implementation of innovation policies difficult and contested. In the innovation policy literature, the EU proves troublesome for analysts. The EU is distinct in that it is not a national system of innovation, yet neither is it a fully fledged regional system (Kuhlmann 2001). In innovation management, as in other areas, EU policies and institutions must be understood as a complex negotiated order among national, supranational and local actors (Elgström and Smith 2000). The Commission's involvement has been governed by the principle of subsidiarity: that the role of Brussels was to augment and catalyse efforts at the regional or nation state level (Kuhlmann 2001: 963). In sum, in marked contrast to issue areas like trade and competition policies, the Commission enjoys relatively little power or autonomy. The Commission lacks effective tools to force through policy changes, even if agreement could be generated on the nature of the problem and the response. This has left the Commission in the position of advocating networking and mobility among research institutes and firms, not because networking and mobility do much to aid innovation, but because such limited policy tools are about the only ones the Commission has (Dosi *et al.* 2005).

EU R&D policy thus continues to operate at the margins of influence. This limits its ability to develop and enforce policy directions and instead makes it prone to backsliding. The Kok Report, a high-level review of EU innovation policy chaired by former Dutch prime minister Wim Kok, observes that European states cannot develop solutions in isolation – and only coordinated action will benefit Europe. UNICE bemoaned the inability of member states to meet their Lisbon commitments, noting that the temptation to use public funds for objectives other than enhancing competitiveness seemed hard to resist (UNICE 2006).

The direction of European R&D

Evolutionary perspectives on innovation draw attention to the uncertainty surrounding innovation (McGuire 2006). The innovative process is uncertain (that does not mean it has no organizational logic) and characterized by incremental improvements and developments that are, from time to time, interrupted by dramatic, discontinuous change. Schumpeter referred to a 'process of industrial mutation . . . that incessantly revolutionizes the economic structure from within' (Drejer 2004: 556). Schumpeter's early interest in individuals as inventors and entrepreneurs gave way in time to a recognition that creative destruction could be – and was – carried out in larger organizations. Mowery and Rosenberg (1989) described the American economy of the late nineteenth and early twentieth centuries as one where, in a somewhat paradoxical way, innovation was made routine by institutionalizing activities underpinning invention. These included the spread of secondary and, later, higher education, as well as the creation of in-house research and development units in American firms. Thus, the innovative process may be uncertain and non-linear, but it is not random. Government policies should be able to provide incentives (where needed) to encourage the appropriate conditions for innovation.

If innovation is as non-linear as evolutionary perspectives suggest, then targeted national champion policies are unwise for a different reason: since a state cannot be certain where and how innovations will arise, the best policy is to encourage innovative activity across a range of sectors. Moreover, a key benefit of innovation lies in its diffusion through the economy to medium- and low-technology sectors. This diffusion ought to make less technologically advanced sectors more productive (Navarro, 2003: 12; Robertson and Patel 2007). Thus, targeted policy that comes at the expense of basic, blue-skies research seems problematic (Brusconi and Guena 2003; Dosi *et al.* 2005). Some evidence to back an emphasis on supporting wide-ranging research comes from a comparison of the early development of biotechnology in the United States and Germany. Both countries invested considerable sums in this new technology, with German government support dating from the 1960s. Yet by 1997 the United States biotechnology sector was larger by a factor of ten (Giesecke 2000: 207). The crucial factor is that diffuse US support for basic research allowed the organic development of the sector. German efforts, by contrast, were hampered by the dominant pharmaceutical firms, which resisted greater competition, and weak incentives in the university system to transform basic research into patentable innovations (ibid.).

By and large the Commission's pronouncements on the trajectory of research and development policy reflect an evolutionary economics perspective, stressing the need for basic research. Central to the Lisbon Agenda is raising the amount spent on R&D by member states to 3 per cent of GDP, though as some academics note, most of this increase is to come from industry (Archibugi and Coco 2005). By 2004 there were several states spending at this level. The Commission's own funding streams, principally the framework programmes and structural funds, were also tilted toward basic research and designed to catalyse innovation. However, these efforts are small in comparative terms: the €10.5 billion of Structural Funds earmarked for innovation from 2000 to 2006 were roughly equivalent to Sweden's annual R&D expenditure (Potočnik 2007). An additional obstacle was the tension between allocating research money on the basis of the excellence of the proposed research, and awarding money to less technologically capable partners in poorer member states. Plans for the European Research Council to centralize and coordinate long-term basic research were developed and accepted in 2006. In a departure from previous practice, 'scientific merit' would be the overriding criterion for awarding funding (European Commission 2004c: 21). There is a persistent tension between cohesion and innovation underpinnings of EU R&D policy (Sharp, 1998). The former implied the need to direct R&D support to poorer member states even if this was unlikely to produce cutting-edge research; the latter suggested that the best ideas needed to win out in a process of competition if EU science was to progress. By 2004, the Kok Report offered indications that the latter view was prevailing (European Commission 2004c). This plan is generally welcomed in member states with strong university systems that can be expected to win the greatest share of money, but other actors prefer to retain a 'developmental' aspect in EU-level research policies.

All that said, governments and the Commission are only partly responsible for the problem: European businesses invest less in innovation than competitors. Business R&D investment – particularly in the major European economies – remains low compared with the United States and Japan (Figure 6.2). In Europe, businesses conduct 64 per cent of R&D expenditures, whereas in Asia

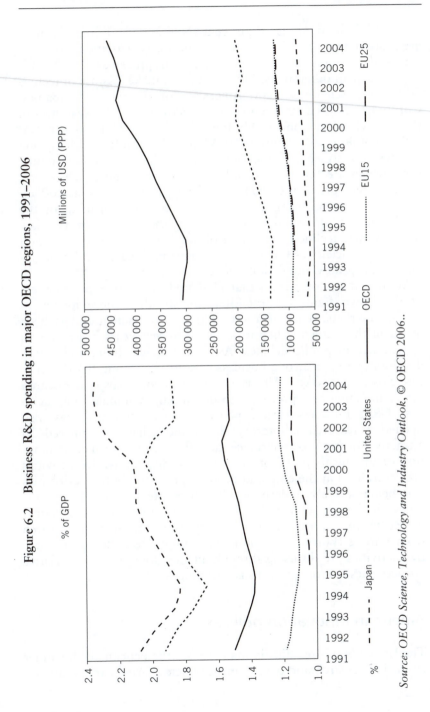

Figure 6.2   Business R&D spending in major OECD regions, 1991–2006

Source: OECD Science, Technology and Industry Outlook, © OECD 2006..

and the US the figure is 70 per cent (NSF 2007d). European firms are more reliant on public funds for innovative activities – and this leaves them more vulnerable to political processes that favour expenditure in other areas. European firms make less use of technicians and scientists than American or Japanese companies. Corporate research staff represent 80 per cent of all researchers in the US, while the comparable figure in the EU-25 is 49 per cent (OECD 2006b: 36) (Figure 6.3). What is the problem with lagging business investment? In the United States, high-technology industries, which are the main spenders on research and development, are a larger part of the economy (European Commission 2007c). For some, the problem remains a lack of pump-priming of the small and medium sized business sector, the sector seen as a key driver of new technologies. The Kok Report called for the creation of new tax incentives for SMEs to engage in research and development (European Commission 2004c).

Another fear, however, is that EU-based firms are expending less of their own funds because they are spending more money in foreign markets. The diffusion of innovative activities has been noted in the academic literature but in recent years has made an appearance in public debates. As countries like India and China develop, there is a strong business case for relocating R&D activities closer to market. Airbus has opened an aerospace research centre in China as a precursor to developing manufacturing facilities. GSK, Europe's largest pharmaceutical company, has also opened a research laboratory there. India has also proved an attractive location for pharmaceutical firms to locate. The assumption of the linear model of innovation – that innovative activities are centralized at the core and product produced in the peripheries – is being severely undermined by corporate activity. As the EU notes, the US has increased its share of foreign affilitates' spending on R&D, to a large extent by taking a greater share of research from Europe (European Commission 2005a: 36). Though innovative activities are diffusing throughout the globe, Europe's relative attractiveness to foreign firms is declining.

American innovation policies

The United States remains in many senses the benchmark for other countries' research and development policies. Gross expenditure on

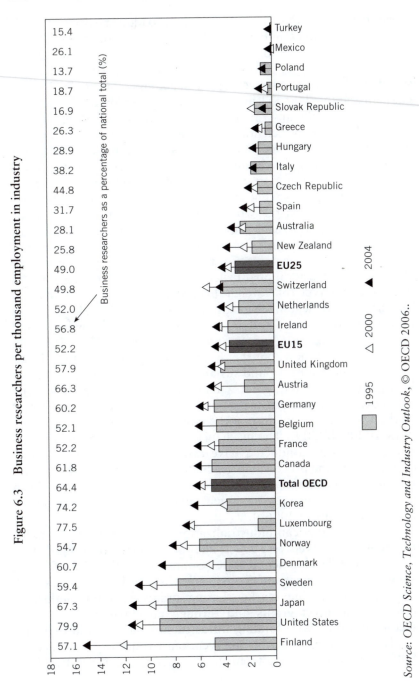

Figure 6.3 Business researchers per thousand employment in industry

Business researchers as a percentage of national total (%)

Turkey	15.4
Mexico	26.1
Poland	13.7
Portugal	18.7
Slovak Republic	16.9
Greece	26.3
Hungary	28.9
Italy	38.2
Czech Republic	44.8
Spain	31.7
Australia	28.1
New Zealand	25.8
EU25	49.0
Switzerland	49.8
Netherlands	52.0
Ireland	56.8
EU15	52.2
United Kingdom	57.9
Austria	66.3
Germany	60.2
Belgium	52.1
France	52.2
Canada	61.8
Total OECD	64.4
Korea	74.2
Luxembourg	77.5
Norway	54.7
Denmark	60.7
Sweden	59.4
Japan	67.3
United States	79.9
Finland	57.1

▲ 2004
△ 2000
1995

Source: OECD Science, Technology and Industry Outlook, © OECD 2006..

research and development (GERD), the broadest measure of R&D spending, was $312 billion in 2004. The US accounts for 44 per cent of all research and development expenditures in the OECD (OECD 2006b: 208; author's calculations). In 2003, its R&D spend was equal to the combined spending of Canada, France, Germany, Italy, Japan, Russia and the UK. (NSF 2005). The US dominates virtually any ranking of knowledge production, whether measured in patents, scientific citations or rankings of universities. For example, the United States gains 40 per cent of all revenues from so-called royalty, licensing and fee (RL&F) activity (WTO 2006). RL&F is an important measure of how intellectual property is used, as it captures what international firms are prepared to pay for. The US remains the world's second largest patenter, trailing Japan. Leading American universities are widely regarded as the best in the world, both in terms both of the sheer research they produce, and of their success in translating this into products and services. This has additional benefits for the American economy, as it affects the type of foreign firm that enters the US market. Technologically leading foreign firms often locate close to top American universities, and in so doing generate knowledge and economic spillovers (Alcácer and Chung 2007). This American dominance is not new, but the result of decades of evolution. It has come from both a heavy and sustained commitment by government in support of research and a willingness of firms to invest heavily in innovation. American firms conducted 64 per cent of all R&D in the US in 2003; in Europe the equivalent figure is 53 per cent (OECD 2006b: 209). The mechanisms through which this innovative activity was conducted have evolved over time; government dominance of the process had gradually been supplanted by greater reliance on firm-level expenditure – until the George W. Bush administration, when government expenditure gained renewed importance (OECD 2006b).

During the American industrialization of the 1800s the US political economy looked very much like the German social market or the Japanese developmental state (Gourevitch 1996: 239–40). The American government intervened extensively in industrial development by sanctioning market-sharing practices, aiding industrial research via direct grants and through an expanding university sector, and otherwise funding infrastructure such as railways and roads (ibid.). However, this interventionist trajectory was successfully and spectacularly altered in the early years of the twentieth century. In a number of industries, the government reversed its policy bias toward business in favour one oriented toward the consumer. The Standard Oil Trust was broken up in response to a public campaign. Banks were offered the choice of operating as either investment or retail banks, thus destroying the American version of the German universal bank.

However, this shift of trajectory did not impede US economic advance; indeed, it may have been vital to it. In a useful reminder of the overlapping nature of policy areas, American scholars have drawn attention to the important role played by competition policy as a *de facto* technology policy (Hart 2001). Antitrust legislation acts as a technology policy by changing the incentives for firms in two ways: first, it influences the organization of R&D activities; and second, it affects the types of products and processes that are researched. As Mowery and Rosenberg argue, antitrust legislation made it difficult for firms to abuse market positions and stifle innovation. Firms also chose to merge with rivals rather than attempt to form cartels. Thus, American firms gained economies of scale and scope which formed the basis of their global dominance after 1945 (Mowery and Rosenberg 1989: 106). It also reinforced a characteristic of US firms even before the Sherman Act: American firms tended to rely more for R&D on their in-house laboratories and less on government funding than their European counterparts. That said, early American interest in using the state to establish the infrastructure for a technologically advanced economy remains a signal feature of that country's development. As US firms emerged from World War II dominant in their industries, it was easy to forget the early role of the state and ascribe American success to free market economics. Thus was born the myth that the US lacked an industrial policy. The benign environment that US firms found themselves in after 1945 made it easy for American firms to believe in the superiority of this arm's-length relationship with the state. Non-Americans too came to regard America's success as a confirmation of the value of laissez-faire, non-interventionist government.

By the mid-1980s however, faith in America's innovative capabilities was undermined. The principal agent of this loss of faith was Japan, which was succeeding in using a type of state-led capitalism to erode American dominance in sector after sector. In American eyes, the Japanese succeeded in assaulting sectors of traditional US dominance – cars being the prime example – as well as newer, knowledge-intensive sectors such as semiconductors. This success owed a lot to the Japanese adaptation of American innovations and the application of these to successful products. Thus US firms and policymakers become concerned at the inability of the US to apply technological advances to products in a timely and effective manner. One alleged culprit was the basic research infrastructure – US universities and research institutes – which were seen as unwilling to exploit the commercial potential of their discoveries, along with a confusing and fragmented patenting regime (Bremer 2001; Mowery 1998). In 1980, the Bayh–Dole Act was passed by Congress with the clear aim of creating incentives for institutions to not merely discover new things but also make money from them. It did so by allowing organizations (universities, but also charities and small business) to patent inventions developed with federal research funds. Additionally, the act gave federal government agencies greater discretion to grant exclusive licences on technologies to firms (GAO 1998).

Americans were also concerned that their industries not merely were the victims of successful competitors but also were being targeted by foreign firms operating with the express support of their home governments. Japan's entry into segments of the computer chip market looked like a predatory effort to drive out all American firms. '[A] classic strategy of infant-industry protection "worked" to create a competitive Japanese industry capable of challenging American supremacy' (Tyson 1992: 86). The European aircraft maker Airbus Industrie was likewise seen as a direct attack on an industry where American firms enjoyed overwhelming dominance. The Airbus episode is a reminder that many economic policy areas eventually make their way into the trade domain.

The late 1980s and early 1990s saw the US continue to develop an industrial policy that sought to improve the competitive position of US firms. One thrust of these policies was to lesson the grip that military applications had on the national system of innovation. Critics pointed out that while the US military had provided funding for a large number of knowledge-intensive products that underpinned US competitiveness, military R&D was no longer as useful to civilian applications as it once was. Military applications required that products have properties that were simply not relevant to the civilian economy: stealth technology for example may be very useful for military aircraft, but has no relevance to civil aircraft design.

The US search for competitiveness

Concerns about the declining competitiveness of American industry did not start with the outsourcing controversy of the early part of the new millennium, but are a persistent feature of American post-1945 political economy. America is the world's largest and hence most attractive consumer market, so penetrating it is the goal of any foreign firm seeking international success. During the 1950s, with Europe and Japan still rebuilding after the war, the American market was dominated by American firms. Indeed, the economy was remarkably self-contained, with relatively little international trade. That situation has changed over the years with first European and Japanese and then Chinese and other South Asian firms gaining market share. American firms began to complain about international competition in the 1960s and protectionist sentiment has been an enduring feature of the American trade policy arena. However, what is relatively new is the view that the US government seeks to actively enhance the competitiveness of US domestic firms through technology policy.

The Clinton administration strengthened the US state's commitment to an active industrial policy, partly in response to the perceived failure of American industry in areas such as semiconductors, advanced materials (such as carbon fibre) and supercomputers (Branscomb 1993). This policy was manifest in the creation of a National Economic Council to oversee the competitiveness of the economy. The Council was deliberately modelled on the existing National Security Council and was meant to convey the message that 'economic security' was as important as conventional military issues (Peterson 1996: 81). The appointment of Laura Tyson as chairman of the Council of Economic Advisors was also seen as a manifestation of the new interventionist mood. Tyson herself had long advocated industrial policy measures as a means of countering the unfair trade practices of Japan, the European Union and some LDCs.

Perhaps the most dramatic illustration of the new, interventionist attitude was seen in the American volte-face in the Uruguay Round on the matter of state subsidies. Here, longstanding American opposition to the very principle of state funding gave way to an acceptance, indeed an embrace, of the idea. European negotiators did not know quite what to make of the Clinton administration's eagerness to accept state subsidy. Commerce Undersecretary

Garten proposed a subsidy regime that was considerably more lax than the one under consideration at the talks, with an extremely generous ceiling on government support for all types of research (Paeman and Bensch 1995: 160). US negotiators in the GATT Uruguay Round talks sought exemptions for R&D subsidies from the proposed WTO subsidy agreement; the exemption was fought for so as to 'accommodate planned new [R&D] programs by the Clinton Administration' (Ostry 1997: 182).

The George W. Bush administration's approach to R&D has been characterized by two trends. First, there has been a dramatic 'remilitarization' of government support, the military budget again assuming the role of key sponsor of high-technology innovation. Military spending accounted for over over 50 per cent of all federal research and development expenditures in 2003, and this rose to about 60 per cent by 2007 (NSF 2003: 3; NSF 2007c). Given the trauma of 11 September 2001, it would have been surprising had US R&D spending not shifted toward military and intelligence spending. The three areas where research spending is concentrated are military spending, homeland security and space; these three got the lion's share of the $132 billion the federal government allocated to R&D in 2005 (Segal 2004). However, as with other OECD states, the percentage share of R&D supported by the federal government has been in long-term decline; in 1964 federal spend was 67 per cent of all R&D spending, while in 2003 the share was 30 per cent (NSF 2005).

Heavy reliance on military R&D spending has been criticized in the US, generally for skewing spending priorities and increasing the risk of American firms being led away from promising commercial applications. However, these fears seem to be reduced by the willingness of US firms to spend their own money, with or without government help, in support of innovation. US firms remain relatively heavy spenders on R&D and there is considerable evidence that US leadership in information technology and its application to business processes owes a lot to the dramatic increase in business-level research and development spending. Beginning in the mid-1990s, industrial R&D spending increased and more than compensated for declines in government funding. Between 1994 and 2000, business R&D grew at an annual rate of 8.8 per cent (NSF 2003: 11). The greater propensity of US-based firms to spend more on research and development than their European counterparts is one area of clear contrast between the trans-Atlantic partners.

There is considerable evidence to support Gourevitch's suggestion that the US has rediscovered the Hamiltonian tradition of political economy (in Berger and Dore 1997: 256). The US has moved away from the free market orientation that characterized its public policy during the early post-war period. The US government has reacted to perceptions that its partners were trading unfairly, especially in sectors characterized by Schumpeterian competition. The reaction was to try and develop a more interventionist and discriminatory industrial policy than previously. That said, another theme that emerges from the survey of US policies is the key role of business-level research and development to American success. American firms have historically invested more in corporate research and development, employed more technicians and scientists and been more willing to invest in innovations as a means of improving productivity. In the past two decades the willingness of US firms to invest heavily in IT is merely the latest example of the propensity of American managers to innovate. It stands in contrast to the lagging investment by European firms. Moreover, it has made American firms the preferred partners for international corporate alliances where technology development is central to the relationship. European firms have been increasingly drawn to the United States as a base to conduct R&D, whether within the firm or as part of a corporate alliance (Archibugi and Coco 2005).

American anxieties about China are not confined to monetary relations; American legislators and commentators have over the past few years grown increasingly alarmed at the growth of innovative capabilities in the world's fifth-largest economy. One manifestation of this has been sluggish growth in exports. Baily and Lawrence note that US export growth has slowed dramatically in recent years, though export growth slowed in the 1990s: 'The weakness in US export performance has been particularly problematic since 2000. US exports grew at only 3.3 per cent a year from 2000 to 2005' (Baily and Lawrence 2006: 5). The same authors note that much of the export problem is a function of the exchange rate, and the depreciation of the dollar, which began in the middle of the 2000s, may help. However, they also note that across a range of industries American firms face formidable competition, including in high-technology sectors. This perception that America is slipping in the innovation leagues is fuelled also by the declining numbers of American citizens pursuing science and engineering careers. Though Europe's difficulties make American problems in this regard look minor, American commentators note that the generation of scientists and engineers that brought America innovative leadership in many fields is not being replaced. American R&D is, as one study noted, increasingly reliant on immigrant labour (Cohen and Noll 2001).

In 2007 the Congress passed legislation designed to address the innovative infrastructure. The 'America Creating Opportunities to Meaningfully Promote Excellence in Technology, Education and Science Act' (COMPETES Act) sought to increase the supply of specialist teachers in science, technology and engineering through enhanced scholarships; more early-career research funding for university scientists was also made available though a doubling of the National Science Foundation scholarship budget (US Congress 2007). The Act provides an insight into the extent to which the United States and Europe share common problems in respect of innovation. Both economies have 'supply problems' in terms of skilled teachers and researchers; Americans tend to eschew science careers, while suitably qualified Europeans often prefer to pursue their careers outside Europe – generally in the US (thus filling the jobs lacking American candidates). Though American universities are lavishly funded by European standards, shifts in US funding patterns – particularly at state-funded institutions – toward less government funding and higher tuition fees made science subjects relatively expensive to teach. Universities in America have responded by essentially rationing places on science and engineering courses (Cohen and Noll 2001). It remains to be seen whether the legislative initiatives such as the COMPETES Act reverse this trend.

The renewed emphasis on innovation comes against the backdrop of stagnation in median wages in the United States, and a growing public perception that middle-class American families are not making the kind of material gains seen by earlier generations. Rising inequality is a feature of many industrialized states, including European economies, but the relatively deregulated American economy, with its low level of welfare and income support programmes, has seen the fastest rises (Burtless 2007). While average incomes have been rising, this is a consequence of the spectacular growth of incomes at the upper end of the income distribution, not a rise in the general level of income (Luce 2006; Piketty and Saez 2006). Several studies have noted that the offshoring of jobs, once confined to low-skilled sectors of the work-force, was now happening to highly skilled workers (Baily 2007; Scheve and Slaughter 2007; see also Blinder 2007). The share of national wealth owned by top earners, having fallen back in the first half of the twentieth century, was now back at 'Gilded Era' levels. Faced with a political backlash against globalization, political debate among some US policymakers and academics focused on the role that a renewed emphasis on science and technology policy can play in generating quality jobs and incomes for American workers.

From transatlantic to global innovation space?

The application of science and technology to economic activity first arose in German and American firms early in the twentieth century and was part of the set of characteristics that allowed the transatlantic economy to dominate the global system for most of the past two hundred years. Though governments devote considerable resources to capturing the benefits of innovation for their own firms through a variety of policies, in fact innovative activity does tend to diffuse across borders. Firms not only create their own intellectual property, but also scan the competitive environment for knowledge that might yield a competitive advantage. Firms were diversifying their innovation activities some years before it became commonplace to talk about the globalization of research. American firms invested abroad earlier than many foreign competitors, with much of this investment going to Europe. For much of the past twenty years, the 'globalization' of innovation was, in fact, the regionalization of R&D among the US, the EU and Japan. These three actors accounted for the bulk of global R&D, and when the research was conducted outside the home country it was located in one of the other two economies. In 2002, US firms placed 61 per cent of their foreign research and development investment in the European Union, worth about $15 billion (OECD 2006b: 123). Over half this investment went to two sectors: automobiles and pharmaceuticals. The United States was a next exporter of research and development activities to Europe until the turn of the millennium, when European firms expanded their activities in the US. Trade in ideas as represented by flows of royalties, fees and licence income from industrial processes was

Box 6.1   GSK: the growth of global R&D

GlaxoSmithKline (GSK) is one of the world's largest pharmaceutical firms, and presents a good example of how corporate evolution and the globalization of innovation change the research and development patterns of Western companies. GSK was formed in 2000, when the British firm Glaxo Wellcome merged with its American rival Smith Kline Beecham. The merged group is formally based in London – as is the chairman – but the executive offices are in Philadelphia, the home of Smith Kline Beecham.

The combined company has numerous laboratories around the world, but they are clustered in Western Europe (11 sites), the United States (4 sites) and Japan (2 sites). However, the company announced in mid-2007 that a new laboratory in Shanghai would open under the direction of a Chinese-born and-educated director. This laboratory will have responsibility for research and development in the area of neurogenerative diseases, which include ailments like Parkinson's Disease.

The important point here is that the Shanghai laboratory is not confined to conducting research primarily aimed at the Chinese market. Rather, like the company's sites elsewhere its task is to undertake work in a particular clinical field on behalf of the entire company. That the new laboratory is located in China is a reflection of that country's growing technological capabilities.

Source: http://www.gsk.com/ControllerServlet?appId=4&pageId=402&newsid=1043, accessed 4 June 2007.

remarkably balanced, with the US generally running only a modest surplus on its trade with Europe (NSF 2007d).

The US was by the early 2000s the favoured location for foreign OECD-based multinationals, many keen to capitalize on US leadership of the information technology sector. The US attracted the bulk of all foreign R&D activity conducted in the OECD, foreign firms began to locate their research facilities in the United States, perhaps to take advantage of basic research done at US universities. By the mid-1990s the share of patents granted to foreign firms was about 45 per cent (Mowery 1998). Access to the American science base was particularly important for sectors like pharmaceuticals, with European firms coming to rely on their US operations for much of the basic research work (Brusoni and Geuna 2003). Indeed, fully half of EU R&D investment in the US was concentrated in chemicals and pharmaceutical sectors (OECD 2006b: 123), and in the pharmaceutical sector it is no exaggeration to describe US–EU links as a fully fledged transatlantic innovation area. Such corporate cooperation was underpinned by broad congruence between the EU and the US on various regulatory matters, not least contract law and intellectual property.

Innovation is now even more globalized and, as outlined above, Europe and America are both experiencing a relative decline in their dominance of the area. It is notable that Europe is becoming relatively less important as an R&D hub for American firms, which are increasing the amount of their research work done in Asia. In 1995, Europe accounted for 70 per cent of all US firms' overseas research and development expenditures: by 2002, this had dipped to 58 per cent (NSF 2007b, figure 22). Though American firms did increase their R&D expenditures in Europe during 1998–2002, the rate of growth (4.8 per cent) was dwarfed by the rate of growth of American R&D investment in Asia (28.6 per cent) (NSF 2007b). It is not hard to understand the interest of American firms in this regard. China has produced a stunning increase in its innovative capacity, with R&D intensity (research spending as a percentage of GDP) rising from 0.6 per cent in 1995 to 1.3 per cent in 2006. China's pool of researchers grew 77 per cent to 926,000 in the same period (OECD 2006a). Smaller developing states are also accounting for more innovative activity, with the share of global patenting accounted for by Brazil, China, India and South Africa increasing from 0.15 per cent in 1991 to 0.58 per cent in 2004 (OECD 2006a) – a small part of the total to be sure, but a dramatic increase and an indication of creative talent that has not gone unnoticed by European and American multinationals. What is good for firms, and indeed the overall economy, may not be good for individual European and American workers however; hence the keen political interest in the globalization and relocation of research and development activities. Innovation policy may yet come to have a political dynamic like that in trade policy: the diffuse benefits of open trade attract little attention compared with the concentrated losses in industries. Consumers gain from innovation, wherever it is created, but skilled workers are not as mobile as their jobs and fear losing out to competitors. Both Europe and America are struggling to devise policy responses that accommodate these conflicting pressures.

Overview and conclusion

This chapter has argued that changes in the international business environment have presented the US and the EU with the same problem: how to ensure the competitiveness of national firms in high-technology sectors. Firms in these sectors offer states the promise of high-paying jobs, a vibrant research base and, if new trade theory is to be believed, the accumulation of economic rents. These attractions offer states powerful incentives to develop discriminatory industrial policies designed to favour home firms. Both the US and the EU have developed such programmes, but so have developing economies like China. In contrast to other policy areas, there is a notable absence of networks: innovation policies are crafted – for better or worse – on the assumption that economic growth is zero-sum. Politicians routinely refer to other states as 'our competitors', disregarding Krugman's (1994) observation that states and national economies do not compete with each other the way firms do. However, the absence of complex relationships in innovation arises too because other policy areas act as proxies. For example, the diffusion of corporate R&D facilities is caught in debates about foreign direct investment.

The enormous costs of R&D push firms to co-operate as a means of spreading the cost – and the risk – of R&D. Increasing complexity also means that firms are incapable of developing all the requisite technologies for certain products. Thus, products are developed by networks of firms with each company bringing some technology or other asset to the group. In this circumstance, firms are attractive because they possess specialist knowledge, and national economies attractive for the innovative capacity they contain. The worst outcome for a firm is to be cut off from technology, even foreign technology. As Ham and Mowery point out, technological interdependence is now well established and unwinding it both improbable and damaging (Ham and Mowery 1995: 92). Thus, an open international business environment is the preferred option. For Europe, the situation is more precarious than for the US. Europe continues to lag in the production and diffusion of technology and is becoming a less attractive place for American firms to invest their research and development money. European firms invest less than American and Japanese firms, and there are indications that when they do undertake R&D a significant amount of that work now takes place in the United States.

A number of conclusions emerge from this chapter:

- First, the European Union and the United States both face increasing competition from developing states in high-technology and high-skilled services and industries.
- Second, both the actors seek to enhance the competitiveness of their economies through enhanced support for innovation. The European challenge is much more structural; the Commission has relatively limited powers to develop and implement technology policies and relies very much on member states to create their own.
- Third, European and American firms have dense research linkages with each other's economies. This made the Euro-American area the dominant scientific hub for most of the last century. These corporate ties are fostered and maintained by political and regulatory networks in areas like intellectual property and legal regimes, that make the trans-Atlantic economic space a familiar and attractive place to conduct research. However, there is accumulating evidence that the European 'leg' of this relationship is becoming weak.
- Fourth, European and American firms increasingly use developing states as bases for their research and development efforts. Traditionally, developing country research was confined to downstream tailoring of products to local markets: this is changing. The development of competitive scientific bases in China and India, among others, means that firms are diffusing their important R&D functions across the globe.

Chapter 7

Regionalism and Interregionalism

The European Union is a regional as well as a global power. It is indeed the most richly developed, complex and successful regional political arrangement in existence. The United States too is a regional and global power; its regional relationships are constructed differently from the EU's but both actors have sought to develop a complex web of geographically defined economic, political and – in the broadest sense – security relationships. Some of these owe their existence to history, while the new regionalism of recent years owes a great deal to both actors seeking to maximize their access to markets and secure foreign policy goals in the post-cold-war world.

The international system is often less globalized than commonly thought – or at least differently globalized – with distinct regional political and economic arrangements surviving and indeed thriving in this age of the global (Gamble and Payne 1996; Hettne *et al.* 1999; Schirm 2002; Payne 2004). That large entities like the US and the European Union have policies tailored to specific regions is not a surprise. However, there has been something of a renaissance in the use of region-specific politics in recent years, partly out of frustration with multilateralism at the global level but also as a reflection of the important historical and cultural realities that shape and constrain policy choice. As power in the international political economy has shifted away from Europe and America and towards Asia, both the EU and the US have relied on regional or bilateral pacts where their bargaining power is significant. There is however an important point of contrast in the manner in which the EU and the US engage regionally. In the regional sphere the EU is clearly the civilian superpower; both within Europe itself, and on the broader global plane, EU leaders have forged a series of powerful but essentially diplomatic and commercial arrangements (Edwards and Regelsberger 1990; Alecu de Flers and Regelsberger 2005). Despite possessing substantial and growing leverage in these contexts, the

Union has limited abilities to use coercion or force and prefers not to. The EU also has a distinctive approach to issues of regional development, preferring to use aid as well as preferential trade agreements in its regional policies (Feinberg 2003). This reflects the 'civilian superpower' status of the Union (and also consolidates it), but also arises from a European political economy tradition not so convinced of the efficacy of market-based solutions for development problems. By contrast, the United States as a military as well as political and economic superpower is much more willing to use the full range of policy tools – including military force – to attain goals. American policies at the interregional level also reflect a more overt commitment to market-based solutions, and often also entail the use of development policies for political ends.

European and American regional policies are thus different in important and obvious ways at the level of mechanisms and motivations. They also contrast in terms of their regional focus. It is unsurprising that the US takes a keen interest in its Latin-American neighbourhood in the same way that the EU devotes considerable energy to relations with Eastern Europe and Turkey. However, at the broadest level, both actors are motivated by similar desires and beliefs: that economic liberalization is good for all countries and makes for more peaceful relations; that regional policies can be used to promote good governance and the rule of law in developing states; and that regional policies must be multifaceted rather than reliant on single policy tools.

The US and the EU also compete with each other in respect of regional policies. This is particularly true where trade is concerned, as any regional trade agreement presents a potential threat to the party left outside the agreement. European firms, for example, have to wonder if the successful conclusion of a free trade agreement of the Americas might be injurious to them by privileging competitor firms inside the zone. This was exactly the experience of Japanese manufacturers after the negotiation of the North American Free Trade Area (NAFTA) in 1994. Suddenly, the new, continent-wide rules on sourcing and local content made Japanese cars ineligible for tariff-free status. The resulting adjustment cost and dislocation so angered Japan's manufacturers that it was central to Japan's negotiation of its own regional pacts (Manger 2005). So too for Europe, which looked to conclude bilateral deals with Mexico, Mercosur and South Africa at least partly in response to American initiatives.

The growth of regionalism and interregionalism alongside pressures for globalization can be seen in two main dimensions. First, regional trade agreements have exploded in popularity in recent years, partly out of frustration with the slow progress of WTO multilateral talks but also out of recognition that some regional arrangements are necessary to accommodate dramatic new growth in areas of the world – and that states (and their firms) cannot risk exclusion. Japan and Korea for example have embraced the regional trade agreement path, both having been staunch advocates of an exclusively multilateral path in the past. Both did so for a mix of reasons: Japanese firms were very angry at efforts to handicap their operations in NAFTA through complex local content requirements, while the Koreans see a free trade area with the US as an important bulwark to the increasing presence of China. Both states are relative newcomers to the regional game: the same cannot be said for the US and the European Union. The WTO now estimates in excess of 300 agreements of varying membership, scope and complexity are in existence (WTO 2007, website) (see Figure 7.1).

Given the problems with the multilateral level negotiations, many states have opted for restricted, regionally defined arrangements. Some critics have opposed these arrangements, and see in them the potential for a stalling, if not a rolling back, of the gains made from trade liberalization over the past several decades. There are several attractions of regional trade agreements, ranging from specific economic gains to more political goals such as satisfying domestic constituencies. There is a view that regional integration represents an important stepping-stone on the route to larger, multilateral economic and political arrangements. This argument disagrees with the view that regional and multilateral arrangements are somehow in conflict, instead asserting an essential complementarity. There are several reasons for this. First, regional arrangements typically feature a smaller set of negotiating partners, and all other things being equal, it seems easier to conclude an agreement among a limited group of states. The very difficult Doha negotiations (see Chapter 3), to say nothing of the increasingly fraught internal politics of the European Union, would be cited by many as illustrative of the diminishing ability of ever-larger groupings to come to meaningful agreements.

The second area of change and development at the regional and interregional levels is that of security. During the cold war, as noted in Chapter 1, there had grown up a network of regional

Figure 7.1 Growth of regional trade agreements, 1948–2006

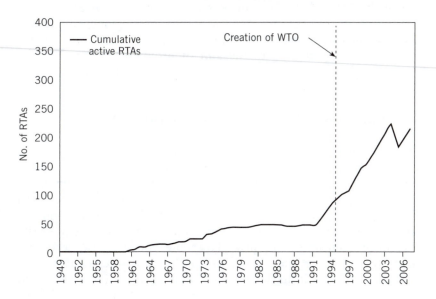

Source: Adapted from WTO website, http://www.wto.org/english/tratop_e/region_e/regfac_e.htm, accessed 27 August 2007.

security pacts focused on Europe (especially in the form of NATO) and other regions where the threat of Communism was seen as pressing, such as South-East Asia and Latin America. Not surprisingly, the USA was at the core of all of these arrangements, but they progressively collapsed as the needs of American diplomacy and the impact of regional conflicts fluctuated. In the wake of the collapse of the Soviet Union, security pacts associated with the USSR also disappeared – but that did not mean that regional security needs had disappeared. In the post-9/11 environment, many existing regional arrangements have taken on new security aspects, reflecting the expanding conception of security itself in the context of the 'war on terror' and concerns over issues as diverse as migration and the environment. This means that in this area, the EU and the US have had to adjust to new security needs, to reflect these in a new generation of regional and interregional agreements, and above all, in the context of this book, to address a series of issues in which they are both entangled.

This chapter will explore these issues by assessing the ways in which the EU and the US can be seen as regional powers, and by evaluating their respective approaches to interregionalism. It will then go on to investigate the impact of competition and convergence in this context, with the aim of providing insight into the ways the EU–US system has evolved and may continue to evolve.

The European Union as a regional power

One of the key motivations in the setting up of the European Communities during the 1950s was connected with 'regional power'. To put it simply, the aim of many of those involved in the European project was to create a 'zone of peace' in western Europe, which would make the recurrence of general war impossible and which would use economic and political means to create a form of 'security community'. For some, this was also accompanied by a broader aim: to create a 'European regional power' which could exert influence on the broader international level, and which might ultimately rank alongside the two 'superpowers' – the United States and the Soviet Union. The two aims were in principle complementary, since a successful regional community in Europe could act as the base for projection of a distinctively 'European' identity and European priorities in the global arena. During the 1950s and 1960s, the most determined proponents of such a view were the French Gaullists, who were in turn resisted by others with a more regionalist or even 'Atlanticist' point of view (see Chapter 1). The consolidation of the Communities saw in turn a consolidation of regional power, such that increasingly they became seen as an 'anchor' of stability in a changing Europe, but progress on the broader global level appeared less impressive – both to its supporters within the Communities and to those outside who might have been threatened or supported by it.

A major factor in the growth of the EU as a regional power, if not a 'regional superpower', is thus clearly the growth of the Union itself. As will be seen in Chapter 8, the enlargement and the 'deepening' of the EU has given it an extraordinary amount of structural power in the European continent, both by reason of its own internal development and because of the attractions of membership (Keukeleire 2003; M. Smith 2007). The Union exercises a magnetic force within the continent of Europe, engaging not only potential members but also those in the 'European neighbourhood' who have to adjust their politics and policies to the presence of the EU. The power thus achieved and exercised, however, is essentially civilian: it depends upon the institutional strength, the commercial weight and the diplomatic leverage that emerge from the development of the European integration project. In many ways also, the power is 'unconscious', reflecting not so much a grand strategy for the exercise of power over the continent as the implications of the EU's dominant presence. Where the power is exercised more self-consciously, it is also subject to important internal restrictions imposed by the 'division of powers' within the Union between the Member States and European institutions. Other limitations emerge from the impact of history: from the longstanding connections of individual Member States with 'outsiders' within Europe, and from traditional alliances and alignments.

Despite these limitations, the EU can rightly be described as a 'civilian superpower' with a dominant regional role in Europe. The EU can also be described as a 'trading state', in the sense that its collective concerns are predominantly commercial and diplomatic, with the diplomatic closely linked with commercial interests and preoccupations (M. Smith 2004; see also Chapter 9 below). The Union does not deal in the 'harder' end of coercion and force, but this does not mean that it is easy to ignore or to resist the incentives or possible penalties that it can offer or impose. These incentives and rewards are clearest in the case of EU enlargement, but there has also grown up in and around Europe a series of arrangements designed to create a regional order centred on Brussels. The 'neighbourhood policy' has come to encompass countries ranging from the Arctic to the Mediterranean, and has generated a complex web of civilian agreements covering not only commercial concerns but also questions of governance, human rights, the environment and migration – questions that in the twenty-first century are unquestionably linked to security (Dannreuther 2003; K. Smith 2005b).

From the 1960s onwards, the EU and its predecessors have thus clearly reflected the growth of European integration as the basis for regional power. For the EU in its region, this has generated a web of new relationships, which have been continuously adjusted and renegotiated in line with both regional and global changes. There has also emerged a series of broader strategies, aimed at key regions or groupings outside Europe. Sometimes, these strategies have a global reach, as with the Lomé and later the Cotonou Agreements setting up trade and development links with the African, Caribbean and Pacific (ACP) countries, which were first established in the 1970s and have been renegotiated several times since (Holland 2000, 2002; Lister 1999). Other such agreements are more 'continental' in character, setting up broad arrangements between the EU and Latin America, Asia and Africa (see below). A third group of agreements is more restricted, establishing what might be described as 'privileged partnerships' between the Union and individual countries or groups of countries from other parts of the world. We shall deal with these in more detail in the next section, but it is important to note here that all of these arrangements reflect a complex mixture of motivations and pressures: historical ties between EU member states and other regions, commercial needs, political ambitions connected with the need to establish the EU as a 'presence' in other parts of the world, and increasingly the need to ensure security in terms of resources, political stability and other, broader aims (Teló 2001; Aggarwal and Fogarty 2004; Alecu de Flers and Regelsberger 2005; Soderbaum et al. 2005).

Another vital aspect of the EU's assertion of its regional power is that it brings the Union inevitably into contact with the United States. Indeed, for some European leaders, the development of regional and interregional policies has been a core element in a global competition with the USA, in which the Union is seen as having a kind of comparative advantage. The increasing range and scope of the EU's regional and interregional links has thus extended its global reach but has also brought it into a new kind of relationship with the USA. We shall see below how this has impacted upon specific interregional relationships, especially where the 'US factor' has been accompanied by increasing politicization and 'securitization' of the relationships in question.

The European Union and the new regionalism

The end of the cold war, as noted above, created a new dynamism in respect of the EU's position in the wider Europe. As described in Chapter 8, this led to substantial enlargement of the Union itself, and to a broader set of strategies relating to broader European order, including the 'neighbourhood policy' embracing countries in eastern Europe, the former Soviet Union and the Mediterranean. The concern here is with the global implications of the Union's development during the post-cold-war period, with the ways it has intersected with new regional developments, and with the growth of a wide-ranging interregional dimension to the EU's external relations. This has been a salient but less well-recognized aspect of the EU's global role, and as noted above it has brought the EU directly into contact – or collision- with the USA. The drive to establish new interregional arrangements reflected a number of forces, not all of them pointing in the same direction (Teló 2001; Aggarwal and Fogarty 2004: Chapter 1; Alecu de Flers and Regelsberger 2005). First, the increasing self-confidence of the Union arising from its pursuit of the single market programme in the early 1990s, and from the institutional changes embodied in the Maastricht Treaty of 1991, gave it a new impetus towards involvement in global order and thus generated a search for new partners. At the same time, though, this was accompanied by a second and less positive motivation: the desire to avoid being excluded from new and dynamic regions as the US and Japan extended their own global reach. The 'triangle' of the EU, the US and Japan understandably preoccupied many EU policymakers as they pondered how to make the most of the post-cold-war world. A third force operating on EU policies was the desire to create or reinforce an image for the Union as a 'world partner', one that did not carry with it the baggage associated with the US and Japan in specific regions of the world.

In developing a strategy – or rather, a set of strategies – the EU was not starting with a blank sheet of paper. There had been inter-regional arrangements with countries in South-East Asia and Latin America since the 1980s, and the Lomé Conventions had set in place a wide-ranging economic partnership between the EU and the African, Caribbean and Pacific (ACP) countries which had in its time been hailed as a revolution in relations between rich and poor countries (Edwards and Regelsberger 1990; Holland 2002). Member States of the Union had also in many cases had close rela-tionships with other regions over a period of centuries, in the form of colonial domination – a rather more ambiguous starting-point for a new set of relationships.

The first extensive attempt to form a new sort of partnership focused on the Asia-Pacific region – an area where the EU and its member states have extensive historical and commercial ties, but from which they seemed in danger of being excluded in the early 1990s. In 1994, the Commission published a communication calling for a new Asia strategy, and setting out the broad framework for a new type of relationship with the countries of the Asia-Pacific region (European Commission 1994b). A key motivation in this strategy was the fear of being excluded from the world's most dynamic region. After all, the EU had no real claim to being a major Pacific presence, but it did have many links that might be drawn upon to bolster its involvement. The result was the Asia-Europe Meeting – an umbrella conference between heads of state and government from the EU and (at that time) ten Asia-Pacific countries consisting of the members of ASEAN (the Association of Southeast Asian Nations) plus China, Japan and South Korea (Forster 1999, 2000; Gilson 2004; McMahon 1998). The ASEM met first in Bangkok in 1996, and has since met on a biennial basis alternately in Asia and Europe. The ASEM itself has also spawned a series of economic, administrative and cultural networks, and a number of action plans in such areas as investment and trade facilitation. But it has also found difficulty in dealing with more 'political' issues, such as whether the 'pariah' government of Burma (Myanmar) should be allowed into the ASEM when it joined ASEAN. What the ASEM has done is partly to remedy the absence of the EU from formal Asia-Pacific forums: whereas the USA has excellent Pacific credentials and was a founder member of the Asia-Pacific Economic Cooperation forum (APEC) during the early 1990s, the EU collectively has only from the mid-1990s made the effort to establish a continuous link. The EU has also pursued new interregional agreements with the ASEAN countries themselves and with the countries of the SAARC (South Asia Association for Regional Cooperation) grouping. These are groupings with which the EU and its Member States have a strong historical link (and crucially, in which the link to the USA is rather less prominent). These efforts have gone alongside the development of strategies for the key bilateral relationships with China and India; both of these emerging economic and political 'giants' have massively increased trade and investment links with the EU since the mid-1990s, and in addition they are crucial to the broader security and stability of their regions. As a result, both have been designated as 'strategic partners' by the EU, attracting special political and economic attention and frequent contacts at the highest levels (Allen and Smith 2004, 2005; Zabarowski 2006b). By the early 2000s, it can be seen from Box 7.1, there had accumulated a wide range of EU strategic positions and organizational forms relating to Asia as a whole, both bilateral and multilateral.

The EU has also developed a stronger interregional relationship with Latin America during the post-cold war period (Faust 2004). As noted above, this was not done from a standing start. As early

---

Box 7.1   EU Bilateral and Multilateral interregional Strategies in Asia up to 2005

Bilateral

1973	EC-India Cooperation Agreement
1978	EC-China Agreement on Commercial and Economic Cooperation
1981	EC-India Agreement on Commercial and Economic Cooperation
1985	EC-China Agreement on Trade and Economic Cooperation
1991	Political Declaration on relations between the EC and its Member States and Japan
1994	EC-India Cooperation Agreement
1996	First Asia-Europe Meeting, Bangkok, Thailand
1995	Commission Communication *A Long Term Policy for China–Europe relations*
1995	Commission Communication *Europe and Japan: The Next Steps*
1996	Commission Communication: *EU-India Enhanced Partnership*
1998	Commission Communication *Building a Comprehensive Partnership with China*
2001	Commission Communication *EU Strategy Towards China: Implementation of the 1998 Communication and Future Steps for a More Effective EU Policy*
2001	Commission Communication *Shaping Our Common Future: An Action Plan for EU–Japan Cooperation*
2003	Commission Communication *A Maturing Partnership: Shared Interests and Challenges in EU–China Relations*
2004	Commission Communication *An EU–India Strategic Partnership*

➡

Multilateral

1980   ASEAN–EC Cooperation Agreement
1994   Commission Communication *Towards a New Asia Strategy*
1996   First ASEM Meeting: Bangkok Declaration
2001   Commission Communication *Asia: A Strategic Framework for Enhanced Partnership*
2003   Commission Communication *A New Partnership for Southeast Asia*
2005–6 Commission Communication on New Asia Strategy

as the 1960s, relationships with some of the early attempts at Latin American economic integration had been established by the EEC. During the 1970s and especially the 1980s, these had persisted and had been given new strength by the membership of Spain and Portugal in the EC from 1986 onwards. They had also become politicised, in particular because of the ways in which they cut across US relationships with Latin American countries. During the Reagan Administrations of the 1980s, the Community actively participated in relationships with groupings such as the San José grouping of central American states which put them on the side of resistance to US domination, and this was one of the early manifestations of a distinct 'European foreign policy' (H. Smith 1995, 1998). The late 1990s saw a new drive to establish an inter-continental relationship, rather in the same form as the ASEM relationship with Asia-Pacific countries: biennial meetings were established in 1999, covering both economic and political aspects of the EU-Latin American partnership. At the same time, the EU pursued free trade arrangements both with Latin American groupings such as MERCOSUR (the 'southern Common Market') and with key partners such as Chile and Mexico (Faust 2004; Müller-Brandeck-Bocquet 2000). The latter is a member of the NAFTA grouping, and thus a free trade agreement offers access for EU firms to the North American market via a route different from that offered by bilateral EU–US relations.

Africa is the third key continental grouping which has attracted the EU's attention since the end of the cold war. Once again, there is a history, both colonial and through the EC's Lomé Conventions, which were first negotiated in the mid-1970s (Holland 2002; Ravenhill 2004). A number of key EU member states, such as France and Britain, remain deeply involved through investment and bilateral political links with sub-Saharan African countries. Significantly, until recently the USA and other major non-European actors have been rather less directly engaged in sub-Saharan Africa, and the EU has had a dominant role in many parts of the region. As in the cases of Asia-Pacific and Latin America, the chief innovation in the post-cold-war period has been a series of biennial Euro–Africa meetings, commencing in 2000 and providing the same kind of 'umbrella' as the ASEM and the EU–Latin America meetings. Alongside this has gone the Lomé and now Cotonou Processes, through which a complex set of institutions has been set up to provide a framework for negotiation and for the management of development aid and trade. The Cotonou Process, agreed in 2002, sets out a general framework within which a series of Economic Partnership Agreements are to be negotiated between the EU and either individual countries or regional groupings (Holland 2000, 2002). As in the cases of Asia and Latin America, there has been a process of 'politicization' in respect of the EU's relations with Africa, based on democracy promotion and conflict prevention (Olsen 2002)

The net result of these and other interregional activities conducted by the EU has been the creation of a carefully differentiated system of intercontinental, subcontinental and bilateral agreements, which in turn has created a continuous process of negotiation between the EU and a wide range of partners (Alecu de Flers and Regelsberger 2005). Typically, the 'umbrella' intercontinental agreements focus on broad-ranging dialogue and global issues, while more specific commercial and political issues are dealt with at the subcontinental or the bilateral level. It is clear that over time there has been a growing political and security content to these relationships: the EU has pursued 'conditionality' relating to good governance, human rights and other issues, and has attempted to use its economic muscle (including both access to the EU market and other mechanisms such as development aid) to raise its profile and promote the interests of European firms and other groupings within the regions concerned. The one thing it has not done – and cannot collectively do – is to assert overtly coercive power as a means of pursuing its aims. Although the Union has used economic sanctions in a number of cases (for example against the Mugabe regime in Zimbabwe; K. Smith 2006b), and indeed has sent military, police or observer contingents (for example to the Congo or to Indonesia) during the past ten years (Howorth 2007: Chapter 7), these have been essentially dedicated to political objectives and (in the case of military contingents) severely limited as to their aims and terms of engagement. Although this may be the beginning of a process through which the EU assumes a 'harder' edge to its power projection in interregional relations, the process is likely to be an extended one.

The US as a regional power

The renewed interest in the development of regionally oriented policies should not blind us to the historical reality: both Europe and America have long had regional policies. Both actors have taken keen interest in particular areas of the world and developed specific policies – though perhaps within a broader foreign policy framework – to engage with those regions. In the case of the United States, regional policies mixed with imperial pretensions a mere few years after the founding of the US, with extensive American involvement in Latin American and the Pacific – most notably the Philippines. American interest and involvement in Latin America represents by some measure the most durable US regional policy. American interest in Latin America today owes much to these early experiences of state rivalry in South and Central America. In the first decades of the founding of the United States, efforts to evict the Spanish from Florida and South America were justified on security grounds and, in the latter case, economic ones as well. 'Why should European powers be the sole beneficiaries of the gold and other treasure flowing from Mexico and Peru?', asked Alexander Hamilton in 1799, articulating a mercantilist view of international relations that would have been familiar to many European diplomats (Chernow 2004: 567). American views that 'the Americas' was a region of such importance to the US that special attention should be paid to the region were evident the 1800s, with the Monroe Doctrine chief among these.

The Monroe Doctrine articulated the view that the US had significant economic and security interests in South and Central America that justified intervention if necessary. American policies towards Latin America throughout the twentieth century were informed by the view that no foreign power should be able to exercise sufficient influence as to threaten US interests. The US was not concerned about the domestic policies of Latin American states provided they were friendly to American interests. This has always meant, among other things, the maintenance of economies friendly to American investment. US firms had been significant investors in South American states since the early 1900s and several, such as the United Fruit Company, were sufficiently important to host economies to exercise considerable influence on national policy-makers – and on Washington. After World War II, it was the spectre of Soviet influence in the Americas that provided the ratio-nale for a series of controversial interventions. American support for the military in Guatemala in 1956 resulted in decades of repres-sion – but with an economy friendly to American investment. Anti-communist policies also led to American support for Augusto Pinochet's bloody overthrow of the democratically elected, left-leaning regime of Salvadore Allende in Chile in 1973. Likewise the Reagan administration in the 1980s authorized covert military support for opponents of Nicaragua's leftist Sandinista regime. This support was both controversial – its execution broke US law – and ultimately a failure; the Sandinista regime was eventually replaced not by the gun but by losing elections. The cumulative effect of American interventions in Latin America has left the poli-cymakers and the general public deeply suspicious of American motivations and activities. Yet the economic ties remain strong. Venezuela remains a key supplier of US petroleum; Brazil has suc-ceeded in penetrating selected US markets for aircraft and fruit and is emerging as a potentially important supplier of the gasoline replacement, ethanol. Mexican and Brazilian firms are active investors in the United States (Santiso 2007).

American interest in regional trade and security policies increased in the 1980s, when two distinct developments together provided a powerful case for a foreign policy more attuned to regional devel-opments. On the economic front, the slow and uncertain progress of the Uruguay Round negotiations added to the perception that the multilateral trade system that the United States had done so much to develop was no longer serving American interests. Though the Uruguay Round was eventually concluded in 1994, the US began to embrace regional trade agreements with enthusiasm. This represented a dramatic shift in US foreign economic policy, which had since 1945 been firmly multilateral in orientation. As recently as 2001, the US was party to only two regional trade agreements, though over 130 existed worldwide (Feinberg 2003: 1019). The US began to play the bilateral or regional trade agreement card in the 1980s, with the Uruguay Round at its nadir. The first was a small but significant agreement with Israel, negotiated in the early 1980s. In 1988 the Canada–United States Free Trade Agreement (CUSFTA) was signed. CUSFTA was an important development in the international political economy and its significance was not lost on other states. Canada and the US enjoyed the largest bilateral trading relationship in the world; both were among the largest trading states in the world; and both were original members of the GATT club that signed the San Francisco Charter in 1945. Canada had initiated talks on the free trade agreement as a mechanism for arresting that country's sliding productivity *vis-à-vis* the US and as a way of locking in access to the American market at time of increasingly protectionist sentiment in Congress. However, that the US took up the offer said much about changing American attitudes toward the GATT process. For the United States, CUSFTA was both an opportunity and a threat. The opportunity lay in freeing up trade with its most important trade partner (bearing in mind that external trade was barely 10 per cent of GNP in the 1980s). The threat was implicit: if other GATT signatories did not do more to open their markets to American products, the US could use the leverage of its vast domestic market as a way of sewing up other states with bilateral preferential agreements. CUSFTA was the opening shot; others could follow.

In the 1990s, however, the Clinton administration showed renewed interest in multilateral arrangements – or at least large-scale regional trade agreements – as the best mechanism for achieving US objectives. In 1994, having successfully passed the NAFTA agreement through Congress, albeit with last-minute concessions to environmental and labour lobbies, the president sought to expand trade liberalization through the twin tracks of the WTO and a hemispheric trade agreement. The WTO track consisted mainly of allowing the new Uruguay Round settlement to bed in, and the US did not press for a new round of WTO talks until late in the Clinton presidency. Even then, the American preference was for a limited round, addressing some of the unfinished issues of the Uruguay settlement (like agriculture) but not envisaging major new negotiations (in contrast with the EU, which preferred a comprehensive negotiation). In respect of a trade agreement for the

Western Hemisphere, with NAFTA safely passed, the Clinton White House looked for a quick expansion of the agreement via an agreement with Chile, long the most liberal and open of the major South American economies. The timing seemed propitious, as many South American states had begun to embrace neo-liberal economic reforms, such as selling off state owned-enterprises, budget and monetary discipline and greater openness to trade. Indeed, the pressure for an expanded and evolved NAFTA came principally from Chile, and by the turn of the decade even traditionally protectionist Brazil was warming to the idea of an ambitious, hemispheric project.

Gradually, however, the momentum for large-scale liberalization faltered. Argentina's economic crisis of 2001 deeply undermined faith in the durability of economic liberalization in Latin America. Argentina's difficulties in turn caused considerable problems for important trading partners like Brazil, as international investors turned away from Latin America, having piled in during the 1990s. In the US, the ending of the Internet and dotcom economic boom also signalled a more sceptical congressional view of trade agreements. As protectionist sentiment gained ground, the possibilities of American concessions on market access for Latin American goods receded, and with them the rationale for entering talks in the first place. Instead of pursuing grander visions, the Bush Administration pushed for less ambitious proposals for FTAs with selected partners.

George W. Bush and the new regionalism

Though he was disinclined to enter into grand multilateral or regional trade deals, President George W. Bush's regional policies, not merely in Latin America but more widely, have been shaped by two events: 11 September 2001 and the collapse of the Cancun ministerial of the WTO in September 2003. When he became president, there was a widespread expectation that South America would be the focus of regional initiatives; indeed Bush himself indicated as much and made good on this with Vicente Fox of Mexico becoming the first foreign leader to meet the newly inaugurated president in February 2001. In addition to Mexico, Brazil was singled out as a country that would receive special attention, with the aim of repairing the strained relations between the two states

(Hakim 2006: 40). Brazil was South America's largest economy but its relations with the United States had long been contentious, with Brazil suspicious of American overtures – particularly on trade – and Washington impatient with a long list of alleged unfair trade practices by Brazil.

The events of 11 September 2001 quite understandably caused the Bush administration to focus on the Middle East to the exclusion of other regions – but also signalled a shift in the type of policies pursued. In doing so, the Bush administration committed the US to the pursuit of policies of regime change and democratization that were at odds with much of America's diplomatic tradition. Post-1945 US policies had been conservative, in the sense that they sought to maintain the system largely created by US power (Jervis 2006). Though lip-service might have been paid to the importance of democracy and the universality of human rights, the US supported undemocratic and authoritarian regimes when it suited. Jervis notes how much this changed during the Bush administration: 'insufficient attention has been paid to the odd fact that the United States . . . is behaving more like a revolutionary state than one committed to preserving arrangements that seem to have suited it well' (Jervis 2006: 8). American policy shifted to one based on firm belief in the importance of the extension of democracy. Though much emphasis was placed on military interventions in Afghanistan and Iraq, the US also used economic leverage with several free trade agreements being signed with Middle-Eastern states. These agreements were meant to perform two functions. First, they were an element of the administration's strategy of opening up markets for US goods. But with, for example, US exports to Morocco amounting to $475 million per year, such liberalization measures were marginal in global terms (USTR 2004). The second rationale was security-related. Bahrain, Morocco, Oman and Jordan – to name the recent counterparties to US FTAs in the Middle East – are small states in a volatile part of the world; they have broadly pro-Western governments in place; and are all potentially vulnerable to extremists. Offering free trade agreements was seen as a way of insulating these regimes from political instability flowing from religious extremism or social unrest.

As a result of these diverse pressures, the Bush Administration embraced regional and bilateral initiatives to a degree not previously seen in US economic policymaking. In 2002, George W. Bush gained important trade promotion authority (TPA) from Congress, which allows the president to conclude trade agreements and place them before Congress for an up or down vote on the entire package. TPA prevents congressmen and congresswomen from unravelling trade deals by inserting self-interested amendments and is seen as a central element of US trade diplomacy. In the wake of 11 September 2001 it was relatively easy for the president to convince Congress that rapid progress on trade liberalization, with or without the WTO, was a necessary element of US security. Robert Zoellick, the US trade representative, aggressively pursued bilateral deals with a wide range of trade partners. Chile, which had been the target of a larger, NAFTA-based agreement, eventually signed a bilateral pact. Other partners in Africa, Asia, the Middle East and Latin America were also brought into the ever expanding list of American preferential trade partners (see Box 7.2). US business played its part in developing these deals. Like members of the US administration, American business leaders had grown weary of the complex and bewildering machinations at the multilateral level. Moreover, the anti-globalization movement, by focusing so much attention at the WTO, had convinced business leaders that a more conducive and less controversial avenue for liberalization lay with bilateral deals (Drahos 2007).

America's relations with its Pacific neighbours have always been conditioned by the sheer heterogeneity of states in the region. Large, emerging markets like China share the Pacific with longstanding American allies like New Zealand and a range of small island economies. Variety makes policymaking difficult. Nonetheless, we can discern patterns in US regional efforts. First, China has unsurprisingly become the focus of foreign policy in the region. Second, the US has sought to bolster bilateral relations with many states – perhaps partly to check China's expansion in the region. Here, Washington is able to play on fears of Chinese domination held by many other Asians. Finally, the US has sought to develop regional institutions, most notably APEC, as a means of governing economic expansion in the area.

Relations with China have crept up the policymaking agenda for several years, with the most noteworthy aspect being the increasing importance of economic relations in addition to the growing military rivalry. China finally achieved normal trade relations – the granting of US most-favoured nation status – during the Clinton presidency. This development owed a great deal to the persistent lobbying of American multinationals worried that the withholding

Box 7.2   US interregional Trade Agreements

FTAs pending Congressional approval (as at August 2007)

- Peru
- Colombia
- Panama
- Republic of Korea

FTAs in force

- Israel
- NAFTA (Canada and Mexico)
- Jordan
- Chile
- Singapore
- Australia
- Morocco
- CAFTA-DR (Costa Rica, Dominican Republic, El Salvador, Honduras, Guatemala, Nicaragua)
- Bahrain

FTAs pending implementation

- Oman

Other FTA negotiations

- Thailand
- SACU (Southern African Customs Union)
- UAE (United Arab Emirates)

Source: United States Trade Representative, 'Bilateral Trade Agreements', http://www.ustr.gov/Trade_Agreements/Bilateral/Section_Index.html, accessed 16 August 2007.

of NTR status impaired their ability to tap the burgeoning Chinese market. Eager as US firms were to expand their relations with China, the expanding Chinese trade deficit – discussed in Chapter 5 – provoked Congressional anger amid the perception that China was trading unfairly by manipulating its currency. Other politicians also drew attention to China's poor human rights record, which in the eyes of several politicians demanded an American response.

Relations with Beijing were of course coloured by the recognition that China represented the only realistic threat to American military dominance of the Pacific. Tensions have been rising over time as China has sought to expand and modernize its military capability. The expansion of Chinese military spending started in the late 1990s and by the turn of the millennium China was among the world's largest spenders on military hardware. The type of capability it sought was also concerning US policymakers. Chinese commissioning of frigates and submarines conveyed the impression that the country aimed at developing a 'blue-water' navy capable of fighting in support of Chinese interests in any ocean. Tensions over Taiwan persisted for this reason. Formally the US is committed to the defence of Taiwan, a territory the Chinese consider a renegade province of China, not a separate state. In its relations with China, the US response bears some similarities with Europe. Both players believe that China's rise is best managed if the country is included in developing governance structures, such as the WTO. Both believe that involvement in the international system will exert steady pressure on China to strengthen the internal rule of law and develop a more pluralistic vision for Chinese society (Shambaugh 2005).

Bilateral relations with other Asia-Pacific states have been a key element of America's regional policy, acting both as a viable policy in their own right and as a bulwark to Chinese influence in the region. Relations with Japan have always been a key to American activities in the Pacific. The Japanese for their part have set great importance on the relationship as the best means of providing Japan with the security it needed. Even as the military side of the alliance was strong, bilateral economic relations were fraught in the 1980s as Japanese firms gained considerable shares of US markets. Bilateral, sector-specific agreements, such as the US–Japan semiconductor agreement of 1986 ameliorated these concerns, but the more profound reason for the decline in economic tension was the differing performance of the two economies. While the 1990s will be remembered as the decade when America boomed and dominated the new, networked economy, Japan stagnated, saddled with a creaky financial system and an ageing population disinclined to spend the Japanese economy back to health. Concerns about China and, more keenly, North Korea and its nuclear programme, meant that the military side of the relationship remained central. An internal Japanese debate about the nature of its self-defence doctrine in the face of threats such as that posed by North Korea's development of a nuclear capability and the continuing potential for disputes with China over longstanding territorial claims did not threaten the relationship, but did signal that future Japanese policy may be more self-reliant.

As with other regions of the world, the Asia-Pacific has seen considerable US efforts at aimed at developing bilateral trade agreements. Singapore and Australia are two of the most important to date, and negotiations with Korea began in 2005. Trade-dependent Singapore has always, like Hong Kong, been seen as a key advocate of the multilateral trade process, so its willingness to enter into a bilateral agreement was met with some concern. For the US, by contrast, it was evidence that its policy of competitive liberalization paid considerable dividends. The US–Singapore Free Trade Agreement provided more indications that the US was succeeding at gaining concessions at the bilateral level that it could not gain at the WTO level. In this case, Singapore's willingness to enhance provisions relating to the protection of intellectual property were a key part of the package for the United States. The same was true of the Australian–American pact signed in 2004. Critics were concerned that Australia's ability to develop and implement its own IP regulations were being constrained. This, and a view that Australian negotiators did not gain enough access to America's markets – especially in areas like sugar – made for a lukewarm reception for the pact among Australians (Thurbon and Weiss 2006).

Competition and convergence in a regionalized world

As with other aspects of the relationship, European Union and American relations with other regions of the world are characterized by a mix of competition and convergence. In the area of trade and commerce, preferential trade agreements (PTAs) raise concerns among business that they will be excluded or disadvantaged. Hence both America and Europe tend to follow a 'me-too' pattern where one actor will negotiate a PTA in response to the success of the other. European efforts to develop a network of Latin American agreements were clearly motivated by concerns that US firms would enjoy all the advantages of a growing South American economy; in similar fashion, EU links with Asia–Pacific have grown at least in part because of a desire to prevent exclusion from a region where the US is influential if not dominant. Rivalry also explains some of the interest of both parties in developing relations with southern Africa. Yet cooperation is seen across the globe too. Though the EU's relations with China are less fraught than those of the US, it is the case that both Brussels and Washington share a belief in the importance of encouraging progressive Chinese engagement with the world. Both share a view that economic development is not an end in itself, but will help catalyse changes within China, including enhancing human rights and the rule of law (Wan 2007). Likewise even areas where competition seems to be the defining element of the relationship both actors move from similar motivations. Both believe that the best way to secure the economic development of South America and Africa is through trade liberalisation and the evolution of democracy – and both the EU and US use aid and trade as mechanisms for encouraging this (for an example relating to EU and US relations with Mercosur in Latin America, see Box 7.3)

As well as engaging in this process of 'competitive cooperation' in the sphere of trade and development, the EU and the US have been affected by processes of politicization and securitization in pursuing their interregional ambitions. We noted at the beginning of the chapter that the post-cold-war context has lent a strong security tinge to the development of interregional relations in general. For the EU and the US, the events of 9/11 have underlined this dimension of their engagement in Asia, Latin America and Africa. In addition, the longstanding and continuing mutual engagement of the EU and the US in the Middle East has always had a major security component, and the EU has seen this as a regional arena (very close to home in geopolitical terms) in which it might develop a meaningful foreign and security policy role (Ortega 2003; Youngs 2006). The result is an emerging competition between the EU and the US in terms of regional security, which is likely to be shaped by the distribution of (for example) energy resources, environmental challenges and human rights issues (see Chapter 9 for further discussion of this in terms of world order). Box 7.4 provides a summary of some of the areas in which this interregional security competition might arise.

Box 7.3   The EU, the US and Mercosur

In 1991, four South American states, Argentina, Brazil, Paraguay and Uruguay, agreed to create Mercosur (Common Market of the South), one of the world's largest regional trade agreements. The agreement is a customs union, meaning that trade is meant to flow freely among members and all member states adopt a common set of trade instruments. This process takes time. The new grouping was in some sense the culmination of efforts to move South American states away from economic nationalism, and spur economic growth through regional integration. Argentina and Brazil were the two main actors in Mercosur, with Brazil alone accounting for almost 73 per cent of Mercosur's exports in 2005 (WTO 2006).

Though much smaller than either the European Union or the North American Free Trade Agreement (NAFTA: Canada, Mexico and the United States), Mercosur was large enough in world trade terms to merit attention. In the late 1990s, Argentina and Brazil in particular were seen as promising emerging markets and foreign investment, notably from the US and Spain, poured in. As with all regional trade agreements, firms often prefer to invest rather than risk remaining outside the agreement, potentially facing discriminatory tariffs and other barriers. Throughout the 1990s and early 2000s attempts were made to bring NAFTA, Mercosur and other Western Hemisphere states into a grand regional grouping, the Free Trade Agreement of the Americas. Such efforts foundered for many reasons, not least the difficulties that Brazil and the United States had in managing their bilateral relationship. Brazil had long attracted American criticism for its nationalist economic policies in areas as diverse as civil aircraft production, pharmaceuticals and citrus production. Brazil, for its part, objected to American trade protection laws, which it regarded as unfair barriers preventing Brazilian goods from gaining market share in the US.

The European Union opened negotiations about a European–Mercosur tie in 1992, shortly after Mercosur's creation and a wide-ranging political dialogue has developed since (For an overview, please see the European Commission's website, http://ec.europa.eu/external_relations/mercosur/intro/index.htm, accessed 10 August 2007.). The EU has offered a range of technical assistance, as well as financial support for Mercosur's secretariat. For some observers, the EU's approach of bundling together economic, political and social issues into a regional cooperation agreement reflects the EU's emphasis on normative power projection, in contrast to the American preference for rules-based agreements that emphasize trade (Grugel 2004). We should also be clear, however, that European firms were concerned that any US–Mercosur tie might affect their access to the market. Moreover, European negotiators were as unwilling as their American counterparts to consider a dramatic liberalization of agricultural markets, a central goal for Mercosur, particularly Brazil (Doctor 2007). As of 2007, the prize of a fully-blown EU–Mercosur agreement remains elusive.

How are we to explain this complex picture of interlocking and intersecting interregional relations? There seem to us to be four potential explanations, none of which captures the whole picture and all of which contribute to a full analysis of competition and convergence. The first potential explanation lies precisely in the fact that both the EU and the US are regional powers. Both of them have developed means of pursuing stability and order within their regions, and this inevitably has an external impact. To put it simply, it may be that both the EU and the US have created 'spheres of influence' in their respective regions, and that this has contributed to an emerging international division of labour between them. This is not a complete or even clear-cut division of labour, but it does mean that the EU and the US have developed certain ground rules for engagement in each other's sphere. At the present time, there is also clearly an unevenness in this division, since the EU does not possess and is unlikely to possess the 'hard power' to which in principle the US can resort (see Chapter 9). The US does not however resort to hard power very readily, despite appearances: where it has done so, it has been largely in areas outside its own sphere of influence, where the ground rules are even less clear. Leaving this issue aside, it seems clear that both the EU and the US as regional powers have an impact on the outside world as well as within their neighbourhoods, and that this inevitably brings them into contact or collision with each other.

The second potential explanation is that in a world characterized by coexisting globalization and regionalization processes, there are ample opportunities for both the EU and the US to inject their presence into new and 'unclaimed' regions. This in turn leads to EU–US 'encounters' which can be both competitive and cooperative – indeed, they can be both at once, with elements of 'competitive cooperation' for example in relations with China or other

Box 7.4   The EU, the US and regional security: issues and cases

The EU and the US either have found or might find themselves in competition in areas such as the following:

- *The Middle East*: Here, the central focus has been the Israel–Palestine issue, but this is accompanied by (1) a series of broader security issues relating to the geo-politics of the 'greater Middle East', such as the politics of the Gulf subregion and the problems associated with Iraq, and (2) a series of cross-regional security issues relating to energy supplies, human rights, democratization and development. The US is engaged primarily at the level of regional stability and security, while the EU through its 'Euro-Mediterranean partnership' and its links with organizations such as the Gulf Cooperation Council has a wider range of organizational connections.

- *Central Africa*: The EU and its member states have strong historical links to central African countries, and have been involved in many of the conflicts that have occurred in this region during the postcolonial era. Most recently, the EU has sent some of its first military contingents to central Africa, especially in relation to the conflicts surrounding Rwanda and the Democratic Republic of Congo. The EU also has a broader interest in development and stability in the region through the operation of the Cotonou Convention which sets the framework for EU cooperation with the African, Caribbean and Pacific countries. US interest has been more distant, but this could be changing because of the coincidence of greater Chinese engagement with Central Africa and the recent discovery of extensive oil reserves in a number of Central African countries.

- *South-East Asia*: Both the EU and the US have important strategic interests in the stability and prosperity of South-East Asia. The EU is engaged through its longstanding cooperation agreements with the Association of Southeast Asian Nations (ASEAN), including its observer status at the ASEAN Regional Forum for security issues and through the Asia-Europe Meeting (ASEM) and its associated economic, cultural and diplomatic networks. The EU has also been actively engaged in monitoring a number of regional conflicts, most recently that in Aceh (Indonesia) where there has been an EU observer mission. The US interest is pursued through bilateral channels and through its engagement with the Asia–Pacific Economic Cooperation forum;

it is also an observer at the ARF, but it has not actively intervened in the management of recent subregional conflicts, possibly
as part of the legacy of its Vietnam entanglement during the
1960s and 1970s. There are, though, some areas in which the US
has high stakes: Taiwan, the Philippines and others that could
become matters of intense concern as the role of China changes.

actors in the Asia-Pacific. The EU's and the United States's interregional strategies are interdependent, and they are bound to create
some uncomfortable episodes as both 'powers' try to assert themselves in new regions or in new relationships. Linked with this is
the third potential explanation: that different regions of the world
become more or less significant over time, and that this creates
changing incentives and risks for both the EU and the US in their
interregional strategies. A case in point is that of sub-Saharan
Africa, where for many years the US did not see a compelling
reason for involvement either bilaterally or at the interregional
level, except where there were fears of Soviet influence. The discovery of new energy reserves in central Africa, the intervention of
China and the occurrence of internal conflicts with associated
human rights questions have changed the calculus for regional
intervention in Africa since 2000, with effects that will be felt over
the next decade at least. The EU has an established interregional
relationship in this region, but it is unclear how that might respond
to the increased interest not only of the US but also of other
external powers.

The fourth and final dimension of competition and convergence
between the EU and the US in interregional relations is linked inextricably to the global system. If there are EU and US 'spheres of
influence', or if there is a growing potential competition between
the two in key regions, then this has repercussions for global institutions and global order. We will deal more fully with issues of
world order in Chapter 9, but it should be noted here that (for
example) trade relationships at the interregional level between the
EU, the US and key regions such as Asia-Pacific are directly related
to issues arising in the World Trade Organization or in key global
institutions dealing with environment, development, energy and
other urgent issues. Indeed, one dimension of growing EU engagement with regions such as Asia–Pacific has been the desire to gen-

erate support for EU positions in trade negotiations or other global issues, while the US has benefited from support from regions such as Latin America in many global arenas. However, such support cannot be guaranteed, particularly in the context of political and other changes within the relevant regions; here, there is another dimension to the interregional question, since it appears that in some respects the EU and the US might be played off against each other by regional actors.

Overview and conclusion

This chapter has added the regional and interregional dimension to our understanding of EU–US relations, and has focused on a number of key policy and analytical issues. In particular, the chapter has argued that:

- Both the EU and the US can be seen as 'regional powers', each with its own characteristic features and priorities. In addition, one way of conceptualizing EU–US relations is in terms of the building of regional systems or 'spheres of influence', which in both cases have long historical antecedents.
- Both the EU and the US have developed systems of interregional relations, embodying historical relationships but also reflecting recent and current policy priorities. Whereas the EU's system of interregional relations reflects the nature of the EU as a 'civilian superpower', and is based on negotiation and institution-building, the US' system reflects the fact that American policymakers can have recourse to 'hard power', and is based more often on strategic priorities such as the 'war on terror'. This is not to ignore the fact that EU interregional policies can have a 'hard edge' to them, or that US policies can place emphasis on negotiation and agreement; it is rather to identify a divergence in the central trend lines of policymaking.
- The intersection of EU and US interregional policies can be evaluated in terms of competition and convergence, with important trends emerging from the fact that both the EU and the US are regional powers and that their policies have different tendencies or mechanisms. The coexistence of tendencies towards regionalization and globalization in the world arena means that the EU and the US will encounter each other in a

variety of regional and interregional contexts, and that in turn these encounters will be reflected at the global level. The encounters themselves – in common with the interregional involvements of both the EU and the US – have become more 'politicized' and 'securitized' during the post-cold-war period.

In this context, it is reasonable to ask, What might the future hold for the EU and the US? Will it be one of increasing interregional competition, one of the building and reinforcement of spheres of influence, or one of a form of global division of labour in which both the EU and the US will play their parts? This question will be taken up again in the conclusions to the book, but meanwhile in Chapters 8 and 9 we will consider issues of European and world order, a number of which have already been suggested in this chapter.

Chapter 8

The New Europe

In this chapter the focus of discussion changes in two senses. First, it is predominantly on the evolution of the post-cold-war order in Europe, as opposed to the largely global emphasis in Chapters 3 to 7. Second, it is primarily on security and diplomacy as opposed to the emphasis on political economy in much of Chapters 3 to 7. In terms of the argument put forward in Chapter 2 the discussion is thus more in the area of 'high politics' as opposed to 'sectoral' or 'low' politics. This does not of course mean that the previous arguments will be forgotten, but rather that we are taking a different 'cut' at the fabric of EU–US relations, and taking up a number of themes largely implicit in the preceding chapters.

Chapter 1 gave an outline of the qualities of EC–US relations during the cold war, specifically as they affected roles in Europe. It explored the nature of US power, its predominance in the security domain and the ways the US could be seen as exercising hegemony over both Europe in general and the European integration project in particular. Chapter 1 also pointed to the ways this hegemony was qualified during the 1970s and 1980s and to some extent undermined as the shape of post-cold-war Europe began to be established. It was at this time that a number of questions emerged that were to become more pointed and a focus of recriminations in the post-cold-war period. Also at this time, the ideology of 'civilian power Europe' was developed and became a key element in the EC's self-perception in international relations.

Chapter 1 also dealt with a number of specific questions that arose for EC–US relations at the end of the cold war, and the ways they found expression. The chapter examined the outlines of the emerging 'new Europe' or 'new Europes' and asked whether the EC or the US was better qualified to act as the guarantor of the emerging post-cold-war order. The answer, of course, is that this was a hotly contested and variable issue, which intersected with the emergence of new ideas about the nature of Europe and European identity, as well as with the changing nature of the European integration project. No less did it intersect with the ways Americans saw their role in the world and the ways they felt they should be able to influence events in Europe (Treverton 1991; Smith and Woolcock 1993: Chapters 1–2; Gompert and Larrabee 1997).

In this chapter, as in Chapters 3 to 7, our argument will follow a common general pattern. First, the chapter will deal with the EU's role or roles in the 'New Europe' that emerged from the end of the cold war. Second, it will deal with the equivalent questions for the US: how did the Americans respond to the 'New Europe', and also to the EU's roles within it? Third, the chapter will explore the ways competition and convergence between the EU and the US in respect of the 'New Europe' has expressed itself since the early 1990s, and with how the intersecting EU and US roles have been managed through the key changes of the post-cold-war era. The concluding section will outline the 'new Euro-American system' in respect of the European order, which seems to have emerged from these developments, and will suggest some possible future developments. In Chapter 9, the focus will shift to pursue a number of these questions in terms of global order, building on the arguments made here.

The EC, the US and cold-war Europe

In Chapter 1 a number of key trends were identified and related to the place of European integration in the cold-war European order. Although it is tempting to see the cold-war period as a unity, it is clear that both the cold war itself (defined as the US–Soviet confrontation) and the place of European integration within it went though a number of different phases. During the 1950s, the integration process was closely embedded into the US-dominated order, in respect of both Europe itself and the broader implications of East–West conflict. This embedding applied both to 'hard security' issues and to questions of political economy or diplomacy. Questions about the European order were permeated by the East–West security confrontation, and the European Communities were in many ways marginal to the overall process, although they played a key role in the reconstruction and stabilization of Western Europe. During the late 1960s and early 1970s, this situation began to change, with the onset of 'European détente', the Helsinki process and the beginnings of European Political Cooperation.

During the 1980s, the impact of the 'second cold war' and the assertiveness of Reaganism intensified the feeling that US foreign policy was replete with risks, and that one means of managing those risks was through development of a more explicit 'European' foreign policy and security identity. Linked with this was the desire to manage a changing European order through European channels and to form new links with the states of central and eastern Europe: a desire that was apparent well before the fall of the Berlin Wall in late 1989 (Allen and Smith 1989). The collapse both of the Soviet Union and of the Soviet bloc between 1989 and 1991 created new opportunities and new risks for the European integration process, and new questions about the continuing role of the US in the 'New Europe'.

By the early 1990s therefore a series of features had come together to provide the ingredients for radical change. Although most of these were not directly associated with the EC, it is important to remember that the changes taking place in European Political Cooperation and the birth of a new EC security policy were a significant additional feature, positioning the Community to take an active role in the events of the early 1990s. At the same time, the Americans had to take on board the reality of an alliance in which there was considerable divergence of views about European security in general, and about the shape of any 'new Europe' that might emerge from the processes of change set in motion during the 1980s.

The EC/EU and the 'new Europe'

It is clear from the argument so far in this chapter (and from those made earlier in Chapters 1 and 2) that although the end of the cold war is well symbolized by the fall of the Berlin Wall from the autumn of 1989 onwards, the process had begun long before. The dim outlines of a possible 'new Europe' in which the EC would play a central role had been discernible for several years, and this had also begun to raise questions about the continuing roles of the US and of NATO. The developments of the period 1989–91, though, raised the issues in inescapable form and are crucial to an understanding of the ways in which the EC/EU and the US have approached the creation of 'new Europe(s)' (Story 1993; M. Smith 2000; Niblett and Wallace 2001).

Three key features of the process should be identified from the outset. First, the ending of the cold war was in many ways an essentially 'European' process, arising from the increasing pressures from newly mobilized groups within Soviet bloc countries and from the crumbling of established institutions both in those countries and in the USSR itself. There is of course substantial debate about the part played in the process by US policies and by the pressure exerted from US imposition of sanctions and other measures during the 1980s, but it seems clear that the radical changes of the late 1980s and early 1990s did have authentically European roots (Alting von Geusau 1993; Story 1993; Laffan *et al.* 2000; Niblett and Wallace 2001). A second feature of the process was that although it could be defined as a series of changes in 'high politics' – the nature of alliances, the control of nuclear weapons, the creation of 'grand bargains' about the future architecture of Europe – it also brought together in potent form all three of the 'baskets' of issues dealt with in the 'Helsinki process': security and defence, economic issues, and human social and cultural questions. The cold war had effectively compartmentalized these issues, giving automatic priority to questions of 'hard power' and 'hard security', but such a compartmentalization was no longer possible. Third, the end of the cold war raised immediate and pressing questions about the institutional 'architecture' of the changed continent, and about the ways in which institutions might have to change to reflect and encourage new forms of political and economic alignment (Keohane and Hoffmann 1993).

Key to all of these general features was the presence and the potential of the EC. For those countries and social groupings pressing for a 'return to Europe' in the ruins of the Soviet bloc, one of the primary objectives was close association and eventually membership of the EC (Nello and K. Smith 1998; Henderson 1999; Smith A. 2000). This was seen as a means of guaranteeing economic and social reconstruction and thus also as a way of enhancing the security – in the broadest sense – of the new or newly liberated regimes. The Community responded initially by creating new programmes of economic and humanitarian assistance, particularly the Phare programme, and by taking the lead in the so-called G-24 countries giving aid to central and eastern Europe (a lead encouraged by the US). But the diplomacy of the end of the cold war in other respects remained on relatively traditional tracks: the 'grand bargains' at the Paris Conference of 1990 and elsewhere that might be seen as the end-of-cold-war 'settlement' were bargains between the members of NATO, led by the USA, and the ex-members of the Warsaw Treaty Organization (Keohane and Hoffmann 1993; Lundestad 2003: Chapter 8). The EC might be associated with these, albeit indirectly, and it might play a key role in practical reconstruction or political stabilization, but this was still confined effectively to the 'civilian power' realm that had been characteristic of EC policy for years if not decades.

There is no doubt however that between 1989 and 1991 the EC became central to the process by which the cold war was ended. The new institutional 'map' of Europe saw the EC and then the EU installed as a central pillar of the European order, with responsibilities going far beyond those purely of market reforms and economic reconstruction. At the same time, it created doubts about the continued existence of NATO, despite continuous attempts to extend new forms of association and partnership to the countries of the former Soviet bloc and the Soviet Union itself (Sloan 2005: Chapters 5–8). As Figure 8.1 shows, this new Europe was one in which a number of potentially complementary (but also potentially competing) organizations occupied the landscape. Some of them included the US and Canada; others did not. Some focused especially on the 'high politics' of alliance and armaments; others did not. Not surprisingly, there was the potential for what has been called 'institutional overcrowding', with uncertainty about which institutions could or should take the lead in dealing with the new range of security issues. These issues themselves linked together military, diplomatic, economic and humanitarian dimensions in new and often unpredictable ways.

One consequence of the crumbling of the cold war order for the EU was in effect its own creation. Between 1990 and 1993, the Maastricht Treaty on European Union first formally created the EU, second endowed it with a Common Foreign and Security Policy (CFSP) and finally laid the groundwork for the establishment of a single European currency through Economic and Monetary Union by the early years of the new millennium. The CFSP can be seen in some ways as a response to the fall of the Berlin Wall, and the desire of other EC member states to create a political framework for the 'containment' of the new Germany after unification in 1990 (Keohane and Hoffmann 1993; Niblett and Wallace 2001: introduction). But it also contained both the legacy of European political cooperation and the seeds of more far-

Figure 8.1   Membership of major security organizations in Europe, 2005

reaching change which was to come to fruition in the late 1990s. The CFSP itself after Maastricht remained largely procedural, in the sense that the framework provided for additional types of collective decision-making by EU member states, but not for the really concrete types of foreign policy action that some might have hoped for (M. Smith 2001). Its institutional and financial basis was still unclear, and subject to a process of 'learning by doing' that gave it an experimental air, especially in areas of crisis such as the former Yugoslavia (see below). None the less, the CFSP did provide for enhanced levels of collective action by EU member states in respect of a wide range of security policies – especially if security was defined in its broader 'soft' sense rather than simply in terms of military action and concerns. Combined with the Single Market Programme and the prospect of economic and monetary union, this gave the EU an air of dynamism and a predominant role in the shaping of European order from within Europe, nothwithstanding the persistence of NATO. If there was a burden to be borne in the 'new Europe', the EU seemed to be an obvious if not *the* obvious candidate to bear it (Allen and Smith 1991–92).

For the EU, therefore, the shape of the 'new Europe' was not a distant ambition: it was and is central to the immediate environment of the Union, and presents immediate problems of management within the 'near neighbourhood'. It also presents the EU with a demand that can never be faced by the US: the demand for member-ship, and thus for the reshaping of the EU itself, not simply its external environment. While in the early 1990s there were those who felt the central and eastern European countries might be kept at arm's length with only the distant prospect of membership, it rapidly became clear that the pressure to open membership negotiations could not be resisted (Nugent 2004: Chapters 1–3; K. Smith 1999, 2005a). It was a question not of whether but of when as many as ten new countries from central and eastern Europe might be admitted. This is in itself a complex story of institutional change, of negotiations and of 'winners and losers' which is still not complete, even after the entry of Bulgaria and Romania in January 2007.

It might be thought that the new, enlarged EU would presage a fundamental shift in the global power structure. While this conclu-sion has not been borne out, it is clear that EU enlargement during the period since 1990 has created a basically new power structure in Europe itself. The EU (once memorably described by the *Economist* as 'the club that swallowed a continent' – see Figure 8.2) has had to reshape its own internal order and institutions at the same time as it has had to take on the implications of its geographical (geoeconomic and geopolitical) dominance in almost the whole of the European continent (M. Smith 2000; Wallace 2000). Although the Constitu-tional Treaty designed to produce some of this reshaping was put into limbo during 2005 by the French and Dutch referendum results, the reshaping of internal institutions and significant parts of external policy is not simply a matter of treaty provisions. External policy has had to be reshaped in the form of the EU's 'neighbourhood policy', which attempts to bring together the 'ring of friends' with which the

Figure 8.2   Map of the member states of the European Union, 2007

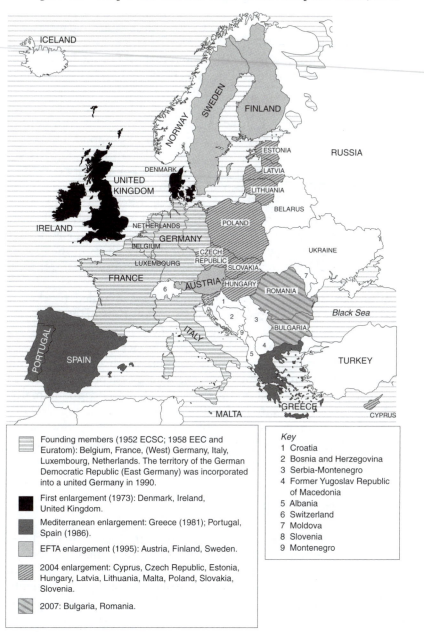

	Founding members (1952 ECSC; 1958 EEC and Euratom): Belgium, France, (West) Germany, Italy, Luxembourg, Netherlands. The territory of the German Democratic Republic (East Germany) was incorporated into a united Germany in 1990.
	First enlargement (1973): Denmark, Ireland, United Kingdom.
	Mediterranean enlargement: Greece (1981); Portugal, Spain (1986).
	EFTA enlargement (1995): Austria, Finland, Sweden.
	2004 enlargement: Cyprus, Czech Republic, Estonia, Hungary, Latvia, Lithuania, Malta, Poland, Slovakia, Slovenia.
	2007: Bulgaria, Romania.

Key
1 Croatia
2 Bosnia and Herzegovina
3 Serbia-Montenegro
4 Former Yugoslav Republic of Macedonia
5 Albania
6 Switzerland
7 Moldova
8 Slovenia
9 Montenegro

Source: Nugent (2004); reproduced with permission with slight changes.

union wants to surround itself (Aliboni 2005; Dannreuther 2003; White *et al.* 2002; Sedelmeier 2004; K. Smith 2005a, 2005b). At the same time, the extension of NATO through new arrangements with Russia and other states of the former Soviet Union as well as through the admission of states from central and eastern Europe has created a new institutional architecture in which the EU and the US remain implicated (Webber 2007; see also below).

We should not forget here that although it is tempting to cast the EU's roles in the 'new Europe' in terms of geopolitics and political influence, there is a highly significant political economic story to be told as well. The 'return to Europe' for Central- and Eastern-European states was certainly motivated by key security considerations, but it was driven also in large measure by the desire for shared prosperity within the EU (Faini and Portes 1995; A. Smith 2000). The redirection of trade and investment flows within and between the states of the former Soviet bloc, to produce an overwhelming focus on the EU, was one of the key shifts in the international political economy of the 1990s, and its results echo into the twenty-first century.

A further dimension of political economy is added by the fact that the expansion of the EU and its absorption of many former Soviet bloc states has brought the Union into ever more direct contact with Russia as the key former Soviet state. The growing trade between the EU (especially certain EU member states) and Russia – particularly the growing energy dependence of EU members on Russian oil and gas – is not just an economic matter: it can be seen as a matter of political and economic vulnerability, exemplified indirectly by the political use of the energy weapon against the government of Ukraine during 2005–6 and the Belorussian regime in early 2007.

The US and the 'new Europe'

In the immediate aftermath of the fall of the Berlin Wall, the US through the administration of George H. Bush made it perfectly clear that they saw the EC and European integration as a key building-block of post-cold-war Europe. As early as December 1989 Secretary of State James Baker had made a speech calling on the EC to respond through economic and political support and then through enlargement to the needs of the Central- and East-

European countries (see Chapter 1, Box **1.6**). This met a ready response in Brussels, at least at the level of general policy direction, although at an early stage there were doubts voiced by some member states about the desirability of major enlargement (Allen and Smith 1991–2; Smith and Woolcock 1993: Chapter 2). We have already noted the ways the economic reconstruction of the Central- and Eastern-European states was led by the EC and then the EU. But the diplomacy of the end of the cold war in other respects remained on relatively traditional tracks: as noted above, the United States as NATO member states were key actors in the post-1990 bargains that framed the end of the cold war. American policy and policymakers were also central to the process of German unification (see for example Zelikow and Rice 1995), although it must be noted that the absorption of the former German Democratic Republic into the EC, through a process of 'enlargement without accession', was also a crucial part of the process (Spence 1991). The EC's impact was thus still confined effectively to the 'civilian power' realm that had been characteristic of EC policy for years if not decades. In terms of the arguments made in Chapter 2, therefore, the US remained structurally dominant in terms of the broad security architecture that emerged from the end of the cold war in Europe.

Despite this apparent continuing dominance, the end of the cold war division in Europe was greeted with a mixture of sentiments in Washington. On one hand there was a tendency to assume that the job was done, and that the time had come to reap the 'peace dividend' and to retire from direct involvement in Europe. But this was countered by an equally if not more powerful desire to retain political leverage in Europe and to prevent the development of a 'European foreign policy' that would deviate from that of the US – not only in Europe but also in the wider world (Smith and Woolcock 1993; Peterson 1996b). Thus as noted earlier the attempts by US leaders in the early 1990s to define the parameters of a new world order had direct implications for the nature of the anticipated new European order. The George H. W. Bush administration that ended in January 1993 laid the foundations for this, by calling for the EU to assume the burden of financing reconstruction in central and eastern Europe, and by also calling for rapid and wide enlargement of the EU (Peterson 1996b; Guay 1999). In this way, it might be argued, the EU was to become 'America's European pacifier', a channel for the stabilization of the new

Europe and for the extension of market economies, the rule of law and western liberal ideas into the former Soviet bloc.

When the Clinton administration took office in January 1993, it did not repudiate this perception of the EU's role, but it did embed it into a wider national security strategy of 'engagement and enlargement' – engagement with both allies and adversaries, and enlargement of the zone of peace and democracy. In this, the EU was seen as an invaluable prop, but predominantly in its 'civilian power' manifestation, partly because of the unproven nature of the CFSP but also because of the continued assumption that NATO was the primary channel of US influence in the security and defence domain. This assumption was also fed by key EU member states such as the UK, which had a distinct interest in maintaining the 'special relationship' with the US and which used this and the NATO dimension to balance against the more enthusiastically 'European' of its EU colleagues (Niblett and Wallace 2001).

A key focus of the ways US attitudes evolved during the 1990s was the enlargement process. We have already noted that this was a compelling feature of the policy context for the EU. But it is also of fundamental importance that this was a game into which the USA could not enter directly, and in which the resources, the magnetism and the structural power of the EU were key factors in producing the eventual enlargements of 2004 and 2007. This is not to say that the USA did not try to influence the process; its perception of likely costs and benefits to the US economy (and especially to US farmers as a result of the extension of the CAP) ran alongside its acute awareness of the potential consequences to the US's position in European security and diplomacy (Asmus 1997; Baun 2000; M. Smith 2005c). One manifestation of this was the persistent and at times strident US insistence that negotiations should be opened for Turkish membership of the EU – an extension that could be seen as benefiting the US through insertion into the union of a major NATO ally and one with a key geostrategic position on the eastern edge of the 'new Europe' (Buzan and Diez 1999). Another symptom was the US effort to make sure that new Central- and East-European member states recognized the benefits they could gain from membership in NATO as well as in the EU, and the recognition that such countries as Poland would if anything add leverage to US positions and preferences in the enlarged Union (Bugaski and Teleki 2007). We will see in Chapter 9 that this could lead to tensions and recriminations in time of broader global crisis.

It must be re-emphasized, however, that although both the EU and the US are implicated in these arrangements and in the broader architecture of the 'new Europe', their impact on and significance for the EU is of a different order than for the US. While it would be both inaccurate and unfair to say that the US has been a bystander in many of these processes, it has clearly approached them from a very different perspective both under the Clinton and the George W. Bush administrations. While the Clinton administration wished to pursue 'engagement and enlargement' within the context of a changing European order (and as we shall see below, became directly involved in European crises and conflicts), the George W. Bush administration after the 2000 presidential election was immediately concerned not with Europe itself but with a far broader view of global order in which Europe – at least initially – rated a relatively low level of attention.

The EU, the US and European order: competition or convergence?

Does this mean that there is an open confrontation between EU and US ideas of 'Europe' and of European order during the early twenty-first century? It certainly appears that the predominantly geopolitical conception of Europe held by a number of policy-makers in the George W. Bush administrations elected in 2000 and 2004 was in direct contrast to the more intimate, subtle and complex conceptions of Europe that have resulted from the processes of EU enlargement and of the recognition that the 'neighbourhood' is of prime concern to European policymakers (Peterson and Pollack 2003: introduction). There is also more than a hint of competition between the gospel of free-market, neo-liberal ideas preached not only by the US government but also by a burgeoning range of American non-governmental organizations in the former Soviet sphere, and the more restrained ideas encapsulated by the EU in the shape of a social market economy – but it must be remembered that there is considerable divergence of views on this question within the EU itself, so the competition is more complex than it might appear. There is certainly institutional and policy competition, often muted but often more overt, in security matters between the growing European security and defence apparatus and NATO, not to mention the US defence establishment (Howorth

2003; Dannreuther and Peterson 2006: introduction and conclusion). But again this is moderated by the close links between EU member states and the US, whether in the context of NATO or in their bilateral 'special relationships'. On the whole, the picture within Europe is one in which EU member states agree on the key architectural features and can act collectively; we will see in Chapter 9 that this is not the same outside Europe. We will now explore the extent to which it is true in the context of conflicts and crises within Europe itself.

While we have been concerned up to now with the ways in which the European order broadly defined has been reshaped, and the roles that the EU and the US have played in that process, such a treatment needs to be accompanied by recognition that specific conflicts and crises may show a very different picture, as they engage not only the broad preferences of European and American governments but also their specific capacities to act or to influence events in particular circumstances. In this section we therefore focus on conflicts and crises in post-cold-war Europe, with the aim of identifying the ways they have impacted on EU–US relations and of exploring their impact on the complex balance between competition and convergence in EU–US relations. First, we deal with the conflicts in former Yugoslavia, and then we explore the conflicts and tensions that have emerged from the collapse of the Soviet Union, in both Eastern Europe and the Caucasus–Central Asia.

The EU, the US and the management of conflict in the 'new Europe'

Former Yugoslavia

It is clear that the collapse of the Yugoslav Federation during the 1990s started some time earlier, after the death of President Tito in 1980. Throughout the 1980s, the increasing economic and political tensions within the multinational federation intensified, bursting out into the open with the ending of the cold war (M. Smith 2001). There followed four main phases of conflict, leading to the dissolution of the Yugoslav Federation: in 1990–1 Croatia and Slovenia claimed their independence; between 1991 and 1995 Bosnia-Herzegovina experienced a bloody civil war the effects of which are still felt in the early twenty-first century; in 1999, there was further conflict over the status of Kosovo; and the final phase, still unfinished, centred on the stabilization of Macedonia as well as continuing reconstruction in the other areas of earlier conflict. Each of these phases created specific patterns of opportunities and challenges for the EU, and each of them brought the EU and the US into close proximity with each other in an often uneasy partnership (Zucconi 1996).

The declaration of independence by Croatia and Slovenia in mid-1990 was followed by short-lived but intense fighting. Significantly, both of the defecting republics expressed their wish to join the EU, and this underlines the ways in which the EU was seen as a model for stability in the post-cold war context. But the crisis also found the EU locked into a debate about its own role, and in particular about the qualities and instruments of the nascent Common Foreign and Security Policy. The EU was therefore trying to establish its own set of foreign policy directions at the same time as it was facing the challenge of conflict in the Balkans – a conflict in which different EU member states had different stakes and expectations (Crawford 1996). At the same time, US policies were pulled in the direction of more global challenges, especially the Gulf crisis of 1990–1 caused by Iraq's invasion of Kuwait. Not surprisingly, there was an inclination in Washington to see the EU as the key channel for conflict management, especially since US public opinion was still hankering after a withdrawal from all but the most pressing global commitments (Smith and Woolcock 1993: Chapters 2, 4).

As the conflicts developed, these pressures led first to a series of tensions within the EU, and then to pressures on the US for more active intervention. EPC gave the EU member states a mechanism for establishing broad solidarity at the declaratory level, but events on the ground could and did lead to fragmentation. While the twelve were able to establish an international conference on the former Yugoslavia, and to work on the ground in an observing and mediating role, the product often seemed to be 'cheap talk', since the EU had no enforcement power, and thus no capacity to back up its diplomatic efforts with the credible threat of force. The same was true of the diplomatic and economic sanctions declared by the Union: the local combatants were determined to fight, and could ignore the best efforts of the EU. The Union also spent a lot of time and effort developing criteria for the recognition of the former Yugoslav republics, but the commitment of the Germans especially to early recognition of Croatia meant that these efforts bore little real fruit (Nuttall 1994; Hoffmann 1996). As a result, the EU arguably wasted its most potent weapon – that of recognition –

without achieving the effects on the ground that it had set itself to pursue. Meanwhile, the Americans stood in the background: they had no desire to intervene directly, and confined themselves to going along with broader international commitments such as those to the United Nations.

While Croatia and Slovenia tested the internal solidarity of the EU, and also the level of US commitment, it was the war in Bosnia-Herzegovina between 1992 and 1995 that provided the sternest examination of their ability to work together in a situation of crisis and violence. While the EU was initially still seen as a significant diplomatic actor, it was progressively marginalized as the conflict intensified. Its diplomatic representative, David Owen, the former British foreign secretary, was both active and committed, and in 1993 was the joint progenitor with Cyrus Vance, the UN representative, of the Vance–Owen plan. The Plan, though, depended for its implementation on the availability of large numbers of US troops, and Washington was less than enthusiastic about the prospect in the face of domestic opposition and military reluctance. From the EU point of view the failure of the plan made it clear that not only did the Union not have the capacity to implement or enforce the plan itself, but it also suffered from major divisions among the member states as to how and whether the plan could be implemented at all. Achieving the active commitment of the US became a central plank of ideas that foresaw a need for forcible resolution of the conflict, but US domestic opposition and global priorities stood in the way.

After the failure of Vance–Owen, the diplomacy of the Bosnian war was dominated by three processes, none of which included the EU as an integral part. The first process centred on the Contact Group composed of the US, Russia, Britain, France and Germany (with Italy added later), and was effectively a form of old-fashioned 'concert diplomacy' among the relevant 'great powers'. It pursued a peace plan modelled in part on Vance-Owen, but with an implied possibility of the use of force if the parties refused to comply with it. Alongside this process was a gradual process of engagement by the US, not only through the Contact Group but also through bilateral diplomacy both with partners on the ground and with the Russians, who had special links with the leadership of Slobodan Milosevic in Serbia. Of all the potential 'peacemakers', only the US could really muster an effective and credible threat of the use of force. The final process, in 1995, was one of direct military intervention through NATO, with US leadership but also with the active participation of several leading EU member states. Throughout these developments, the EU position remained solid at the declaratory level, but increasingly leading member states were engaged in other types of diplomacy or military activity.

In the final Dayton Agreement of 1995, which established the basis for the future consolidation and reconstruction of Bosnia-Herzegovina, the EU played the part of an observer; but it also had a potentially key role as the coordinator of the economic and social reconstruction processes that were to last for years if not decades. Some drew the conclusion from this that there was an emerging 'division of labour' between those who did the fighting (the US and NATO members) and those who provided the longer-term reconstruction and 'peace-building' efforts, such as the EU and the OSCE (Hoffmann 1996; Peterson 2003). This analysis could also be supported from studies of the EU's impact on the conflict in former Yugoslavia during the early 1990s, which showed significant influence in these longer-term and 'structural' areas (Ginsberg 2001: Chapter 4).

The third phase of the conflicts in former Yugoslavia, as noted above, centred on the fate of Kosovo. This enclave in Serbia, populated largely by ethnic Albanians, had been largely subdued during the earlier phases of conflict, but unrest in Albania itself during 1996 and 1997 played its part in raising the political temperature. Significantly, although the EU had attempted to play a central role in handling these earlier Albanian conflicts, it had eventually been reduced to allowing a 'coalition of the willing' led by Italy to intervene. While Kosovo itself was internationally recognized as part of Serbia, it could be argued that escalating Serb repression of the Albanian majority there created a threat to the stability of the western Balkans as a whole, and thus could provide the basis for active if not forcible intervention. The negotiations that took place in 1998 and early 1999 under the aegis of the Contact Group, in an attempt to resolve the issue peacefully, thus took place in the shadow of NATO threats to intervene (Gow 1997; Weller 1999). This made it appear that the EU had been marginalized right from the start, although this was a somewhat misleading impression, given that it was recognised from the outset that the Union could play a major role in post-conflict reconstruction and in the diplomacy of the crisis. The role it was already playing in Bosnia-Herzegovina thus played into the EU's capacity to remain an active player on Kosovo. As the conflict continued, the role of the EU's special representative, Martii Ahtisaari, also became significant as he exploited the need for negotiations between Serbia, Russia and others (Ginsberg 2001: 245–52).

These features of the situation meant that although NATO – and by implication the US – dominated the headlines as conflict escalated, the EU became important in plans for the final resolution. One significant aspect especially was the search for a regional solution, and the injection into this of a 'membership perspective' for those local entities seeking membership of the Union. During the Kosovo conflict, the EU proposed the idea of a 'stability pact' for the Balkans, through which peacekeeping, economic reconstruction and regional cooperation would be developed under the aegis of the Union (Friis and Murphy 2000). On the basis of performance within the proposed 'stability and association agreements', regional entities could then be considered as potential EU members. This proposal not only gave some broader context for the treatment of Kosovo (and also Serbia's), it also created a framework within which the fourth phase of the former Yugoslavia conflicts could be dealt with. When violence erupted in Macedonia during 2000, the Macedonian government was actively engaged in negotiations for its own stability and association agreement with the EU, and this arguably gave the Union significant leverage in practising a form of 'coercive diplomacy' to bring the situation back to a stable basis. EU involvement in Macedonia also led in March 2003 to the first operational deployment of EU forces, Operation Concordia. In its turn, Concordia was supplanted in December 2003 by an EU policy mission, Operation Proxima, and in late 2004 the EU took over responsibility for supervision of the Bosnia-Herzegovina settlement through what became known as the European Union Force (Eufor), giving itself a significant military presence in the Balkans for the first time (Howorth 2005, 2007)

From the above outline of the developments in former Yugoslavia, it seems clear that the EU managed between 1991 and 2004 to develop a substantial role as a diplomatic and then eventually as a military actor. This does not gloss over the fact that there were periods of failure, particularly in light of the high expectations encouraged during the early phases of the conflicts. It is also clear that the EU's engagement in the Balkans fed directly into the moves that took place from 1998 onwards to develop a Common European Security and Defence Policy (ESDP). The motivations of leading member states such as France and the UK were strongly shaped by the need to avoid marginalization in future conflicts, whether within Europe itself, in the 'new neighbourhood', or further afield. This reflected a broad feeling that the US should not be relied upon as the 'stabilizer' of post-cold-war Europe – and as we have seen it also corresponded at the time to US preferences for a reduction in its global military commitments. This did not mean that the Clinton administration, in power throughout this period, did not have an interest in maintaining US leverage in Europe; indeed, Secretary of State Madeleine Albright while welcoming the moves towards ESDP in 1998–9, made it clear that these must not lead to what were described as the 'three Ds': decoupling, duplication and discrimination (Albright 1998). Successive secretaries of state have supported the ESDP, but with these caveats never far from the surface, and EU member states have generally been anxious to explain that the aim is not to replace US influence but rather to provide a means whereby EU member states and others could act collectively in situations where the Americans were unable or unwilling to lead. In this sense, the western Balkans have provided a laboratory for the development of a new EU–US division of labour, in which the EU itself has added a hard edge to its 'soft power'.

The broader European 'neighbourhood'

Any discussion of EU–US relations in relation to European order would be incomplete without consideration of the ways 'non-EU Europe' enters into the relationship. For the purposes of this chapter, 'non-EU Europe' is taken to mean the constituent parts of the former Soviet Union (some of which are part of wider Eurasia and extend to the Russian Far East and into Central Asia), and Turkey (which in turn borders on areas of continuing EU concern in the Middle East). As noted earlier in the chapter, these are areas in which the United States, as the sole remaining superpower and a key interlocutor of governments and other groups, has a strong and consistent interest. They are also areas which in most cases are unlikely to become candidates for full EU membership; even Turkey, at long last given candidate status and then the opening of negotiations in the early 2000s, is unlikely to join the Union until around 2015 at the earliest. As noted earlier, the EU has developed an extensive 'Neighbourhood Policy' to pursue its aims in areas extending from the Mediterranean to the Arctic, expressed particularly in terms of partnership and cooperation mechanisms (Dannreuther 2003; Batt *et al.* 2003). These areas engage both the EU and the US in terms of key security interests, as well as presenting economic challenges and opportunities. So there is much for both the EU and the US to play for, but also an unpredictable political and economic context in many of the areas concerned. These are also areas in which for obvious reasons the EU and the US are competing more in terms of traditional international instruments, given the lack of the 'membership perspective' and the strong gravitational pull of American political and economic resources.

Let us look first at Russia. During the cold war, although there had been differences between European and US policies – particularly during the early 1980s in relation to sanctions imposed in the wake of Poland's declaration of martial law and over US attempts to impose controls over technology transfers to the Soviet bloc – there had generally been agreement, or at least compliance, among EC member states to US policy preferences. The end of the cold war removed what has been described as the 'security overlay' that had muted differences of view both among EC member states and between them and the US, and this has had a series of important consequences for their approaches to common problems. As a preliminary to discussion of these problems, we must first note that as with the Central- and East-European countries, Russia stands in a different geopolitical and geoeconomic relationship to the EU from that which it enjoys with the US. Large parts of Russia are European, and even though the Russian Far East may seem a long way away from western Europe, there are substantial (though often submerged) elements of common culture and experience. Not only this, but the process of enlargement discussed above had to pay continuous attention to the 'Russian dimension', given the previous status of many of the countries involved and the closeness of Russian territory (part of it, in the case of Kaliningrad, surrounded by EU member states). For obvious reasons, the US experience with Russia has been more distant and more clearly defined in terms of strategic competition, and this has been a key element in the management of both EU and US relations with Moscow since 1990 (Allen 1997; Light *et al.* 2000; Webber 2000).

The EU's strategies towards Russia have thus been shaped by a combination of broad interests (for example, in Russia's adoption of democratic institutions and peaceful means for the resolution of disputes) and more immediate or tangible pressures created by the economic needs of member states, the consequences of the enlargement process, or the handling of conflicts in Europe and beyond. These are issues on which EU member states themselves have often been divided: for example, even before enlargement took place, there were clear differences between German or Finnish attitudes, shaped by geographical proximity and economic dependence (for example, on energy supplies from Russia) and those of Spain, Portugal and the UK. After enlargement, with the accession initially of eight and later of ten countries that had either been members of the Soviet bloc or (as in the case of the Baltic states) part of the Soviet Union itself, it is clear that this dispersion of preferences among EU member states has increased. The net result has been that it has often been difficult to discern any kind of EU collective strategy towards Moscow (Allen 1997; Light 2003), and that European positions have been pushed and pulled around by an uneasy mixture of ideological and material forces.

Nonetheless, the EU has developed a policy framework for dealing with Russia, based on a series of agreements and also on the Common Strategy adopted by the European Council in the June 1999. The Partnership and Cooperation Agreement was concluded in June 1994, but it came into force only in 1997, having been delayed as a consequence of Russian actions in Chechnya (Light 2003: 74). At the same time, the TACIS (Technical Aid to the Commonwealth of Independent States) programme has provided key elements of support for democratic transition. Tellingly, though, despite occasional Russian claims that they would wish to be EU members, there has been no move towards including a 'membership perspective' in any of the main EU–Russia agreements. These have been designed to establish an arm's-length relationship, with the key aim of stabilization and furthering democratic transition but without pushing so hard on the latter that material aims are jeopardized. The formal agreements have been supplemented by the growth of regular dialogues and consultations, and not least by the deepening of private investment and other ties between the EU and Russia. This process has been especially intense with respect to energy, where the increasing price of oil and gas and the political risks associated with energy supplies at the global level have created a political dilemma for the Europeans. European oil corporations have been among the leading participants in exploration and exploitation in the Russian context, and key EU member states such as Germany are particularly dependent on supplies from the former Soviet Union, so there is a very strong set of forces tending towards accommodation with whatever regime is in power in Moscow. In October 2000, this was formally expressed in an EU–Russia Energy Partnership. But at the same time Russian policies in Chechnya and elsewhere have created opposition in the EU, and have added to the pressures on EU member states to take punitive measures. Not surprisingly, these have not been forthcoming on any significant scale, either in the cases noted here or in those of the Ukraine and Belarus (see below).

At the same time, Russia occupies a key position in EU thinking about the emerging European order, and about EU international strategy. Sometimes this is a very immediate consideration – for example, the historic links between Russia and Serbia have been a factor in EU policies towards the Balkans, especially in the Kosovo conflict. As we shall see in Chapter 9, the Russian position on global conflicts and the War on Terror has also been a key influence on the thinking of EU member states. More generally, though, Russia is important to the kinds of 'structural diplomacy' in which the EU seems to specialize (Keukeleire 2003), through which the Union has set out to provide collective regional and interregional agreements with the aim of enhancing stability and institutionalizing cooperation. Thus, the Union has set out to construct a jigsaw of agreements with countries of the former Soviet Union, and to balance in this context between their relationship with Russia and the desire to promote the independence and stability of other, often fragile, states. Equally, the EU's strategy towards Russia in security terms has been shaped by the European Security Strategy of 2003, with its emphasis on 'effective multilateralism' and broad international order considerations; but it has also had to adapt to the development of the European Security and Defence Policy (ESDP) and the complex coexistence between ESDP and NATO (Webber 2001). Russia's emphasis on maintaining and if possible enhancing its great-power status has led it to exert considerable pressure on the EU for recognition of that status, and to try to exert influence through not only diplomatic but also other means, including the 'energy weapon'.

As noted above, EU strategies have also been conditioned by the ways in which the international politics of the Soviet 'successor states' have been conducted (Webber 1996, 2000). While the Baltic states have been successfully incorporated into the Union (albeit

with some remaining tensions over the treatment of Russian populations in these countries), the 'near neighbours' Ukraine and
Belorussia, along with a number of states such as Georgia,
Azerbaijan and Armenia in the Caucasus, have no immediate
prospect of EU membership, but are clearly vital to what might be
described as the EU's 'security perimeter' (M. Smith 2006b). They
are also incidentally in several cases vital to the flow of oil and gas
to western Europe. Here the EU comes up against the diverse pressures caused by (1) local desires for greater independence from
Russia (in the case of the Ukraine and Georgia especially, also
linked with a desire for EU membership, particularly in the case of
Ukraine), (2) continued authoritarian rule and dependence on
Moscow (Belarus in particular) and (3) local or regional antago-
nisms (in the Caucasus especially, often mixed with Russian intervention). Many of the tensions noted above, between ideals and
self-interest, can be seen at work here: the 'orange revolution' in
Ukraine and the apparent triumph of pro-western forces in Georgia
have led to Russian retaliation, and to consequent hard choices for
EU member states, often creating the kind of divergence that has
typified many EU policies towards Russia itself. The perceived
attractiveness but also insecurity of energy supplies from the
Caucasus that have to transit Russian territory is a further key
geopolitical consideration.

While EU policies towards Russia and the former Soviet Union
have thus been characterized by tensions and often 'lowest-
common-denominator' policy outcomes, US policies have often
seemed likely to create open conflict since the end of the cold war.
One source of this latent conflict is the structural reality of the US
as the 'only superpower', dominating the global military scene and
capable of intervening in ways Russia cannot contemplate. Another
source is the ways, in the immediate aftermath of the collapse of
the USSR, the US did intervene both economically and politically in
Russia. As Margot Light has pointed out, this created a high level
of anti-Americanism since it became associated with economic
instability, with the iniquitous privatization of major state industries, and with a feeling of national humiliation against which the
later policies of the Putin regime can be seen as a reaction (Light
2003). Much of the feeling at the diplomatic level became concentrated on responses to the enlargement of NATO and the military
intervention of the US in the Balkans, both in the Bosnian conflict
and in the Kosovo crisis. Although the Clinton administration

between 1993 and 2001 made efforts to counter this by attempting to engage Russia in a variety of diplomatic contexts – including making special arrangements for the relationship between Moscow and NATO (Larrabee 1997) – this was not true of the George W. Bush administration from 2001 onwards. The unilateralist tone of much US diplomacy, and the commitment of the administration to major developments in nuclear weapons, missile defence and related policies meant that there was little prospect of major advances in US–Russian relations.

At the same time as the diplomatic landscape of US–Russian relations has been 'frozen' for much of the George W. Bush period, there has also been evidence of increasing intervention by the US through 'private' channels in Russia and former Soviet states. In contrast to EU policies, which were often unavoidably conservative, those of the US regime could be described as radical or even revolutionary in nature. Private religious or political groups were encouraged to become involved in reform movements in Russia and elsewhere, and to provide financial and logistical support to civil society organizations working against the incumbent governments. Such groups were influential in encouraging the 'revolutions' in Ukraine and Georgia, and were active despite efforts to ban them in Russia and Belorussia. When combined with the distinctly unilateralist posture of the administration itself in respect of Russia, they created a sense of continuing tension between Washington and Moscow, which was if anything exacerbated by the globally interventionist policies of the George W. Bush government. These chimed badly with Russian sensitivities about the maintenance (or the recreation) of great-power status, and arguably contributed to the more abrasive Russian stance on European issues in relations with the EU.

Further evidence of the uneasy balance between EU and US attitudes in respect of the EU's 'neighbourhood' can be found in the handling of Turkey's attempts to start accession negotiations with the Union in the late 1990s and early 2000s. Turkey had had an association agreement with the EC and then the EU since the 1960s, had initially applied for membership in 1987 and had agreed to establish a customs union with the EU in the mid-1990s. On the other hand, it had been a member of NATO, and a key element in the US's preferred 'security architecture' for the Black Sea region since the early 1950s. So there is a lot of history on all sides to this relationship. Since the Turkish application for membership in the late 1980s, US support for Turkish accession to the EU – essentially on geostrategic grounds – has been constant, while within the EU there have been distinct differences of opinion leading to a succession of attempts to put off the time at which any decision might have to be made (Buzan and Diez 1999). Thus during the 1990s it became almost a ritual for the EU (and especially members such as France or Austria) to express grave doubts about the Union's capacity to absorb Turkey, while US representatives pressed privately (and often not so privately) for Turkey to be granted candidate status. At the Helsinki European Council of 1999, where major decisions about mode and timing of accession negotiations were made, the Turks were consigned to a 'waiting room' constituted by a 'European Conference'. US pressure for active negotiations continued, to the irritation of President Chirac of France in particular, coming to a head in late 2002 when US intervention in the run-up to the Copenhagen European Council meeting, in the form of demands for an opening of accession negotiations with Turkey, led to strong condemnation by the French and the Germans. Maybe it was not a coincidence that within the following three months the French and the Germans in particular were among those most solidly opposed to US intervention in Iraq (although the Turks themselves refused permission for US forces to enter Iraq via their territory – see Chapter 9).

A new Euro-American system?

The issue of Turkey encapsulates what some might see as fundamental differences in the style and purpose of EU and US policies on European order after the cold war. On the one hand, the immediacy and material nature of the stakes for the EU have clearly conditioned attitudes towards Turkish membership – as they have attitudes towards the former Soviet Union and conflict in the Balkans. For Europe, these are not notional issues to be dealt with in a broad strategic fashion: they are issues relating to the immediate environment within which the Union operates, and they also intersect with internal divisions within the Union. In the same way, EU enlargement is about the very essence of the Union itself, engaging deep cultural and ideological issues as well as major substantive interests in economic and other matters. While it would not be accurate to claim that the US has no such immediate interests in the 'new Europe', it is possible to draw a distinction between views and actions in the US and in the EU. Back in the 1970s, in his 'Year of Europe' speech (see Chapter 1), Henry Kissinger attracted European ire by asserting that European interests were regional while those of the US were (and had to be) global, concerned with the shape and future direction of the international system as a whole. If anything, the aftermath of the cold war, with EU enlargement, regional conflict, political and economic reconstruction and the building of new institutions, has underlined both parts of Kissinger's statement: the EU has become deeply entangled with the politics of the continent in a way not possible before, while the US as the 'only superpower' has been led into renewed global interventionism.

Something else has also happened, however. Because of the enlargement of the EU, and its diplomatic activism in the wider Europe, the Union has extended its reach and its grasp – to such an extent that it is no longer entirely fanciful to talk about the 'Euro-American system' as an 'EU–US system' (as suggested in Chapter 2). To be sure, the continued claims of Russia to great-(European) power status, and the continued existence of NATO, dilute this claim to a degree, but they cannot dispose of it. The consequences of this for the EU–US relationship are likely to be substantial, and arguably already are. In terms of the mechanisms discussed in Chapter 2 – transatlantic governance, 'hard' and 'soft' balancing and crisis management – it can be seen that the scope of these mechanisms has expanded, and to some extent the room for manoeuvre around them has decreased as the EU has come to fill up the European end of the 'transatlantic space'. Does this make transatlantic governance more effective (because of the greater scope of the EU's authority in many matters of 'low politics'), or does it make it more difficult (because of the raising of stakes in governance disputes)? Does it create a situation in which 'soft balancing' by the EU may increasingly 'harden' as its defence capacities expand and as the stakes are raised both by US policies and by greater policy competence in Brussels? Finally, does it mean that crisis management, which has been a pervasive feature of EC–US and EU–US relations for fifty years, has become more difficult if not impossible given the lack of 'ways out' within an increasingly polarized Euro-American system, or does it mean that crises will be less frequent because of the development of 'early-warning mechanisms' and continuing dialogue between the two partners?

Overview and conclusion

As can be seen from the discussion above, there are many unanswered questions about the developing roles of both the EU and the US in the 'new Europe'. This chapter has attempted to provide a framework for consideration of such questions as these by exploring EU–US relations in respect of the 'new Europe'. The following conclusions can be drawn:

- First, the transition from cold war to post-cold-war saw the coming together of a series of potent factors that continue to condition relations between the EU and the US. Some of these were inherent in EC and EU–US relations, others were generated by the emergence of a new European order, while others still reflected broader international change (see Chapter 9).
- Second, EU and US responses to the challenges posed by post-cold-war Europe have been conditioned by the nature of the perceived stakes, the immediacy or 'distance' of challenges and the internal politics both of the EU and of the US. The 'regional–global' dichotomy is one way of expressing this, but reality also reflects a series of different levels of engagement and response feeding into broad patterns.
- Third, the challenges of conflict in the Balkans and of the politics and economics of the former Soviet Union have evoked distinct patterns of response from the EU and the US, reflecting not only the broad strategic postures noted above but also particular patterns of preferences or 'governmental style'.
- Finally, the expansion of the EU and its predominant position in terms of the 'European architecture' have changed the dynamics of EU–US relations as much as they have the European order itself, and they will continue to do so. This poses a continuing challenge for analysis and for evaluation.

In Chapter 9, we will explore a number of these and related issues in respect of world order – that is to say, the broader global arena beyond the transatlantic and the European orders. While we can expect to find strong traces there of the issues raised in this chapter, there are also major elements of difference and distinction to be explored.

Chapter 9

World Order

One of the consequences of the EU's growing international presence and activity, and of the extension of its policies into new areas such as foreign and security policy, has clearly been a growing concern with what might broadly be described as 'world order': the ways in which the global system is structured and operates, and the ways in which it changes. For the United States, this has been a preoccupation since the beginning of the twentieth century, as the US became a world power, and particularly during the cold war and its aftermath, when the US was either one part of a superpower duopoly or (in more recent years) 'the only superpower'.

In this chapter, the focus is on the ways the European Union and the United States approach issues of world order, and on how their distinct approaches come together when they are dealing with questions of order and disorder in the world arena. The chapter thus intersects with many of the issues discussed in previous chapters, both those chapters that deal with particular areas of policy and those such as Chapters 7 and 8 that are more concerned with order at the interregional and the European levels. It also develops several of the key themes identified in Chapter 2 – specifically, those dealing with the processes of EU and US policymaking, the impact of change, and the tensions between the 'politics of power and security' and the 'politics of interdependence and integration'. One of the key focuses of this chapter is what might be seen as fundamental conflicts between the EU and the US views of world order, and the ways in which these seem to be expressed in a variety of arenas. Another key theme is the changing nature of security in the post-cold-war and post-9/11 era, which has greatly broadened the notion of 'soft security' as opposed to traditional military 'hard security'.

The chapter is thus wide-ranging, and centred on the study of changes taking place within and between the EU and the US in a complex world arena. It is also centred on the discussion of power,

and of the ways the EU and the US have developed distinct perspectives on the nature and use of power in international relations.
This question has of course pervaded earlier chapters, with the
notion of the EU and its predecessors as a centre of 'civilian
power', and of the US as a major centre of 'hard power', recurring
in many policy arenas and sectors. During the cold war period, as
noted in Chapter 1, this distinction was not only easy to discern,
but also part of the way the cold war was 'organized'. The United
States took responsibility for the protection of the 'free world',
assisted by a number of key allies in Europe and elsewhere, and in
Europe particularly by NATO. At the same time, the European
Communities could develop economically and politically towards a
notion of 'civilian power' which took as one of its key assumptions
that the EC would not and could not develop the kinds of 'hard',
coercive power attributes that characterized the United States and
the USSR. This 'civilian power' was increasingly influential in the
management of the world economy, and led also to an increasingly
active 'European' diplomacy conducted through the European
Political Cooperation (EPC) process, which was influential in the
management of interregional relations as well as the management
of the changing European order (see Chapters 7 and 8). But it was
all essentially conducted within the confines of the bipolar world
order at the head of which stood the two superpowers.

The end of the cold war, as we have seen in Chapters 7 and 8
especially, gave rise to new opportunities and new challenges for
the EU and for the US. It is on the challenges and opportunities at
a global level and on the EU and US responses that we focus during
this chapter, but it is important here to remind ourselves about
some of the key characteristics of the post-cold-war era. It is these
characteristics that have created new opportunities, new challenges
and new risks for the EU and the US, and which have shaped their
mutual relations in a significant way.

The first such feature is the end of bipolarity: the disappearance
of the Soviet Union and of its 'empire' in the early 1990s created
new areas of uncertainty and of flux in the world arena, and also
established the United States as the predominant 'power' in the
international system. At the same time, these changes underlined
the changing nature of power and security themselves. Specifically,
the established focus on 'hard' military power and 'hard security'
was joined by a growing focus on what have become known as
'soft power' (Nye 2004a) and 'soft security'. Whereas the former

types of power and security reflected the ability of states to muster military resources and to defend themselves against predominantly military threats, alone or with allies, the 'soft' variants emphasize a very different set of qualities: on the one hand, the ability to communicate, to persuade, to form networks and to shape international institutions in a variety of subtle ways, and on the other hand the capacity to counter these in the attempt to provide a more comprehensive form of security. Most importantly, the qualities of 'soft' international politics are not just associated with the state and with the state apparatus of power. So here there is a paradox: the United States in the post-cold-war era has been the unchallenged 'hard power', but its power may not be appropriate to the challenges of 'soft security' (Nye 2002). The EU, on the other hand, reflects predominantly power and the search for security at the 'soft' end of the spectrum, and thus presents a potentially major contrast to the US. Both the EU and the US have been threatened by new forms of security threats and risks, arising from the activities of non-state actors such as terrorist groups, and by the emergence of new types of sectoral challenges such as those relating to the environment, to energy and to human security in its broadest sense.

Some at least of these new challenges can be related to the phenomenon of globalization. Globalization had been identified as an issue during the 1980s if not before, but perceptions of its significance had been shaped by the persistence of bipolarity and of superpower dominance. Alongside the end of bipolarity and the sharpened impact of globalization, there has thus gone an increased demand for mechanisms of global governance – institutions and rules that enable the impact of change to be managed, and which inevitably involve both the EU and the US in a major way.

Finally, the new world arena has generated new types of crisis, embodying the processes of power-shift, the changing nature of security and increasing global interconnectedness noted above. The most symptomatic of these new crises has been that crystallised by the events of 11 September 2001, when the attacks on New York and Washington DC precipitated the 'war on terror' and new types of both global and local conflict (Halliday 2001). Once again, this was not a totally unprecedented set of events, but it has given the post-cold-war period a very specific tinge during the new millennium.

In confronting and responding to these developments, the EU and the US have brought to bear very different predispositions, resources and strategies. Indeed, it has been argued that the two entities live almost in two different worlds when it comes to issues of world order in the new millennium, with the EU pursuing negotiation, multilateralism and 'soft power' while the US has espoused coercion, unilateralism and the massive deployment of 'hard power' (Kagan 2003; M. Smith 2004; Lindberg 2005). The purpose of this chapter is to explore this general assertion, to arrive at an assessment of the extent to which the EU and the US live in different worlds and to discuss the implications of their mutual relations for world order in the future. As in previous chapters, we shall examine first the EU's approach to world order, then that of the US, and then the implications for the relationship. These implications will then be examined in two key areas of policy: first, the ways the EU and the US relate to each other in matters of global power and security, and then how they relate in matters of global governance. The chapter argues that there are important differences between these two areas, especially in the extent to which the EU can take a leading role, that relate to the key differences on world order issues noted above.

The European Union and world order

In confronting the 'new world' created by the end of the cold war, the European integration project and its leaders have not been concerned solely with external policy developments. It is important to remember that the fall of the Berlin Wall and the end of the Soviet Union occurred alongside (and often intersecting with) institutional and policy developments in European integration – the very developments, in fact, that created the European Union itself and gave it a new range of institutional and policy resources. Thus, between 1990 and 1995 the European Union was set in place, a Common Foreign and Security Policy was established, and Economic and Monetary Union was put in motion with its projected completion date the turn of the millennium. The first question we must address in relation to these developments is, What motivated them? What predispositions in Europe and in the EU did they reflect, and how can we see these in relation to broader world order questions?

One way of engaging with these questions is to cast them in

terms of the nature of the European project, and the kinds of underlying orientation towards world order that it reflects. It is thus important to understand that the EU is a kind of 'trading state', whose original impetus drew upon cooperation in the commercial and economic fields, and whose institutions were profoundly shaped by this fact. Trading states, as Richard Rosecrance has argued (1986, 1993), pursue characteristic policy aims, centred on stability and on the pursuit of commercial advantage. True to its underlying character, the EU thus pursues essentially conservative international policies, aimed at creating forms of 'negotiated order' in the world arena. At the same time, these policies are also 'civilian', using diplomatic and commercial devices to establish and maintain a predictable international setting and valuing these almost as ends in themselves. The EU's diplomacy is based also on reciprocity, a process of give and take which sees international order as centred on the exchange of rewards and the granting of incentives. The objective is to create a set of international structures that engender stability and enable the EU to carry on its international business (M. Smith 2004: 107–11). The EU thus presents a long-term attempt to engender 'soft security' and use 'soft power', but it must not be forgotten (see Chapter 1) that it was also established within the framework of the cold war, in which 'hard security' was the key area of confrontation between the United States and the Soviet Union.

This focus on 'soft power' and 'soft security' can be observed throughout the life of the European project; although individual EU member states might take a more martial line in particular circumstances, they all subscribe to these assumptions for matters where the EU is the central focus of their activities. In the post-cold-war world, however, these assumptions have come under severe strain, for a number of reasons. First, the end of bipolarity has created for the Union a much more unpredictable international context, in which tensions and conflicts can flare up suddenly and in which 'civilian' issues such as trade can become very closely linked with political or military activities through processes of 'politicization' or 'securitization'. Second, this has been added to by the impact of globalization, through which the impact of shocks in one part of the world arena is transmitted very rapidly to other parts. This is not a world in which it is easy to establish stability or predictability, and thus the EU has come under pressure from a number of sources. As a result, the EU has become engaged (as one

would expect) in a number of important efforts at global governance, in areas such as the environment, development and human
rights, but has also had to contend with the essential unmanage-
ability of many of the tensions and conflicts that surround them.
We shall see in later parts of this chapter what this might mean in
specific conflict situations. Finally, the Union, as might be
expected, makes policy in what might be described as a 'negotiated' or 'deliberative' way, having to take into account the needs
and preferences of member states and of the 'European' institutions
as well as the 'European interest' (Elgström and Smith 2000), but
this is not on the face of it a very efficient way of responding to the
unpredictable and interconnected crises that have erupted in the
post-cold-war era. To put it crudely, this might mean that the EU is
'all talk' when it comes to handling key international conflicts.

The picture on the EU's motivation towards world order issues is
thus at least partly cloudy. Yet at the same time, the changing circumstances of the post-cold-war era have prompted to EU to
develop significant new resources with which to confront world
order issues. Most importantly, the Union has provided itself with
new institutions in the field of foreign, security and defence policy
that have moved it at least in principle away from purely 'civilian'
power (M. Smith 2001). In the Maastricht Treaty of 1991, which
entered into force in 1993, the Common Foreign and Security
Policy (CFSP) was a major feature; it was then added to in the
Amsterdam Treaty of 1997 and the Nice Treaty of 2000, so that
by the beginning of the new millennium there was a complex institutional structure, supported by growing budgetary resources and
by activities that seemed to integrate more than ever before the
wide range of interests that the Union had in the world arena
(Vanhoonacker 2005). From 1998 onwards, the development of
the European Security and Defence Policy (ESDP) created an
embryonic military dimension to the Union's external policies, and
by 2007 there were established 'battle groups' bringing together
contributions from many EU member states (Howorth 2005,
2007). The Constitutional Treaty of 2004 would have gone even
further down this track, by providing for a Union 'foreign minister'
and for the creation of long-term mechanisms for ensuring the
resources necessary for foreign policy activities. Box 9.1 summarizes these developments.

The Union's institutional development since the end of the cold
war has thus been dramatic, and in precisely those areas where the

Box 9.1   CFSP and ESDP from Maastricht to the Constitutional Treaty

Maastricht

Establishes Common Foreign and Security Policy, with eventual possibility of European defence policy and 'European defence'. New instruments: Common Positions (from EPC) and Joint Actions. Possibility of QMV, limited Commission power of initiative. Some budgetary provision. Association of Western European Union with CFSP. Remains essentially intergovernmental.

Amsterdam

Further extension of QMV, introduction of Common Strategies and possibility of 'constructive abstention'. Incorporation of 'Petersberg tasks', further linkages with WEU (eventual merger). Establishment of high representative supported by Policy Planning and Early Warning Unit. Further budgetary regularization. Still largely inter-governmental.

Nice

Incorporation of ESDP agreements from St Malo to Helsinki: includes new Political and Security Committee (COPS), Military Committee and Military Staff. Consolidation of proposals for rapid reaction force based on 'headline goals' of 50–60,000 troops, focused on Petersberg tasks.

Constitutional Treaty

Establishment of European Union foreign minister and External Action Service. New provisions for crisis management (beyond Petersberg Tasks) and for 'enhanced cooperation' among sub-groups of member states. Solidarity clause against military attack and terrorist action. Creation of European Armaments Agency to coordinate national arms procurement policies and (long-term) bring them into EU framework.

Note: the Constitutional Treaty was rejected in referenda in France and the Netherlands in 2005. In 2007, it was agreed that a revised 'reform treaty' should be negotiated, containing most of the above provisions relating to foreign and security policy

EU was previously lacking as an international actor – diplomacy and security/defence policy. In a sense, this can be seen as a direct response to the challenges posed by the end of superpower bipolarity. The disappearance of the Soviet Union created a need for imaginative initiatives in Europe (see Chapter 8), but it also created both challenges and opportunities in the rest of the world. The emergence of the CFSP and then the ESDP reflects in part a recognition by EU member states that a collective EU presence was essential in order to spread the risks and take advantage of some of the opportunities created by the new world situation (Ginsberg 2001). Clearly, however, there are strict limits on this set of developments, emerging both from divisions between member states and from the fluid nature of the world arena itself. The EU is thus still limited in its external defence activities to what are called the Petersburg tasks – essentially conflict prevention, peacekeeping and peace-building, aligned to post-conflict reconstruction and the creation of effective government – although aspects of crisis management have been added to these.

Added to this set of 'harder' resources, the Union of course has substantial and long-established resources in the economic and commercial fields, which can be brought to bear on world order questions through trade policy, development policy and the like (see Chapters 3 to 7). In this way, it can be seen, the Union has added considerably to its resources during the period since the end of the cold war, but it is not always clear how they can be deployed to deal with world order issues in a globalized world. There is a gap, it might be said, between the multilateral institutional level at which the EU can be effective on the basis of its role as a 'trading state' and the essentially confused and dynamic situations in which the Union might need to deploy its security and defence resources.

One answer to the critique outlined above might be in the development of EU strategies, which would establish the principles for 'European foreign policy' and link it to the pursuit of world order. The Union has for a long time had many strategies, whether towards individual international partners or on specific international issues, and thus in a way it is easy to discern the principles of 'European foreign policy'. Such principles would include multilateralism, dialogue, negotiation, the use of international institutions and the promotion of 'global civil society' including such aspects as human rights and good governance. It is only since the end of the 1990s that the Union has attempted to set these out in terms of its explicit commitments and objectives with respect to world order. In particular, in 2003 the Union agreed the European Security Strategy, which brought together a wide range of world order objectives with the more specific interests of the Union itself, and set out how these should be pursued (Council 2003; Howorth 2007: Chapter 6). It is this document that encapsulates the Union's commitment to conflict prevention, crisis management and the pursuit of 'effective multilateralism' through channels such as the United Nations (see Box 9.2). The document in effect sets out what it means to be a 'trading state' in the new post-cold-war world, and by so doing reveals that 'civilian power' is no longer enough to protect and promote the Union's interests. The EU's security requires the development of a 'harder' or more martial strategy, and the deployment of different types of resources, while retaining the broad commitment to multilateral means and civilian priorities (Dannreuther and Peterson 2006: Chapter 1; M. Smith 2006b). This might be a source of regret, that the Union is losing its 'unique selling point' in the pursuit of international order, but in many ways it can be seen as a logical response to the nature of the post-cold-war world (Manners 2006; K. Smith 2000, 2005c).

Does this development of a new strategic focus and (at least in part) a new 'strategic culture' (Cornish and Edwards 2001) in the EU provide it with a good basis on which to pursue world order? In a world where the oddly reassuring presence of two super-powers has gone, there is a clear need to develop some idea about what a European identity and European interests might add up to (Manners and Whitman 2003; Whitman 1998). There is also a need to bring together the commercial and economic interests of the EU with the 'harder' security interests that are increasingly linked to them. In a globalizing world, the increasing politicization of the commercial is a key point of reference (as we have noted in many of the previous chapters in this book), and the EU seems well placed to respond to it. But the development of strategic visions, and even an EU 'grand strategy', is limited by the institutional and other constraints noted earlier in this chapter. It is both a strength and a weakness of the EU that it is not a state in the conventional meaning of the word: a strength, because it can generate among its member states a normative consensus that goes beyond purely national interests and provides a strong basis for the extension of European to global governance; a weakness, because the EU is in no position at present to guarantee that its stance on world order

BOX 9.2 The European Security Strategy (extracts)

In a world of global threats, global markets and global media, our security and prosperity increasingly depend on an effective multilateral system. The development of a stronger multilateral society, well functioning international institutions and a rule-based international order is our objective . . .

It is a condition of a rule-based international order that law evolves in response to developments such as proliferation, terrorism and global warming. We have an interest in further developing existing instruments such as the World Trade Organization and in supporting new ones such as the International Criminal Court. Our own experience in Europe demonstrates that security can be increased through confidence building and arms control regimes. Such instruments can also make an important contribution to security and stability in our neighbourhood and beyond . . .

A number of countries have placed themselves outside the bounds of international society. Some have sought isolation; others persistently violate international norms. It is desirable that such countries should rejoin the international community, and the EU should be ready to provide assistance. Those who are unwilling to do so should understand that there is a price to be paid, including in their relationship with the European Union . . .

There are few if any problems we can deal with on our own. The threats described above are common threats, shared with all our closest partners. International cooperation is a necessity. We need to pursue our objectives both through multilateral cooperation in international organizations and through partnerships with key actors.

Source: *A Secure Europe in a Better World*. European Security Strategy, Brussels, 12 December 2003.

issues can be backed up with the 'hard power' that is sometimes required to make diplomacy or negotiation more effective. It is also important to note that in the area of 'hard security' the EU does not possess the institutional dominance that is a feature of its engagement with some areas of 'soft security'; quite simply, the density of the institutional arrangements surrounding 'hard security', with NATO and a range of other bodies playing active roles and actively involving the USA, means that the EU has to proceed with acute awareness of its institutional limitations (Cameron 2007: Chapter 5; Howorth 2007).

If we look at the record of EU engagement with world order issues since the end of the cold war, this paradoxical situation becomes clearer, especially in the case of global security. The Union has been relatively effective over those issues and processes that give maximum leverage to its 'civilian power', for example the building of institutions to deal with global problems such as environmental change or sustainable development, and it has become a significant presence in the United Nations and related bodies through the capacity of its member states to coordinate their positions (Sbragia 1998; Holland 2002; Vogler 2005; Laatikainen and Smith 2006). It has also taken an effective stand on questions such as those of land-mines or so-called 'dual-use weapons', where its member states can readily agree on the priorities. As we saw in Chapter 8, there are also examples in Europe of conflicts where the EU has taken an effective collective stance, within the limits set by Member State agreement. But in situations where the demands are more urgent, where the likelihood of violence is higher and where major state interests are engaged, the EU is (maybe not surprisingly) markedly less effective, and other organizations such as NATO become more salient. Such characteristics have been especially marked in the period since 9/11 – an event that marked a coming together of a new set of security threats, and led to responses across the spectrum of 'hard' and 'soft' security measures, challenging the EU's capacity to maintain solidarity and to muster its institutional resources in a variety of areas (see below) (Gnesotto 2004; Hill 2004). This is a reflection of the fact that whatever its institutional development, and however apparently strong the commitment of member states, the centre of gravity of the EU is still in its nature as a 'trading state'. The likelihood or the actual use of force is still not something on which the Union and its members are effectively 'integrated'. In fact, it can lead to the opposite, to forms of fragmentation and disintegration. Thus in the Middle East, or the Persian Gulf, the Union can become involved but seems unable to move beyond a presence and into purpose or impact (Crowe 2003; Ortega 2003; Youngs 2006: Chapter 1). This judgement may seem harsh, but it corresponds with the record of the post-cold-war period as a whole.

We can conclude that while the EU has had problems in finding a stable role in matters associated with global 'hard security', it has been arguably much more effective in dealing with issues of global governance, where 'soft security' is the central focus. The foundations laid by the development of the Common Market and the Single Market have been exploited to produce EU policy not only in the 'old agenda' of trade (where the EU plays a leading role in the World Trade Organization; see Chapter 3), but also in a number of 'new-agenda' areas such as the environment and humanitarian matters. In such areas, the EU has developed new areas of competence, at the same time as the US (for example) has encountered difficulties of its own. We will return to this issue later, but it is important here to register the EU's significant and growing contribution to the institutions and rules of global governance.

The United States and world order

As noted in the introduction to this chapter, the United States has been integral to world order since the beginning of the twentieth century, and a leading if not the dominant member of the world arena since at least 1945. During the cold war, the US was one of the two 'superpowers', existing in an often uneasy state of 'adversarial partnership' with the Soviet Union and dominating the 'western alliance' of which the European Communities were a subordinate part. Since the end of the cold war and the disappearance of the USSR the United States has been in the position of unchallenged predominance in terms of 'hard power' at the global level, simply being able to do things that no other power – or even combination of powers – can do. But this does not make for an easy relationship between the US and world order: the 'only superpower' can often seem the 'lonely superpower' without a near rival, and the management of predominant power can be as challenging as the management of subordination (Ikenberry 2002; Daalder and Lindsay 2003; Held and Koenig-Archibugi 2004). This means that we can ask the same questions about the US and world order as we did in the preceding section about the EU and world order: What predispositions does the US bring to questions of world order? What motivates US policy? What resources do they deploy in pursuit of world order? What strategies do they pursue? And what does the record say about the relationship between the US and world order since the end of the cold war?

It is fair to say that US policymakers have more often than not approached issues of world order with a 'vision' of how that order should look (Daalder and Lindsay 2003; Lieven 2004; Ikenberry 2006). The notion that the US is an exceptional country, with a mission to bring its form of democracy to as many of the world's peoples as possible, has been integral to US foreign policy during the cold war and beyond (and indeed since the beginning of the twentieth century, when the US first became a global power) (Lieven 2004: Chapter 1). But alongside this notion of 'American exceptionalism' there has gone a more pragmatic or 'realist' strand to US policies, especially when they were locked into the context with the Soviet Union for cold war predominance; this realism has often combined with elements of liberalism to support a US commitment on pragmatic grounds to multilateral institutions and principles (Ikenberry 2006: Part one). There is also a third strand: the persistent tendency among some Americans to hanker after various forms of isolationism, to withdraw from the world and cultivate the perfect democracy, insulated from the grubby dealings of the world (and especially of Europe, at least in the past). This set of coexisting tendencies is backed up by an acute awareness in the US of the merits of 'hard power', and of the need to back up the US vision with muscle, especially military muscle, in order to promote the hardest possible security perimeter. It can readily be seen that this interaction between vision and muscle might take three distinct patterns: when power is aligned with 'exceptionalism' it can lead to a form of crusading foreign policy; when linked with 'realism' it can lead to a search for international primacy and alliances, and to qualified support for multilateral institutions; and when linked with isolationism it can lead to a policy centred on 'fortress America'. In contrast to the EU, this gives the US the character not of a 'trading state' but of what might be termed a 'warrior state'; even when it wishes to back away from the world, the role of 'hard power' and military capability is central to US policies on world order (M. Smith 2004).

None of these strands in US foreign policy have gone away in the post-cold-war period, but they have been present in a markedly new type of international structure. The disappearance of the Soviet Union instantly gave the United States a position of international primacy that is unprecedented in the modern era, based not only on military power but also on economic leadership (partly expressed through globalization) and 'ideological' primacy centred on ideas of liberal democracy. But the absence of challengers created as many problems as it solved for US policymakers. Where 'hard power' is effectively unlimited, as in the case of the United States since the end of the cold war, all other countries in the international system have a problem: how are they going to deal with the predominant power? But the predominant power also has a problem: how can this unlimited power be managed politically, in a situation where it seems that it has only to be applied to prevail? The Clinton and George W. Bush administrations that have led the US since the end of the cold war have had to grapple continually with the problem of political management of power, and while their solutions to the problem have often been different in detail they have reflected essentially the same underlying question: How do you adjust to a world in which you have no rivals and in which you can apparently act unilaterally as often as you want? While the Clinton administrations generally came down in favour of multilateral action and coordination with allies, the George W. Bush administrations generally came to a different conclusion: that there was no compelling case for multilateralism, especially when the vital interests of the US were at stake. Such a position was crystallized by the events of 9/11 and was pursued through the 'war on terror' and then the war in Iraq (Daalder and Lindsay 2003: Chapters 6–11; Halper and Clarke 2004: Chapters 7–9; Kaldor 2004).

One of the reasons for this unique position, in which the United States could effectively define its own interests as equivalent to those of the world community, and impose its vision of world order on its allies as well as its adversaries, lay in the resources the US was able to apply. Particularly in the area of military resources, the US is theoretically capable of prevailing over almost any conceivable combination of other countries in the world arena. This predominance reflected the massive investment that had been made in military capabilities during the later stage of the cold war – in this respect, George W. Bush was the principal legatee of Ronald Reagan (M. Smith 2004). Whether on land, in the air, at sea or even in outer space, the US was technologically dominant and apparently invincible. As 9/11 showed, however, this apparent invulnerability could be challenged dramatically by those such as Al-Qaeda practising 'asymmetric conflict' and effectively operating in a different world of power. Economically, the United States is not so unchallengeable: the existence of major competitors such as the EU and the emergence of new economic powers such as China and India has made the post-cold-war global political economy a much more complex place, and the need for collective management is necessarily more apparent in this area. Although the US might be seen as the progenitor of globalization, that does not mean that American leadership is easy to establish or to maintain in the global economic arena. In the area of political ideas, resistance to US attempts to extend the 'free world' has been widespread and often effective. Although this might be seen in terms of a global 'clash of civilizations', it can also be interpreted in terms of imperialism, domination and resistance – a relationship with a long historical tradition (Ikenberry 2006: Chapter 9; Todd 2003).

The post-cold-war world has as a result been a much more complicated place to manage than some US policymakers have been able to admit. Unilateralism and the deployment of 'hard power' can achieve spectacular results in the short term, but this does not guarantee success in the longer term. The most dramatic demonstration of this problem is to be found in the invasion of Iraq, and the subsequent inability of the United States to control the insurgency that then followed (Woodward 2006). The 'war on terror' itself does not require simply the application of massive military power; rather, it demands long-term planning and the application of a wide range of political, legal, administrative and other measures as well as force. The US has very large 'hard-power' resources, and the capacity to deliver them to many parts of the world, but the need to apply these in a complex, globalised and crisis-ridden context places unprecedented demands on the US political and administrative system as well as on its armed forces. Not only this, but the frequent resort to 'hard power' can have the result of reducing the credibility of US 'soft power' and making it much more difficult to bring other along with US international initiatives (Nye 2002, 2004a).

World order is thus not a simple problem for the US. Power and resources are available, but their impact and their relationship to political objectives are not predictable. One way of attempting to deal with this problem is through the development of 'grand strategy', and this has been a characteristic feature of US foreign policy during the post-1945 period (Kupchan 2002; Lieber 2007). While during the cold war the centrality of the contest with the Soviet Union provided the core of such 'grand strategy', the post-

cold-war period is not so easy to cope with. The Clinton administrations of the 1990s generally pursued a strategy based on the
interrelated concepts of 'engagement' and 'enlargement' – engagement with both allies and adversaries, enlargement of the zone of
freedom and democracy – a strategy which reflected a broadly mul-
tilateralist approach but which was accompanied by the willingness
to use force if necessary, as in Bosnia and Kosovo (see Chapter 8).
The George W. Bush administration after 2000 adopted a posture
based much more closely on the exercise of 'hard power' at an
early stage, pre-emptively if necessary. The National Security
Strategy of 2002, adopted immediately after 9/11, focused almost
exclusively on the need to prevent challenges to the US and to use
force in this cause (see Box 9.3). Engagement with allies as an end
in itself was marginalized; in the words of US Secretary of Defense
Donald Rumsfeld, 'the mission determines the coalition, rather
than the coalition determining the mission'. Although this message
was moderated somewhat in the National Security Strategy of
2006, and there was recourse to NATO to manage conflict situations in Afghanistan and elsewhere as the 'war on terror' wore on,
there was still no doubt about the strategic priorities and the
'weapons of choice' of the administration. Such preferences
extended beyond international conflict and violence, into the realm
of global governance, where the administration was quick to reject
attempts at multilateral management of environmental issues and
at the international application of various aspects of human rights.

The 'grand strategy' of the George W. Bush administrations was
thus moulded by exceptional conditions in the international order.
It was also conditioned by exceptional circumstances at home, with
the ascendancy of a small group of 'neoconservative' politicians
determined to make US supremacy count and take the opportunity
to reshape global and regional orders (Daalder and Lindsay 2003;
Halper and Clarke 2004; Lieven 2004). By the start of 2008, the
last year of Bush's second term, these circumstances have changed
perceptibly, with the intractability of events in Iraq and elsewhere
leading to mounting opposition at home, and creating a much less
permissive policy context. Above all, the record of unilateralism
and a focus on 'hard power' in actually restoring a stable international order was sharply questioned. One view of the George W.
Bush administrations is that they were dominated at least in the
early stages by 'utopian radicals' who were determined to overthrow the existing international order in the cause of creating con-

BOX 9.3   The US National Security Strategy of 2002 [extracts]

The United States possesses unprecedented – and unequalled – strength and influence in the world. Sustained by faith in the principles of liberty, and the value of a free society, this position comes with unparalleled responsibilities, obligations, and opportunity. The great strength of this nation must be used to promote a balance of power that favours freedom . . .

The United States is fighting a war against terrorists of global reach. The enemy is not a single political regime or person. The enemy is terrorism – premeditated, politically motivated violence perpetrated against innocents . . . Our priority will be first to disrupt and destroy terrorist organizations of global reach and attack their leadership; command, control, and communications; material support; and finances. This will have a disabling effect on the terrorists' ability to plan and operate . . .

We must be prepared to stop rogue states and their terrorist clients before they are able to threaten or use weapons of mass destruction against the United States and our allies and friends . . .

The United States has long maintained the option of preemptive actions to counter a sufficient threat to our national security. The greater the threat, the greater is the risk of inaction – and the more compelling the case for taking anticipatory action to defend ourselves, even if uncertainty remains as to the time and place of the enemy's attack. To forestall or prevent such hostile acts by our adversaries, the United States will, if necessary, act preemptively.

Source: National Security Strategy of the United States, September 2002, accessed at http://www.whitehouse.gov/nsc/print/nssall.html

ditions for the spread of democracy worldwide (Jervis 2005, 2006). If this version is accepted, then stability was not an intended outcome; but the consequences of destabilization were not so easily calculable or controllable as the radicals may have imagined. While Bush administrations had self-consciously rejected the 'politics of limits', it appeared by 2007–8 that they might have to accept at least some of that logic as a means of exerting effective influence on world order as it actually existed.

While we can conclude that the US has faced major problems in coping with its own 'hard power' and security, American administrations have also encountered difficulties in dealing with the growth of demands for global governance in the post-cold-war era. Though it would be simplistic to argue that the EU has been much more ready for these demands given its internal structure as a kind of governance system itself (see above), it is clear that successive US administrations since the late 1980s have had their attention fixed much more on 'high politics' than on the more technical aspects of many global governance issues. In addition, the demands of domestic politics in such areas as environmental policy or the practice of international human rights have given US policies a distinct twist, through which sovereignty and power (including the power of US example) have been emphasized at least as much as global cooperation. Thus, international collective efforts have frequently been spurned either on the grounds that they would unacceptably limit US freedom of action or because they would in any case be ineffective (the latter of course often seeming like a self-fulfilling prophecy, because US participation is central to international cooperation itself); only after several years did the use of NATO as a device for sharing the burden of 'hard security' commitments begin to seem a suitable option. We will see in the final section of the chapter how this feeds into EU–US relations.

The EU, the US and world order: power and security

It is evident from the discussion in this chapter so far that although both the EU and the US have a persistent interest in issues of global power and security, they approach them from markedly different positions and with markedly different resources and strategies. In this part of the chapter, we look at the ways in which these different approaches have intersected or collided in the post-cold-war world and at the ways they have contributed to broader changes in the world arena. As noted at the beginning of the chapter, it has been argued that the EU and the US exist in 'separate worlds' when it comes to the establishment of international order, but self-evidently this is true only at the most abstract level. As might be expected, the pursuit of world order by the EU and the US has several dimensions. Here we will look at four of them: the management of power; unilateralism and multilateralism; institutions and cooperation; and bargaining and problem-solving. The argument will be illustrated by reference to key cases: the 'war on terror' that ensued after the attacks of 9/11, the Iraq War and occupation, and the problem of Iranian nuclear intentions.

It is clear from what has been said above that both the EU and the US have to confront problems emerging from the management of power. The EU experiences the continuous need to manage American power, since the US is a dominating feature of the external environment for European integration. Since the end of the cold war, this problem has taken a new form, and the EU has had to deal with a United States that is itself searching for an appropriate role in world order. In those terms, it was rather easier for the Union to come to terms with the Clinton administrations than with those of George W. Bush, since the Clinton years saw at least an attempt by US leaders to use the institutions and mechanisms that might channel or contain their power (Smith and Woolcock 1994; Peterson 1996b). The George W. Bush administrations had a different view of American power: they wanted to use it, and to demonstrate their primacy as well as to assert it in the cause of global democracy. This, not surprisingly, created pressure on the EU and its member states, and made collective action by the Union much more difficult in areas where the US took an assertive position (M. Smith 2005a).

The attacks of 9/11 provided a catalyst for many of these underlying tensions in EU–US security relations. In one sense, the fact that the attacks reflected a novel, transnational and non-governmental form of violence seemed to play to some of the strengths of the EU: this was a problem that demanded cross-national coordination, often by non-military means, to preserve economic and social structures in the face of a broad and often ill-defined threat (M. Smith 2001; Nye 2004b). Thus, the EU collectively could respond with statements of support and with economic and diplomatic measures. But the 'war on terror' as it developed faced the EU with a different challenge, as US forces led the move into Afghanistan during 2001–2 with the aim of deposing the Taliban regime that had harboured Al-Qaeda. This pushed EU solidarity beyond the limits of sustainability, and leading members of the coalition that led the Afghan campaign, such as the British or the Dutch, acted much less as members of the Union than as allies of the US; there was also a tendency among the larger member states to take on a special role in the crisis, as for example when the French, the

Germans and the British met separately before the European Council meeting of October 2001 in Ghent, or when British Prime Minister Tony Blair convened a meeting of those who had committed themselves to military engagement in Afghanistan, without inviting Javier Solana, the EU's high representative for common foreign and security policy (Cameron 2007: 32–4). In the longer term, however, the EU could play a role, in organizing the reconstruction effort and coordinating financing – areas that played into the 'soft-power' resources of the Union. In the same way, the EU could provide support for the 'war on terror' through its developing responsibilities for 'justice and home affairs': a category of activities that was greatly extended with the need to exchange information and coordinated intelligence in the aftermath of 9/11 (den Boer and Monar 2002; Monar 2004). Thus the EU was able, for example, to promote a pan-European arrest warrant, measures to promote transport and data security, and regulations to deal with the financing of terrorist groupings. The Union was also able in some areas to resist US policies, for example where conceptions of human rights differed between the two sides of the Atlantic (see below). Not only this, but it could be argued that new areas of European foreign policy cooperation were made possible, not in the classic collective foreign policy mode but through the emergence of new potential coalitions within the EU and through their interaction with NATO and other security organizations to address shared problems (Hill 2004; M. Smith 2006b).

Whereas the 'war on terror' saw strains but also new forms of solidarity within the EU, the use of force against Iraq was clearly opposed by a number of leading EU member states, and was not seen by them as part of the response to 9/11. Thus, as the US moved towards war with Iraq during 2002–3, it was effectively impossible for the Europeans to keep their act together; a number of countries such as the United Kingdom, Spain and Italy defected from any common position on the ground that they must support the United States, while others such as France and Germany attempted to maintain solidarity around resistance to immediate use of force and full use of the United Nations (Lindstrom 2003: Chapters 1–2; Gordon and Shapiro 2004; Peterson 2004a). The particular issue of 'weapons of mass destruction' and their presence or absence in Iraq saw a fundamental divergence between those within the Union who supported a multilateral, UN-based approach (and who suspected the WMD issue of being a cover for 'regime change') and those who espoused a more coercive military approach. This created a position of considerable internal crisis within the EU, and led Donald Rumsfeld to identify a division between what he termed 'old' and 'new' Europe (see Box 9.4).

While Rumsfeld's division was simplistic (and referred to the enlarged NATO as well as to the EU), the wounds opened by the Iraq crisis did lead to a proliferation of efforts to form more partial 'European' caucuses and to express difference or convergence between European and US positions. In many of these initiatives, the EU institutions themselves seemed likely to be marginalized; thus in the months before the invasion, the French and the Germans took measures to increase their cooperation in resisting US and British pressures; in January 2003, the leaders of eight EU member states or soon-to-be member states signed an open letter supporting US policies without consulting other member states or candidate members, and in February the so-called 'Vilnius Group' of Central- and East-European countries (including seven candidate EU members) pledged support for the US in a letter published in the *Wall Street Journal*. Only with difficulty was a position reached

---

BOX 9.4   Donald Rumsfeld on 'old' and 'new' Europe

Q: Sir, a question about the mood among European allies . . . If you look at, for example, France and Germany . . . it seems that a lot of Europeans rather give the benefit of the doubt to Saddam Hussein than President George Bush. These are US allies. What do you make of that?

A: What do I say? Well, there isn't anyone alive who wouldn't prefer unanimity. I mean, you just always would like everyone to stand up and say, Way to go! That's the right [thing] to do, United States . . . Now, you're thinking of Europe as Germany and France. I don't. I think that's old Europe. If you look at the entire NATO Europe today, the center of gravity is shifting to the east. And there are a lot of new members . . . They're not with France and Germany on this, they're with the United States.

Source: US Secretary of Defense Donald H. Rumsfeld, Briefing at the Foreign Press Center, Washington, DC, 22 January 2003.

in the Council of Ministers that allowed the EU as a whole to state a common position on the humanitarian and related aspects of the conflict, while maintaining an uneasy silence on the war itself. Although tensions arising from these events persisted in the EU for several years, threatening to make it much less easy to undertake security initiatives in other areas, there was a gradual process of repair (Lindstrom 2003; Peterson and Pollack 2003; Lindstrom and Schmitt 2004; Peterson 2004a; Pond 2004). The issue of relations between the EU's defence identity and other defence organizations also persisted; in February 2005 German Chancellor Gerhard Schroeder suggested that NATO was no longer the appropriate forum for discussion of transatlantic security issues (Cameron 2007: 86), and although not many other EU leaders would have agreed with him then, the question still lingers as the ESDP develops further.

The divisions within the EU and between the EU and the US over war in Iraq were also responsible for one of the more notable transatlantic debates during the early 2000s. In 2003, arising directly out of the buildup to the war, Robert Kagan published an article and then a book dealing with what came to be known as the 'Mars/Venus' problem (Kagan 2003; see also Lindberg 2005). In Kagan's view, the US had not fully come to terms with its preponderance of 'hard power', but had (as noted above) a tendency to resort to coercive solutions even where others might work. On the other hand, the Europeans emphasized the use of 'soft power' and resistance to military solutions, partly as a rationalization of their military weakness but also because of historical experience with the use of force. To put it in the terms used by a popular American self-improvement book, 'Americans were from Mars and Europeans from Venus'. In various forms, this debate came to encapsulate not only a political but also an institutional and cultural difference between the two sides of the Atlantic. This difference was not absolute – the British, for example, looked more like Martians than Venusians on many occasions – but it came to stand as a metaphor for the EU–US divergence on 'hard-security' issues (Cox 2003; M. Smith 2004; Forsberg and Herd 2006). The key question is how much this difference constitutes a fundamental and lasting rift in EU–US security relations (Andrews 2005: Part III; Lindberg 2005; Zabarowski 2006a).

How much does this difference over the management of power and the pursuit of security reflect broader differences over the utility of unilateral and multilateral approaches to world order? One example that can help to illuminate this question is that of EU and US responses to fears that the Iranians would pursue and obtain a nuclear weapons capability. Coming alongside the war and insurgency in Iraq, this challenge represented for some American neo-conservatives an extension of the problem that had led to US intervention in the first place – an extension to which the remedy might be 'more of the same' in the form of the use of force against Iran. The European analysis differed: there was a consensus within the Union that the Iranian problem was not only distinct from that of Iraq (although it had become entangled with it partly as a consequence of US intervention in Iraq) but also that it should be dealt with diplomatically, using the EU's 'soft power' in the form of potential partnership and cooperation agreements. During the period 2003–7, the EU developed a mechanism for pursuing a diplomatic solution through the so-called 'EU-3' (France, Germany and the UK), which maintained diplomatic contact with the Iranian government and which was able to put together successive packages of measures to present to the government in Tehran (Everts 2004; Posch 2006; Youngs 2006: Chapter 3). This did not prevent the Iranian government from making moves towards the production of the raw materials for a nuclear device, but it did preserve a diplomatic linkage and prevent the taking of pre-emptive military action. Perhaps surprisingly, the US went along with this diplomatic strategy; but it should be noted in this context that the growth of the insurgency in Iraq between 2004 and 2006 and the consequent growth in domestic opposition to US interventions would have made any unilateral American action difficult in any case.

Each of the examples referred to thus far has contained at least elements of 'hard security'. But as noted earlier in this chapter, there are many current issues between the EU and the US that are predominantly if not entirely of a 'soft security' type. The notion of 'soft security', as noted earlier, relates to the preservation of economic security, environmental security, energy security and what has come to be termed 'human security' in the broad sense. What has happened in the post-cold-war era is that many of these areas have become newly or increasingly 'securitized': that is to say, they are presented by governments as questions relating to the preservation of national security (or EU security) in the face of new threats and risks. They are also used by some if not all governments as weapons in their relations with others, through the manipulation of dependencies (for example, on supplies of oil or gas or technical assistance) and consequently vulnerabilities. The EU and the US are thus bound together by their status as rich countries or groupings in dealing with these problems, but this has not prevented the emergence of significant conflicts between them. In the context of this argument, the important question is: to what extent do these differences betray different fundamental perspectives on the use of 'soft power' in the search for 'soft security'?

The first case we should examine is what we can term 'economic security'. Since the 1970s, as indicated in Chapter 1, there have been differences between the US and the European views of economic security, if by that is meant the preservation of economic stability and the pursuit of economic growth and prosperity, for example through trade and the management of the currency. The US economy remains the single largest national economy in the world, and thus there is a historic tendency among US policy-makers to stress the ways in which growth and prosperity depend upon national initiatives and national instruments. During the 1990s and 2000s, there have been variations in the stances of successive administrations (see Chapters 3 and 4 above), but these have been variations around a fairly consistent tendency to prioritize national measures and to downplay the prospects of multilateral cooperation. Thus although the US is a leading member of the G-7 industrial countries, which meet annually to coordinate national economic policies, Washington has been reluctant to allow its national economic strategy to be constrained by international action. The EU's stance is different: long experience with coordination and integration within Europe itself has created a predisposition to multilateralize economic security issues, and to search for means of collaboration. Although again there are variations around this trend line, the tendency to prioritise collaboration and multilateralism is evident (Pollack 2003a). It is also difficult in this area for the US to 'divide and rule', since unlike areas of 'hard security' there are much stronger institutional arrangements and a predisposition in the Union to agree on matters of 'economic security', even where there are sharp differences among member states on the specifics.

While there is a long tradition of European solidarity on matters of 'economic security', our second example, environmental security, is less longstanding. Significantly, however, the EU's acquisition of competence in areas of environmental policy during the late 1980s and 1990s coincided with growing awareness of the ways these issues needed to be managed at the multilateral level (Sbragia 1998). The EU has thus had an incentive (through the European Commission) to pursue a leadership role in environmental security, and to create a distinctively 'European' definition of interests, focused (for example) on the adoption of binding targets for reductions in carbon dioxide emissions and on the development of emissions trading schemes. Despite a great diversity of views within the EU on most environmental issues (most recently between some of the less developed new member states and the older-established and richer members), there has been a capacity to collaborate around common positions in international organizations, often in distinct opposition to US views (Vogler and Bretherton 2006). On the American side, while the US has led in some areas of international environmental regulation, there is more of a predisposition to allow market forces to operate, and to initiate action at the national level. This has been particularly the case in the area of climate change, where the US has opposed binding targets for reductions in carbon dioxide emissions (as symbolized by the commitments in the 1999 Kyoto Protocol) and has instead argued for the development of new technologies through market incentives and at the national level. These are not mere differences of detail: some have argued that they betray a basic difference between EU and US perspectives on environmental regulation that emerges as much from cultural predispositions or the relationship between government and society as from government tactics (Bodansky 2003). But it can equally be argued that setting aside the rhetoric on both sides there is a good deal in common between the EU and the US, since both of them share the problems of rich industrialised areas that need to find a way to preserve their standards of living and levels of consumption in a world where others (such as India or China) are seeking to emulate them. In this sense, the question is one that squarely confronts the themes of this book: there is a great deal of overt competition between the EU and the US, but a large amount of common interest arising out of their shared predicament.

The third example that can be examined here is that of energy security. During the 2000s, both the Europeans and the Americans have become more sensitive than at any time since the 1970s to issues of the price for and the supply of oil and gas. Neither the EU nor the US can satisfy its own energy needs from domestic sources, and thus both are heavily dependent on supplies from the Middle East and Persian Gulf, the former Soviet Union (particularly Russia) or Latin America. The impact of conflict in the Middle East and the Gulf during the early years of the twenty-first century has been severe, and has driven up oil prices in general to historic highs. At the same time, the newly assertive Putin government in Russia has tried to use the 'energy weapon' as one means to restore its international status and to make others take notice of its priorities (see Chapter 8). In Latin America, the Chavez government in Venezuela has made it its business to provoke Washington and to use its oil resources as a means of forming new international alliances (for example with Cuba and Iran). Both the EU and the US have thus come under pressure to address problems of energy vulnerability, without being able in the short term to avoid reliance on imported oil and gas supplies (Musu and Wallace 2003). This is an inherently political issue, and one where 'hard power' is not to be relied upon as a means of dealing with it. For both the EU and the US, there is little room for manoeuvre, since they cannot intervene forcibly (the EU because it could never muster the resources, the US because the Iraq precedent has cast its shadow over any future such expedition, and because the one thing the intervention has not done is increase US access to cheap oil). The result in both cases has been uncertain, with commercial and consumer priorities conflicting with national security needs, and no means of squaring the circle. Here, therefore, we find both the EU and the US in a quandary and with no means of reliably ensuring energy security.

Let us look finally at the issue of 'human security'. During recent years there has been growing attention to the combination of regional conflicts, development issues and human-rights issues that clusters around the security of individuals or groups within or across national jurisdictions. The plight of refugees from a great variety of civil conflicts, but now also from a growing range of environmental disasters, is perhaps the most obvious example of a wide-ranging problem. In terms of world order, it is clear that the EU places a much larger emphasis on cooperative solutions to such problems, embodying multilateral principles and inclusive characteristics, while the US (perhaps inevitably as a dominant power) has tended to look for exclusive coalitions and 'special relationships', if necessary rejecting efforts at multilateral management (Kaldor *et al.* 2007). Thus, the European Union has been a strong supporter of United Nations management of regional conflicts, while the US has been much more equivocal about it; equally, the EU has strongly supported the establishment of the International Criminal Court as a means of pursuing and punishing those involved in civil conflicts, while the US has rejected it and specifically attempted to undermine the EU's collective position by concluding agreements with EU member states to exempt US forces from its application. Until recently, the EU has had little capacity to intervene in civil conflicts or regional conflicts that cross-national boundaries, but the development of ESDP during the early 2000s has given it at least some potential instruments in this area (Howorth 2007). As a result, the EU has become involved in Central Africa, in dealing with conflicts involving Rwanda and the Democratic Republic of Congo. The US, on the other hand, has largely remained uninvolved on the ground, reserving its interventions for those areas in which it has a direct strategic interest, such as the Middle East or the Gulf. The EU, it might appear, has a winning combination of assets that can be used in the African context particularly: emerging military capacity (limited as noted in Box 9.1 above to the 'Petersberg' and associated tasks); a long-standing engagement with international development in Africa; and a commitment to the achievement of 'human security' through multilateral action, which might enable it to develop a form of 'burden-sharing' with the United States (Lindstrom 2005). But the dynamics of 'human security' are not so simple. When the crisis in the Darfur region of Sudan emerged in the late 1990s, both the EU and the US described the actions of government-backed militias as 'genocide', but neither was willing to intervene with the requisite force or economic support for the affected areas. Given that other factors also operate in Central Africa – particularly the recent discovery and exploitation of large oil reserves, and the increasing presence in the region of China as an aid donor and oil buyer – it might be suspected that attitudes both in the EU and the US could change rather rapidly, but that is to underestimate the public (and in the case of the EU, Member State) opposition to renewed intervention in the wake of Iraq and Afghanistan. Here, then, we find that what might be in some ways defined as a 'soft security' issue is far from amenable only to 'soft power', and this problem afflicts both the EU and the US.

The EU, the US and world order: global governance

The contrast between the EU and the US over multilateralism and unilateralism in issues of security reflects a broad difference of view on the utility of international cooperation and institutions. As we have seen, the EU places great store in the need for global governance, not least because of its experience with multinational governance in Europe itself (see Ortega 2007). Although there are differences between EU member states, they all share this broad commitment to the management of international order, and to the role of institutions in that process. The Americans, on the other hand, see international cooperation as a matter of choice rather than of necessity: where US interests are served, the cooperation is acceptable, but where international cooperation threatens what are seen as US vital interests, the country retains the right to opt out, to oppose and to undermine such efforts. As Robert Keohane points out (2003), this reflects an attachment to the Westphalian view of sovereignty which has largely disappeared under the impact of interdependence and integration in the EU. Thus when the US opposes the International Criminal Court, it is not merely on grounds of practicality; rather, it is on grounds of underlying attachment to a view of sovereignty that is at odds with any such effort at international management. Likewise, EU support for the Kyoto Protocol on climate change is partly a reflection of recognition of environmental threats, but also a reflection of deep-rooted views about the necessity for international cooperation itself.

The EU has been very active in promoting multilateral institutions and rules, not least because it is through some of them that the EU can maintain and enhance its international legitimacy and status. The EU is itself an example of governance at the continental level, and some have argued that this gives the Union a special role in promoting and defending the mechanisms of global governance. The United States has taken historically a different perspective arising from its emphasis on sovereignty and on its national interests, but has had to take into account the need for management of the globalizing world. During the post-cold-war period there have been many instances in which these different approaches have come to the fore, and here we will present four examples to illustrate this phenomenon (drawing on Smith 2005b).

The first case is the process by which the agenda for the Doha Development Round was established and pursued within the

World Trade Organization during the period 1998–2003 (see also Chapter 3). A number of forces contributed to the initiation of a process that led first to the Seattle ministerial meeting of 1999 and later to the Doha ministerial meeting in 2001, the Cancún ministerial meeting of 2003 and the Hong Kong ministerial meeting of 2005. In Seattle, the presence of thousands of anti-globalization protestors added drama to the ministerial meeting, which failed to set an agenda for a new round of trade negotiations; the EU blamed the US for the failure, and the US blamed the EU. The Doha ministerial meeting agreed an agenda focused especially on the needs of developing countries, and was hailed as an example of the international community working together in the aftermath of the 9/11 attacks. After two years of tortuous negotiations, in which both the EU's Common Agricultural Policy and US farm export subsidies came under sustained attack, the Cancún meeting failed to meet its deadline to agree detailed negotiation processes and targets. Two years later, the Hong Kong ministerial also failed to make significant progress, and again the intransigence of the EU and the US was blamed, especially by the so-called G-20 of large developing exporters. In all of these stages, the participation of the EU and the US was seen as essential at the multilateral level; equally, in all of them there was a strong EU–US bilateral agenda in which the existence of 'competitive co-operation' was apparent (Allen and Smith 2002, 2003; Baldwin *et al.* 2003; Allen and Smith 2004; M. Smith 2005b). In what ways can this be seen as contributing to 'global governance'?

Throughout the buildup to the various ministerial meetings, the EU and the US were active in establishing their own negotiating positions, but also in attempting to have these accepted as the focus for the multilateral process. In areas such as agriculture and the broad 'development' agenda, the EU and the US vied for influence and were also frequently engaged in intense bilateral exchanges. As the Cancún meeting approached, the EU and the US produced on a bilateral basis a key document dealing with agriculture, which aroused intense suspicion among other members of the WTO and arguably contributed materially to the collapse of the Cancún meeting. But the Cancún debacle also revealed other aspects of the negotiation process: while the EU and the US had been mutually absorbed in their bilateral context, the growth of the G-20 developing countries had led to the emergence of a powerful caucus dedicated to resisting any EU–US bilateral stitch-up. Pursuit of the agenda for the Doha Development Round thus involved structured negotiation occasions between the EU and both the US and other WTO members, but also a host of less formal and structured encounters. Arguably, the focus on EU–US bilateral concerns and their projection onto the multilateral arena meant that important signals about changes in the negotiation context were ignored and the 'Cancún surprise' reflected this. It is a moot point as to whether global governance has been enhanced or undermined by this example of EU–US 'bi-multilateralism'.

A second and closely related case is provided by the negotiation of China's admission to the WTO, which was achieved formally at the beginning of 2002 (Allen and Smith 2001, 2002, 2003). For our purposes, the key feature of this process is that both the EU and the US had (and continue to have) a major stake in getting the Chinese into the multilateral trade regime, and that in accordance with the rules of the WTO the Chinese had to negotiate deals with all of the existing WTO members before they could enter. Both the EU and the US were thus negotiating bilaterally with the Chinese, while the result would be a major change in the scope and membership of the multilateral trading regime. What emerged during the latter part of 2000 was a kind of 'negotiation race' in which the respective offers made by the Chinese to the EU and the US generated a competitive dynamic in areas such as financial services, fed by the demands in both the EU and the US of major interest groups – particularly those related to the financial services industry. In the terms proposed by this chapter, here there was a process under way that promised to extend and enhance global governance, but because of the rules and conventions built into the WTO, there was an incentive for major stakeholders to conclude advantageous bilateral deals – and to renegotiate them, indeed, if the opposition seemed to have stolen a march at any given stage. All of the parties at various stages could take advantage of linkage strategies, with uncertain consequences for the WTO regime in general. After the Chinese entered the WTO, they continued to exert this paradoxical influence on EU–US relations: both the EU and the US experienced large and growing trade deficits with China, which led to appeals for protection from industries such as apparel, and which in turn led the EU both to impose unilateral quotas on the Chinese and to threaten complaints against China in the WTO (Allen and Smith 2006); but both the EU and the US preferred to act bilaterally to negotiate with China in the shadow of WTO action, a tactic that appeared to bring some results in at least the short term. The US also tried to get the Chinese to revalue their currency, and thus to reduce the price advantage held by their products, but with little immediate success. Here, we can perceive the tensions built into global governance mechanisms when major members (in this case of the WTO) can see advantage in dealing bilaterally with others, or acting unilaterally against them. In this case, the EU and the US have generally preferred not to invoke the most punitive WTO measures against the Chinese; is this a victory for global governance or for bilateralism?

A third case raising questions about the EU, the US and global governance is provided by the EU–US tensions that emerged in the late 1990s and persisted into the new millennium, centred on the ratification and implementation of the Kyoto Protocol (Allen and Smith 2000, 2001, 2002; Bodansky 2003; Bretherton and Vogler 2006). We have already mentioned this process in the context of 'soft-security' issues above, and this dimension is relevant to its fate in global governance terms. The Protocol dealt with the emission of greenhouse gases and the consequent phenomenon of global warming, and it established a framework for dealing with successive reductions in emission of the damaging gases. The USA was initially supportive of the process, but at the end of the Clinton administration it reversed its position and refused to ratify the protocol – a major problem for its implementation, since the US accounts for a larger proportion of emissions of greenhouse gases than any other country (though China is catching up and may well have overtaken the US by the time this book is published). Through the early years of the new millennium, there was a succession of EU–US bilateral efforts (mediated especially by the UK) to rescue at least part of the deal, with notably more commitment on the EU side than on that of the new Bush administration after 2000. At the same time, the EU set out to establish what can only be described as an anti-US coalition in the context of continuing efforts to achieve multilateral ratification of the protocol – an effort which attracted the lasting hostility of the Bush administration but which also brought to prominence the role of other major players such as Russia (whose ratification was vital to implementation of the protocol). For the EU, the position was complicated further by the need to negotiate emissions trading procedures within the Union itself, while at the same time trying both to deal with the US on a bilateral level and with the rather unruly remainder of the Kyoto coalition in the multilateral arena (Vogler and Bretherton 2006). This problem of positioning had clear roots in the 'bi-multilateral' nature of the negotiation process, in which the bilateral relations between the EU and the US were related strongly to the progress of multilateral efforts to deal with climate change, and meant that particularly for the EU the problem of creating and maintaining a credible posture was especially difficult (M. Smith 2005b). Although the Protocol came into force in February 2005, following Russian ratification in November 2004, the US then proceeded to sponsor alternative international efforts to try and arrive at more flexible targets – efforts that were eventually if reluctantly accepted by the EU, while the Union maintained its commitment to the more prescriptive Kyoto model. This seems to present a clear example of the ways in which competition – in this case between two models of the global governance of climate change – and convergence can and do coexist in EU–US relations. Again, the issue for global governance is whether the EU–US relationship has contributed materially to advances in the multilateral management of climate change issues. Perhaps significantly, the convergence of views that did take place in 2006 and 2007 was reflected not specifically in EU–US actions, but in the different institutional context of the G-8 leading industrial countries (the US, Canada, France, Germany, Italy, Japan, Russia and the United Kingdom), at its June 2007 summit in the German resort of Heiligendamm. The road to effective convergence between the EU and the US on global governance issues can take several routes depending on the subject at issue and the institutional resources available.

Our final case concerns an area in which global governance mechanisms and power and security considerations overlap: the protection of human rights in the 'war on terror'. As noted earlier, the EU has positioned itself in general as a form of 'normative power' concerned to defend and promote a particular perspective on human rights and related issues. By doing so, it has aligned itself with a host of intergovernmental and non-governmental bodies, ranging from the United Nations to Amnesty International, which are concerned with the rights of individuals or groups and their defence against encroachments from 'national security' and other areas (K.Smith 2006a, 2006b). The United States, on the other hand, has historically seen human rights at least partly as an instrument of foreign policy, and subject to the demands of national security; thus, they have tended to align themselves with regimes that promise stability but do not put human rights at the top of their list of priorities, while rhetorically endorsing a vision of international democracy (Halper and Clarke 2004: Chapter 1). These two approaches – one seeing human rights as an end in themselves, the other seeing them as part of the search for security – have been brought out in a sharp form by the conduct of the 'war on terror' since 2001. Some examples will sharpen our focus here. One concerns the demand by the United States that terrorist suspects should be extradited from the EU to face charges that might imply a death sentence. The EU has consistently resisted this demand, on the grounds that its member states have abolished the death penalty and that they cannot extradite individuals to face even the possibility of execution. A second example concerns the holding of terrorist suspects by the United States at its base in Cuba, Guantanamo Bay. The US has defined many of these as 'unlawful combatants' and thus not subject to the humanitarian provisions of the laws of war as set out in the Geneva Conventions. Once again, opinion in the EU has been strongly opposed to this interpretation, although individual member states such as the UK have found it more difficult to resist the US position. Finally, there has been a continuing tension between the EU and the US over the process of 'extraordinary rendition', through which the CIA has allegedly transported terrorist suspects to countries (including, again allegedly, some in the EU itself) where they have faced severe interrogations leading to claims of torture. The EU, and especially the European Parliament, has taken a strong stand against such processes and in favour of the various investigations that have taken place into them (Allen and Smith 2006, 2007). Each of these cases shows the symptoms of 'bi-multilateral' governance processes, in which the EU and the US are linked to broader processes of global governance and to the regimes and rules that characterise a globalizing world.

The balance sheet of EU–US relations in terms of global governance, on the basis of these examples, is decidedly mixed. It is not a case of 'EU good, US bad' (on the grounds that the EU presents itself as being in favour of increased global governance and indeed a model for it, while the US resists it and preaches national self-sufficiency). Rather, it seems to be the case that the EU and the US have fundamentally mixed attitudes towards the establishment and the extension of global governance mechanisms, and that this reflects mixed views on particular areas of competition or convergence. It is not possible to arrive at a simple overall judgement, but the aim of the cases presented here has been to show the ways in which the roles of the EU and the US in global governance might be explored and evaluated.

Overview and conclusion

This chapter has focused on the ways EU and US views of world order can be explored and evaluated, and on the ways they can be observed in action within EU–US relations. A key aid to understanding these issues is an awareness of processes of change, both within the EU and the US and in the broader global context within which they conduct their relations. This is not a new theme in this book – indeed, it is one of the core themes that run through the whole of our analysis. Here, it has a global scale and a connection with key aspects of the approaches to the world on both sides of the Atlantic.

The chapter has argued as follows:

- First, the change from the cold war world to the post-cold-war world created new challenges and opportunities for both the EU and the US, and their responses to these challenges and opportunities reflect a combination of pragmatic, institutional and cultural understandings about the way the world works and the way it should look.
- Second, and more specifically, the chapter has characterized the EU as a form of 'trading state', emphasizing the search for stability, the use of multilateral strategies and the exploitation of 'soft power' based on reciprocity and problem-solving.
- Third, the United States, on the other hand, can be characterized as a 'warrior state', searching for advantage, prepared to act unilaterally and to use 'hard power', particularly military force, in pursuit of national advantage.
- Fourth, in matters of global power and security, the EU and the US represent different responses to the issue of managing the changing global power structure, and these responses are crucial for the management of global power and security as a whole. The relationship between 'hard power' and 'hard security' and 'soft power' and 'soft security' is crucial here, but it is

also complex and does not produce a clear-cut distinction between EU and US positions.

- Finally, in matters of global governance there is considerable evidence of a different balance between the EU and the US, giving the EU a form of comparative advantage in institution and regime-building, but both the EU and the US are essential components of global governance mechanisms. There is also evidence of the impact of competition and convergence between the EU and the US, and significant evidence that each of them subscribes to global governance in ways that are modified by their own interests and internal politics.

The discussion in this chapter reveals that that the EU and the US have differences over world order at three levels. In the first place, they have pragmatic and practical differences about the post-cold-war world, in economic, security and defence issues, which arise out of their mutual interactions and which in principle are susceptible to management through a process of negotiation and problem solving. Many of the economic issues that arise between the two partners are of this kind, but so also are a number of security issues which reflect the broader conception of security that has grown in the post-cold-war era. Often these disputes arise within a framework of shared understandings and expectations, and can be very effectively managed. But there are other differences that emerge out of a kind of competition between the EU and the US to 'sell' or establish their models of economic and political organization to potential converts in the post-cold-war context. Into this category fall a number of 'big-picture' trade and development issues, as well as some questions to do with human rights and the management of international conflicts. The processes of interaction here are those of hard bargaining and the exercise of muscle, rather than negotiation and problem-solving. The final type of difference is much less amenable to either problem solving or bargaining, since it depends upon fundamental differences of culture and assumptions about the nature of power, sovereignty and international order itself. We can expect that in future these three strands will continue to characterize the respective EU and US approaches to world order, and that the result will continue to be an uneasy and shifting set of complex compromises.

Chapter 10

The 'Euro-American System' and Beyond

In Chapters 1 and 2 of this book we presented two linked views of EU–US relations. First, in Chapter 1 we explored the historical development of the relationship between European integration and the United States, charting a number of key themes and points of major change. In Chapter 2 we addressed the notion of the 'Euro-American system' – a structured set of relations involving not only the European integration process and the United States but also the networks, institutions and processes of policymaking in the transatlantic area, of which EU–US relations have been a growing if not now dominant part. We also noted in Chapter 2 that the 'Euro-American system' and EU–US relations must be viewed in the context of broader processes of global change and transformation, to which EU–US relations contribute at the same time as they are affected by them. In both chapters, we addressed the question of change: How much of what was established in the 1950s and 1960s is still recognizable in EU–US relations, how much has been changed, and how much has the relationship been transformed into something fundamentally different from what it was at its origins? The purpose of this chapter is to reappraise these key questions in the light of the detailed examination carried out in Chapters 3 to 9, and to identify a number of key current trends that may point towards different futures for the 'Euro-American system'.

The European–American relationship has dominated international relations and international political economy for most of the last century. The relationship, as noted in Chapter 2 and as detailed by Chapters 3 to 9, is a network of dense and well-developed relationships among a myriad of actors – politicians, officials, military bodies, regulators, corporations, international institutions and, increasingly, non-governmental organizations. Relations among these actors have been underpinned by shared assumptions about the importance of democracy as the best means of allocating political power, and of the market as the optimal means of allocating economic resources. They have also historically been founded on shared perceptions of the key security challenges and of the nature of a desirable European and world order. Europe and America have disagreed about the wisdom of particular foreign policy decisions – and about the extent to which the free market should govern all aspects of economic life – but the basic ideational consensus has proven to be remarkably durable. As EU–US relations have developed and deepened, they have come to comprise the key component of transatlantic relations in general, and to subsume a growing proportion of the key interactions between the many groupings involved in the 'Euro-American system'.

The global impact of the EU–US relationship cannot be exaggerated. For most of the postwar period, it has been central to the global economy. The US in the immediate period after World War II accounted for half of the global economy. Even now the US remains the world's largest national economy by a considerable distance. The EU, taken as a single economic entity, is the world's largest trader, exporting goods and services across the globe; its affluent and open market, like America's, is a magnet for investment. As important, both actors have a substantial role in the management of the global economy. Some functions, like that of the US dollar as the *de facto* global currency, are obvious but others are not. Throughout the world, Euro-American standards and regulations are the benchmark against which other national and regional systems are measured. The World Trade Organization owes much of its structure, processes and substance to successive generations of American and European diplomats, who worked hard to overcome domestic opposition to trade liberalization, motivated by the belief that economic nationalism rarely ends well. The effect is subtle, but important, because it forces other states to play the game according to a set of rules created by others. Thus, when China is accused of breaching international agreements on IP, those agreements are deeply informed by European and American understandings of the desirability of IP protection, and of the importance of enforceable contracts. A signal feature of the international political economy is the extent to which shared understandings of how economic life should be conducted owe everything to Europe and America. It is hegemony in its clearest, yet most subtle form, extending beyond the WTO into the international monetary institutions and into the management of a vast range of international transactions and communications.

In the realm of international relations more broadly conceived, the Euro-American system has been central as well. As we noted in Chapter 2, the components of this system are states, intergovernmental institutions and an increasing array of private actors, such as firms and a variety of groups from civil society, constituting overlapping systems at the intergovernmental, transgovernmental and transnational levels. Thus, the intergovernmental aspects of transatlantic relations, carried on by a growing range of states since the end of the cold war, have a clear impact not only on those states directly involved but also on the broader balance of power in the world arena. Not only this, but the EU has come to perform a range of economic and diplomatic roles not unlike those of many states (operating alongside and coordinating while not replacing its member states in crucial areas). Both the EU and the United States use international organizations as an instrument of state power, though the US has a more durable scepticism about this route and the EU has to work in coordination with its member states in crucial areas such as monetary, development, environmental and security policy. While many EU leaders proclaim the primacy and the desirability of multilateral action through international institutions, many American politicians and commentators are vocal critics of the United Nations and prefer to use multilateral organizations only as a last resort. Both the EU and the US have used unilateral and multilateral mechanisms to advance the rule of law internationally – an often overlooked achievement. The US, more so than the EU, is prepared to use force to attain its goals, but as noted in Chapter 9 this should be placed into a broader historical context and understanding of the roles played by both the EU and the US more generally. Thus for example, criticism of George W. Bush's conduct of foreign policy has focused to a considerable extent on its departure from American norms, while the notion of the EU as a 'civilian power' is in tension with some of the policies adopted by key member states.

Despite the enduring influence of intergovernmentalism and 'state power' in EU–US relations, international organizations exert influence themselves. As we outlined in Chapter 3, the international trading system works – albeit imperfectly – according to rules manifest in WTO agreements, backed up by a disputes process. As with any regime, international organizations work to structure actor expectations and inculcate norms of behaviour. Though they remain, ultimately, vulnerable to state indifference or hostility, they are not empty vessels for preferences of the powerful. Most importantly, the picture drawn in this book is one that emphasizes the persistence of different layers of interaction between and within international institutions. The EU itself is an object lesson in this respect: as noted in all of Chapters 2 to 9, the EU presents a hybrid organization, with aspects of supranational authority and collective action existing alongside intergovernmental coordination and sometimes conflict to present a picture of complex multilevel political and economic activity.

As we expected on the basis of the arguments in Chapter 2, the volume has outlined the important role of private actors in the Euro-American system. In several spheres of economic activity, private organizations provide critical expertise that informs debate and influences policy. For example the European Union's adoption of international accounting standards during the late 1990s relied heavily on private sector efforts to develop internationally agreed rules. American trade policy is deeply influenced – some say dangerously so – by lobbyists from both organized labour and corporate interests – but then, so is trade policy in the EU. Indeed, many influential US lobby groups are prominent in Brussels as they target EU legislation and policy initiatives. In similar fashion, the international community of monetary and financial experts has strong bases both in the EU and in the US, and dominates thinking about the structure and the restructuring of the international financial system. Even in the areas of 'high politics' represented in this book by activities in international security and related policy domains, the transatlantic influence of communities of experts and private industry has come to be a significant factor in the generation of transatlantic policy initiatives.

Thus far, then, our initial expectations about the 'Euro-American system' appear to have been borne out by the discussion in Chapters 3 to 9. We can discern a system founded on multiple levels of activity, demonstrating the presence of markets, hierarchies and networks, and revolving around a form of multi-level politics in 'high', 'low' and 'sectoral' policy arenas. We have illustrated from a variety of policy domains the varying patterns that these political and economic processes take, and the ways they intersect each other to create new challenges and opportunities both for the EU and for the US. One feature that has become very apparent here is that quite apart from the interactions between the EU and the US, it is important to take into account the domestic politics of policymaking and political and economic change; on both sides of the Atlantic, the influence of powerful forces is evident, whether it is the member states and a variety of transnational forces in the EU or the Congress and other parts of the federal system in the United States. Another feature that has become salient is the coexistence of competition – sometimes threatening open conflict – and convergence between the EU and the US.

Competition and convergence

One conceptualization of the post-1945 world was the gradual convergence of the global economy and society towards an American model of free-market economics and democratic government. This view enjoyed particular prominence in the wake of 11 September 2001 among neo-conservative US commentators. This book articulates a different view. Convergence does occur in the EU–US relationship, but it is not necessarily toward an American ideal. The terms competition and convergence suggest polar opposites, but the reality of politics in the Euro-American system is that issues can feature complex *blends* of competition and convergence. Moreover, issues evolve and competition or convergence can arise as one or both – or many – actors alter their policy preferences in reaction to changing circumstances. Despite their shared preferences on many issues, the EU and the US have thus disagreed, and continue to offer up alternative solutions across a range of issue areas. These disagreements reflect deeply held differences informed by history and society, often sharpened by the evolution of the broader world arena. As we argued in Chapter 2, they can in principle be managed through a number of processes: transatlantic governance, balancing – 'hard' or 'soft' – and crisis management.

Competition between the two actors is seen most clearly in the economic realm, where despite a shared preference for the market economy, alternative visions of the extent and operations of that market persist – given added point by the ways in which European integration has shifted the balance of economic power in the direction of the EU since the late 1960s. Europe remains much more attached to a social market conception of capitalism, with relatively higher taxation and a larger role for the state. Extensive state intervention in health care, for example, is a signal feature of most

European states, even that neo-liberal outpost called the United Kingdom. Yet even here convergence on some issues can be seen. Across policy areas, developments push both actors towards not so much a common solution but more a consensus about the general way to tackle the issue. In competition policy, for instance, European practice has become more American-like, thanks partly to the controversial performance of the Merger Task Force in the 1990s. In financial services regulation, Europe appears to be setting the pace, for a more complex set of reasons to do with the Lisbon Agenda and the unintended consequences of American legislation. In respect of innovation, the development of transnational industrial structures and processes of exchange within industries has made the structure of competition and convergence complex and thus regulation more challenging; the notion of 'national' or 'European' champions is misleading in the era of the global corporation, and as noted in Chapter 5 this has led to new process of 'competitive cooperation' involving both state and EU authorities and private entities.

Processes of competition and convergence are also discernible in the broader world arena, where the search for order and for structure entails not only economic and commercial relations but also those of diplomacy and of security policy. As in more purely 'economic' transactions, here we find competition not only at the level of day to day activity but also at the level of models and values. As noted in Chapter 7, the competition between the EU and the US for 'presence' in major regions such as Asia, Latin America and Africa is often informed by the idea that Brussels and Washington are in a competition for global advantage, based in their contrasting attitudes towards economic organization, political order and the pursuit of values such as security or development. Yet as we have also seen, this inter-regional competition also gives evidence of a common set of EU and US interests centring on stability, market economics and democratic politics. This coexistence of competition and convergence is equally discernible in the pursuit of European and world order, as explored in Chapters 8 and 9. But here there is a key set of differences to be taken into account. Within Europe, the EU can bring to bear a preponderance of structural power based on its economic, institutional and legal order. The mere fact that many of the EU's neighbouring countries wish to become part of it gives the Union a substantial set of resources and gives the 'EU model' an advantage. This advantage, though, remains largely 'civilian', based on 'soft power', and it dissipates the closer events move towards the use of coercion or 'hard power'. As shown in Chapter 9, the pursuit of world order encapsulates this problem for the EU. The Union's capacity to threaten or to reward declines rapidly as it moves away from the European neighbourhood, while the US preponderance in military power and the instruments of coercion becomes more substantial. As noted above, this does not always mean that the core preferences or priorities of the EU and the US diverge, but it does mean that the chosen instruments for pursuit of those preferences and priorities can be markedly different. As we also saw in Chapter 9, and as argued in Chapter 2, it might be supposed that this is a fundamental structural difference between the EU and the US, in which the US is dominant and the Union essentially dependent, but there is some evidence that the 'hardening' of EU security policies during the early years of the new millennium has changed the terms of EU–US engagement. This, though, is only the beginning of what might be a very long story.

What does this mean for the mechanisms of management outlined in Chapter 2: transatlantic governance, balancing and crisis management? As with the presence of competition and convergence themselves, it is clear from our analysis that the mechanisms of management coexist more or less comfortably, and that they are deployed in situations where policy requires a complex blend of qualities. Thus, in the areas of political economy we have explored, there is considerable evidence of transatlantic governance in action, but it is also clear that this often takes place at the global level, through bodies such as the WTO or other international regimes. Governance itself in areas of political economy can often be accompanied by considerable evidence of balancing through the exploitation of international 'institutional opportunities' such as those presented by negotiations on the global environment or energy security, and there is also evidence of the need for crisis management in a rapidly changing global political economy. When the story turns to diplomacy and security, we would expect to find more evidence of balancing and crisis management, and this is borne out by the discussion in Chapters 7 to 9; often, the occasions for crisis emerge from outside the 'Euro-American system' and thus create a demand for imaginative responses in situations where the use of 'hard power' is a possibility. The incidence of crisis is dramatic and threatening, both in general and to EU–US understandings of their respective roles, but it must be placed into the context of the broader balancing between the EU and US 'models' in the longer term, and of the persistence of governance mechanisms even where the competition and conflict seems at its height.

New challenges and opportunities

This book has traced the competition and convergence theme through various issue areas (Chapters 3 to 9). A key theme that emerges from these chapters is the extent to which the EU and the US are both challenged by globalization – ironically, a process of which they have been the major originators. The international system is moving towards a multipolar structure, where the Euro-American system, while still dominant, is no longer so powerful that it can develop and implement policies irrespective of the wishes of other actors. The globalization of economic activity owes much to Europe and America; their belief in rules to structure markets is manifest in the myriad of international organizations that work to facilitate trade and exchange. Yet other states have learned to play the globalization game well, and the liberalization of markets has become an increasing source of controversy in Europe and America, as workers are squeezed while corporate profits soar. At the same time, the globalization of security concerns poses new challenges and creates new opportunities for the EU and the US as they move further into the 'post-post-cold-war period'.

In the international trade realm, the European Union and the United States were central to the creation, development and functioning of the World Trade Organization (WTO). For all the criticism it attracts, the WTO is in many respects an extraordinary success. Both the GATT and the WTO have presided over a dramatic expansion of global trade, which has expanded to embrace virtually all regions of the world. Even if the operation of the WTO cannot be said to have caused this, the symbolic importance of the organization cannot be questioned; the WTO represents an accepted view that international economic activity should be conducted within rules. Its membership of 151 states (2007) means the institution is representative of the global community – and membership is widely sought by states wishing to signal their credibility to international finance and firms. This legalization or constitutionalization of the international economy owes much to Europe and America.

The expansion of the WTO's membership, while reflecting the success of the postwar international economic order, is now posing great challenges to Washington and Brussels. As countries in Latin America and Asia gain in economic weight and strength, the ability of the US and the EU to drive the organization is being curtailed. This is part of a broader evolution of the organization away from its western roots. Canada, a traditional member of the 'Quad' of leading countries in the WTO (along with the EU, US, and Japan), has seen itself clearly supplanted by the emerging powers of China, Brazil and India. Even as the WTO has become the central institution, the sheer heterogeneity of members' demands may yet threaten its viability. The EU and the US can no longer force a settlement, but must negotiate hard with actors holding different priorities. America remains more sceptical about multilateral institutions like the WTO, with the EU seeming more comfortable with the constraining effect that membership brings.

Both the EU and the US have sought to direct the WTO's evolution and both have generally supported the expansion and development of the organization's activities, though precisely which direction these should take is a source of disagreement. The United States has sought changes to the disputes process, to make the activities of the disputes panels more transparent, yet not more invasive to domestic politics than they currently are. Brussels has generally been more supportive of including non-trade activities, such as competition policy and the other Singapore issues, in the negotiations. This reflects Brussels's greater comfort with regulatory solutions – but may well represent an attempt to deflect attention from the highly trade-distorting effects of the Common Agricultural Policy. In trade policy, the two participants' high-profile trade disputes and disagreements in the Doha negotiations represent the inevitable conflicts that arise when two actors have domestic constituencies to satisfy. Brussels's trade negotiators, no less than Washington's, cannot be seen to give in to international pressures. Yet, both actors converge on important 'macro' issues relating to the international system, such as the need for trade rules, for broad currency stability and for protection of investments, reflecting the fact that no other parties to the multilateral system have the same stakes in the international economy. Both have been staunch supporters of a GATT/WTO process that embraces liberalized markets, which are governed by rules enforceable through a disputes process. The WTO's membership may be dominated by developing states, but its essence, the deep structures and norms of the institution, remain distinctly Euro-American. How far this situation can survive the rise of China, India and other major emerging economies is a key question for EU and US policymakers.

The management of the world's financial system is another area where the US and Europe have worked closely together. Though it is true to speak of deregulation in respect of financial markets, it is not accurate to describe the global system as any form of rule-free zone. What has changed is the form of regulation: away from capital controls and other means of directly shaping monetary policy, and towards a greater emphasis on adherence to principles and transparency in reporting. The abandonment of formal monetary controls during the 1970s put an emphasis on transatlantic networks of officials, central bankers and private actors in the international capital markets. The US, Germany and Japan worked together in the 1980s to manage the exchange rate of the US dollar, amid American allegations that both the German mark and the Japanese yen were undervalued, thus presenting their exporters with an unfair advantage. Thirty years later, China became the target of American politicians seeking to address the chronic trade deficit.

If the American dispute with China in respect of the correct value of the yuan represented a degree of continuity with previous eras of international monetary relations, the early part of the new millennium featured a major break: the first indications that the dollar was losing its pre-eminent status as the only global currency. Persistent US budget and trade deficits played their part in eroding the dollar's status; as more and more US-denominated debt circulated, the dollar weakened in the expectation that only more competitive American exports would restore balance to America's national accounts. The prime holders of US debt, the Asian economies of Korea, Taiwan, Japan and China, though long content to hold US treasury notes as a means of maintaining American demand for their goods, nonetheless sought to diversify their holdings. China announced in May 2007 that it would diversify its $1.4 trillion in foreign exchange reserves into equities, including direct investment into private equity firms. During its brief life to date, the euro has gone from a currency no one wanted to one that is rapidly acquiring a global status alongside the American dollar. This is testimony to Europe's economic strength, both as a producer of goods and services and as a market. The advance of the euro also says much about international perceptions of declining American dominance of the global economy, with international investors diversifying their holdings. It may be only a matter of time before the dollar, the euro and the yuan become the three major currencies of the global economy.

That said, there are reminders of continued importance of the Euro-American relationship. The turmoil in international money markets in August 2007 saw the European Central Bank operating in tandem with the American Federal Reserve, as well as other central banks, to provide emergency liquidity for the market, once it became clear that many firms were badly exposed to deteriorating conditions in the international debt market. The ECB was in no way a 'junior' partner in this intervention; indeed, Europe's importance as a financial hub led the ECB to act before the Federal Reserve. The episode blended traditional and new features of the EU–US relationship. It was traditional in that the market intervention in August 2007 was merely the latest intervention by European and American regulators over the past sixty years: co-ordinated action by Europe and America to stabilize markets goes back to at least the collapse of the Bretton Woods system in 1971. The novelty lay in the nature of the problem: complex financial derivatives. European and American financial houses have been in the forefront of developing complex financial products, often tailored for specific clients, such as hedge funds. In spite of the sophistication of these products, and the risk management procedures of the finance houses themselves, risk was not eliminated and only central bankers could act to safeguard the entire financial system. Events of August 2007 illustrated the two themes central to this book. First, Europe and America matter to each other, and matter to the world. Their financial services sectors were the key innovators in this new area of international finance; and their regulators were key players in rescuing the system when things went wrong. Second, it is worth noting that other regions of the world were relatively unaffected. China, with its $1 trillion in exchange reserves, was untroubled. Likewise other economies in Latin America and Asia (except Japan) seemed able to shrug off the problem thanks to their booming domestic market. World economic growth no longer depends on the US to the extent that it did through most of the post-1945 era. The most troubling questions posed by the crisis concerned the inability of the regulatory regime to anticipate the problems that could arise with such complex and customized (hence non-transparent) financial products.

The decline of American dominance is also seen in the broad area of financial services regulation, where a set of disconnected events converged in the early 2000s to place Europe – temporarily at least – at the centre of international financial regulation. The first important event, or more precisely process, was the creation of the Single Market. In a globalizing world economy, Europe offered a smaller yet still significant laboratory to develop new rules and, in the case of the Euro, new money. The integration process has emboldened Brussels, which now sees harmonisation around European standards as a form of 'policy export'. The various financial services standards developing in Europe, whether in accountancy, corporate governance or insurance regulation, remain very 'Anglo-Saxon' in conception, reflecting as they do the pro-market thrust of the Single Market. America has played its part in this process. The changed security environment after 11 September 2001 made the United States seem an unwelcoming place to do business, though it remains one of the most open economies in the world. Likewise the tough auditing provisions of Sarbanes–Oxley, put in place after corporate scandals such as that surrounding Enron, are blamed – perhaps unfairly – for contributing to the perception that America is not open for business. Also, America has run a payments deficit for many years, and it was perhaps only a matter of time before that deficit had to be reduced through a steady and considerable depreciation of the dollar. Finally, at the point when America was most fearful about the outside world, the rising economies of Asia and, latterly, Russia, looked for places to invest. In previous years, New York would have been the automatic choice for initial public offerings, or for debt. Now Shanghai, Hong Kong and, most notably, London are the places where emerging international businesses seek to raise or place their money.

Until it came to a spectacular conclusion in August 2007, the early part of the new millennium saw an era of remarkably cheap money as major economies maintained low real interest rates in the wake of 11 September 2001 and the ending of the dotcom boom in 2000. Both Japan and the US kept interest rates low, in the hope of maintaining (or in Japan's case, stoking) domestic demand. The flow of cheap money manifested itself in various ways. A merger boom made investment banks, hedge fund managers and a few corporate chiefs enormously rich. Europe and America, as might be expected, dominated this boom, in terms both of the companies active in the process and of the location of the transactions. Europe and America have longstanding and extensive regulatory relations in the area of competition policy, and in this issue area (as noted in Chapter 6) cooperation is much more marked than conflict. It is a policy area where the triumph of Euro-American conceptions of economic governance is most evident. The spread of robust competition policies – many using American and European processes as templates – has grown dramatically in recent years. The United States is still more comfortable with an internationalization process that is organic and driven by state preferences; hence its interest in maintaining the International Competition Network as the key multilateral body for the sector. Europe, more comfortable generally with the give and take of multilateralism, may yet convert other actors to the cause of an international competition policy agreement within the WTO.

The globalization of innovation is another area where the previous dominance of the European–American relationship can no longer be taken for granted. China, Singapore, India and other states are developing significant innovative capabilities, not just in downstream customization work, but also in the 'blue-skies' fundamental research where discoveries can lead to applications across products and services. The dominance of Europe – and particularly America – in fundamental research produced the two largest economies in the world. As in other spheres, Europe and America face a challenge posed by states adopting the very practices and strategies that allowed the North Atlantic partners to dominate for so long. China's rise in the innovation stakes has been spectacular, and firms have increasingly recognized that country as a place where leading-edge research can be done. For most of the largest companies in the world, the locus of their research and development activities remains the European–American axis. American universities still dominate any ranking of top research institutions and Europe has significant strengths in advanced manufacturing, pharmaceuticals and biotechnology. Yet the EU in particular faces considerable challenges: European firms tend to invest less than rivals in R&D and, increasingly, when they do invest they tap foreign locations for the work. Concerns about competitiveness in the US take on a different hue. American white-collar workers, the college-educated elite of the workforce, are finding that even they face international competition. From an economic standpoint, the globalization of innovation is to be welcomed: if foreign companies can provide new goods and services at a lower cost then consumers benefit. But the politics cannot be ignored. Globalization's distributional effects are again important. Just as in monetary relations, some European and Americans do well, but many workers have seen their share of the economic pie shrink. European welfare states tend to shield their workers – at least temporarily – from the worst effects, but not so America. In the United States, inequality soared in the late 1990s and early 2000s with all but a handful of people at the top of the income scale essentially going nowhere in economic terms. This fuelled increasing resentment at what globalization is doing to local American economies and society. Europeans will not be shielded from this; inequality is rising there too, although, except in the United Kingdom, it is rising more slowly than in the United States. In terms of the argument in this book, it can be seen that this and the other changes noted above create a whole new set of 'security problems' for the EU and the US: those do to with what can be called 'societal security', relating to the social and institutional foundations of the market economy.

As noted above, regional and inter-regional relations and policies also illustrate how Europe and America can compete and converge at the same time; but they also illustrate the impact of emerging changes in the world economy and world order. Both actors have sought to develop neighbourhood policies to structure their relations with nearby states, and in both cases these emerge from deep historical roots. European enlargement, as well as the EU's complex relations with Eastern-European border states, are both motivated by a history that needs little explication; but they also reflect a current need to navigate an increasingly fraught relationship with Russia. Russia's dominant position over European gas supplies, and the threat of the use of energy as a political weapon, galvanized action at the Community level in a way that even the threat of global warming could not, leading to the call in 2006 for a new European policy on energy security. This was also an unwelcome reminder that American policymakers – years ago, in the early 1980s – warned Western Europe not to rely on the then Soviet Union for energy supplies. At the same time, the EU has had to take on board the need for more security in light of challenges

The European Union and the United States

Competition and Convergence in the Global Arena

Steven McGuire
and
Michael Smith

palgrave
macmillan

First published 2008 by
PALGRAVE MACMILLAN
Houndmills, Basingstoke, Hampshire RG21 6XS and
175 Fifth Avenue, New York, N.Y. 10010
Companies and representatives throughout the world

PALGRAVE MACMILLAN is the global academic imprint of the Palgrave
Macmillan division of St. Martin's Press, LLC and of Palgrave Macmillan Ltd.
Macmillan® is a registered trademark in the United States, United Kingdom
and other countries. Palgrave is a registered trademark in the European
Union and other countries.

ISBN-13: 978–0–333–96851–2   hardback
ISBN-10: 0–333–96851–4   hardback
ISBN-13: 978–0–333–96862–8   paperback
ISBN-10: 0–333–96862–X   paperback

This book is printed on paper suitable for recycling and made from fully
managed and sustained forest sources. Logging, pulping and manufacturing
processes are expected to conform to the environmental regulations of the
country of origin.

A catalogue record for this book is available from the British Library.

A catalog record for this book is available from the Library of Congress.

10 9 8 7 6 5 4 3 2 1
17 16 15 14 13 12 11 10 09 08

Printed and bound in China

Contents

List of Tables, Figures and Boxes

Tables

Figures

Boxes

List of Abbreviations

ACP	African, Caribbean and Pacific states
APEC	Asia-Pacific Economic Cooperation
ASEAN	Association of Southeast Asian Nations
ASEM	Asia–Europe Meeting
CAFTA	Central America Free Trade Agreement
CAP	Common Agricultural Policy
CCP	Common Commercial Policy
CEECs	Central and East European Countries
CFSP	Common Foreign and Security Policy
CNOOC	China National Offshore Oil Company
CSCE	Commission on Security and Cooperation in Europe
CUSFTA	Canada–United States Free Trade Agreement
ECB	European Central Bank
ECJ	European Court of Justice
ECSC	European Coal and Steel Community
EDC	European Defence Community
EEC	European Economic Community
EMS	European Monetary System
EMU	Economic and Monetary Union
EPC	European Political Cooperation
ERM	Exchange Rate Mechanism
ERP	European Recovery Plan
ESDP	European Security and Defence Policy
FDI	foreign direct investment
GAAP	Generally Agreed Accounting Principles
GATT	General Agreement on Tariffs and Trade
G-8	Group of Eight
IAS	International Accounting Standards
IASB	International Accounting Standards Board
ICBC	Industrial and Commercial Bank of China
ICN	International Competition Network
ICPAC	International Competition Policy Advisory Committee
IFRS	International Financial Reporting Standards
IOSCO	International Organization of Securities Commissions
ITO	International Trade Organization
MCR	Merger Control Regulation

Mercosur	Common Market of the South
MFN	most favoured nation
MTF	Merger Task Force
NAFTA	North American Free Trade Agreement
NATO	North Atlantic Treaty Organization
NTM	New Transatlantic Marketplace
OECD	Organisation for Economic Co-operation and Development
OEEC	Organization for European Economic Cooperation
OPEC	Organization of Petroleum Exporting Countries
OSCE	Organization for Security and Cooperation in Europe
PTA	preferential trade agreement
RTA	regional trade agreement
SAARC	South Asian Association for Regional Cooperation
SEA	Single European Act
SGP	Stability and Growth Pact
SMP	Single Market Programme
TABD	Transatlantic Business Dialogue
TACIS	Technical Aid to the Commonwealth of Independent States
TAD	Transatlantic Declaration
UNCTAD	United Nations Conference on Trade and Development
USSR	Union of Soviet Socialist Republics
WTO	World Trade Organization

Acknowledgements

Several people have helped bring this project to its eventual fruition. Willie Paterson, as series editor, provided considerable feedback on earlier drafts, as did an anonymous reviewer, and we are grateful for their input. Chris Nicoll and Da Hao Shang provided valuable research assistance for Chapters 3 to 6. Our publisher, Steven Kennedy, of Palgrave Macmillan, is to be thanked for his patience and support.

STEVEN MCGUIRE
MICHAEL SMITH

The author and publishers would like to thank the following who have kindly given permission for use of the following copyright material: Palgrave Macmillan for Figure 8.2, the Organisation for Economic Co-operation and Development for Figures 6.2 and 6.3, the World Trade Organization for Figures 3.2 and 7.1. Figures 3.1, 5.1, 5.2, 5.3, 6.1 are European Union copyright. The section on European innovation policy starting on page 150 draws on work previously published by Steven McGuire in the *Journal of European Public Policy*, 13(6), 2006, pp. 887–905.

Introduction

The relationship between the European Union (EU) and the United States of America (US) is simultaneously highly significant and immensely challenging, both as the subject of academic analysis and as a subject of policy-making in both the EU and the US. It is significant because the EU and the US are two of the most weighty actors in the world arena, and because they are highly engaged in each other's economic and political processes. What happens between the EU and the US matters, both to those directly involved and to those within the broader world arena by whom the effects of EU–US interactions are felt. The relationship is challenging because in addition to being highly significant, it is complex and dynamic: EU–US relations take place and have their effects in a multiplicity of issue areas and 'sub-arenas' within the world arena, and the openness of the transatlantic relationship means that changes in the world arena will in turn have important repercussions for EU–US relations. This book is an attempt to expose the complexities of the relationship and its impact on the world arena, to subject it to analysis and to evaluate its past, its present and its possible futures.

Relations between the EU and the US are rooted in a history, and have been affected by the development of international politics and the international political economy over a long period, from the 1950s to the early years of the twenty-first century. So one of the first tasks of any book on the subject is to establish this history and the major trends or turning-points within it. A second task is to explore the 'analytical history' of the relationship, and to look at what successive waves of scholarship and commentary have to say about the nature of the relationship, its dynamics and its impact. Only if these two contexts – of historical development and of analytical awareness – are established can effective appraisal of the current nature of the relationship take place.

A third task is to explore the development of the relationship in respect of the international political economy. The establishment of the European Economic Community in 1957 through the Treaty of Rome, and the ways in which this contributed to an emerging 'adversarial partnership' between the EEC and the US during the

1

1960s and beyond, are central to an understanding of the contemporary world economy, and to the analysis of key trends within it. The EU and the US come into contact – or collision – in a multitude of economic domains, and the continuing development of the world economy in its turn shapes the ways in which the EU and the US relate to each other. Thus, EU–US relations have been and are central to the development of world trade, monetary relations, technological innovation and the management of commercial organizations such as large firms through competition and related policies. Both actors have left their 'imprint' on the operations of a variety of international organizations and regimes. The current structure of the global economy and security system owes much to European and American conceptions about the exercise of political power. But the EU and the US are not alone; they are joined on the world stage by an increasing number of strong competitors and potential partners, from Japan to Russia to China, India and Brazil. They are also involved in a growing range of interregional relationships extending to all continents, which will help to shape the international political economy of the future. The international economy thus presents us with a paradox. Though the Euro-American relationship was central to the construction and operation of the global economy over the past decades, the conditions it created have allowed other states to emerge as successful economies and, potentially, political competitors. The increasing reach of this 'constitutionalized' or rules-based international economy is to be welcomed, yet as more and more states integrate into this system, policymaking becomes more complex. Europe and America cannot dominate economic policy matters as they did even a scant ten years ago.

A fourth task, particularly pressing in recent years, is to investigate the relationship between the EU, the US and world order in the political and security domains. European integration was at its origins a matter of security, with the aim of stabilizing Western Europe and of forestalling any possibility of renewed war between the European Powers. For much of its life, it developed within the 'western security community' led by the United States in opposition to the Soviet Union and its allies. Thus, from the outset, the links between European integration and the United States were highly political and linked to the preservation of western security. With the end of the cold war in the early 1990s, the security context was given an entirely new complexion, and one in which the European such as illegal immigration, which has linked the pursuit of 'societal security' to movements of population in the post-cold-war period, both within Europe and between Africa and the EU. This latter problem demonstrates the link between regional and inter-regional policies, since the aim of the EU's African policies is not simply to promote democracy and good governance in the continent but also to forestall pressures such as those from voluntary or involuntary movements of African populations. The more distant inter-regional partnerships of the EU, such as those with Asia and Latin America, can perhaps be seen in a more commercial light, focusing on economic partnership and the promotion of stability, but even so these are shaped by the shifting nature of global security concerns in ways ranging from the control of the trade in illegal drugs to the prevention of human-rights abuses.

For the United States, perceptions of regionalism are filtered through the lens of 11 September 2001, with an increased emphasis not on the opportunities offered by regional trade but rather on the dangers of illegal immigration and the chances of terrorists using porous borders to infiltrate the United States. US-Mexican relations were most clearly affected by this, as American policymakers sought to reconcile economic concerns with demands that something be done about illegal immigration across the border The construction of a wall along part of the border, as well as congressional defeat of a plan to grant amnesty to many illegal immigrants already in the US, did not augur well for any further regional integration. Relations with Latin American states are likewise deeply influenced by security concerns. The American attempts at better relations with Brazil may reflect the increasing economic weight of Brazil in the world, but may have at least as much to do with Brazil's biofuel industry and opportunity it represents to insulate US consumers from the volatile world of international petroleum markets. The same connection between economic advantage and security concerns can be seen in the US relationship with Asia through APEC: this organization, as pointed out in Chapter 7, can be seen not only as a source of regional security and stability for a region of which the US is also a member but in addition as a means of handling economic competition from some of the most important emerging economies, especially that of China. At the same time, the emerging partnership between the US and India projects US policy more firmly into a region of considerable volatility – a volatility underlined by the presence of terrorist groups, failed states and nuclear weapons. While the US has not yet engaged with Africa as closely as with Latin America or Asia-Pacific, the intersecting presences of humanitarian concerns, economic incentives such as those connected with the emerging sub-Saharan Africa oil industry and security concerns such as those generated by the increasing Chinese engagement are likely to draw Washington more closely into the region in the near future.

Both the United States and Europe have used regional and inter-regional policies to gain some of the benefits denied them at the multilateral level. The bundling of non-trade issues with those of a more conventional commercial nature, as in the case of labour standards or intellectual property provisions, is controversial and leads to concerns that Europe and America may exploit their power to gain preferential access to regional markets, while denying equivalent access to their partners. Equally, the attempt to impose different versions of 'political conditionality' on countries within either the 'near neighbourhood' or in broader inter-regional relations can be seen as reflecting forms of hegemonic behaviour both by the EU and by the US. But as noted above, regional relations are not just about economics; both actors share a view that economic stability is part of a broader policy of political and social stabilization, both at the national and at the regional level. This being so, the increasing politicization and securitization of these relationships, as described in Chapter 7, is a key challenge for leaderships on both sides of the Atlantic.

A number of the points made above about regional political and economic relations in Europe can be related to the key challenges of European order for the near and medium-term future. Both the EU and the US have key interests at stake in the 'new Europe' that has emerged and become consolidated since the end of the cold war. But they also face different situations, as noted in Chapter 8. The US retains a strong set of strategic interests (both economic and security-related) in European order, and has managed to resist the threat of exclusion from key areas of European strategic engagement. Indeed, it could be argued that it has extended its reach through the enlargement of NATO and the construction of new relationships with the former Soviet countries, as well as retaining a strong set of connections with many of those countries that are now member states of the enlarged EU. Given that no direct or immediate security concerns emanate from the European order – not a given to be relied upon too heavily bearing in mind the assertiveness of Russian policies in the early part of the new millennium – it might be said that the US stake in European order is relatively well guarded. For the EU, however, the issue is different: after all, the Union has virtually *become* the European order with its expansion and the creation of a new set of strategic relationships within the European Neighbourhood Strategy. For the EU, therefore, the stakes attached to change and threats within Europe are of a different quality from those experienced by the US, and the problems of security and prosperity become attached to the very essence of the EU itself – what it is as well as what it does. This differential experience of change in Europe is one that will continue to characterize EU–US relations for the foreseeable future. All of the points made above feed into the challenges and opportunities facing the EU and the US in relation to world order. In Chapter 9, we made a crucial distinction between world order defined in terms of power and security and world order defined in terms of global governance. The distinction is crucial because it relates to the very status of the EU and the US as global actors. In the case of 'order as power and security' the United States has had and will continue to have a key role. For some this role is defined as that of providing essential global public goods in the form of reassurance in the face of threats, necessary interventions and the guardianship of global security order; for others it is a manifestation of a form of liberal imperialism which creates dangers and instabilities in a globalizing world. In this world of power and security, the EU is less prominent, although some of its member states have taken their own actions, often in concert with the US, on key issues such as Iraq or the 'war on terror'. The key challenges of the early twenty-first century have found the EU either divided or relatively underprepared, and thus often unable to resist pressure from the US even if it has wanted to. A key question to be confronted by the EU in this context is whether it should aim to develop itself as a 'mini-USA', acquiring new military powers and a role in 'hard security', or whether in the absence of consensus among its member states it will be able to move on such issues at all. Events, of course, can have a major catalytic effect in these areas, as with 9/11. On the side of global governance, the EU has positioned itself as a champion of multilateralism and collective action but, as noted above, it is not always easy to maintain this posture in the face of challenges to commercial or political interests, especially where the dominant forces within the Union itself are less than fully committed to multilateral action. The US has been cast as a unilateralist on global governance issues by many of its political and academic critics, but it may be that new US administrations in new circumstances will find it political or economically expedient to move towards a new multilateralism (as has happened in the past, for example in the 1980s). For both the EU and the US, the shifting map of globalization, with the emergence of new major actors and the politicization or securitization of new issues, will be a key challenge in the years ahead.

Moving forward

In a sense, European–American relations in the early years of the twenty-first century present us with something of a paradox. On the one hand, this book has shown how the dominance of the Atlantic area is eroding – across issue areas. The world of the early new millennium is moving rapidly towards a multipolar system, where Europe and America play leading roles but arguably are no longer dominant. This is most apparent in the global political economy, where the centrality of the EU–US relationship can no longer be taken for granted in a wide range of issue areas. In terms of global security, the Iraq conflict has signalled – as did the Vietnam war in the 1970s – that the United States is not guaranteed to dominate, because of the increasing prominence of 'asymmetrical' conflicts where formal military firepower is not the only determinant of outcomes. The impact of Iraq on the EU's collective view of its 'security future' is still being played out, and raises key issues about the EU's role as a 'partial superpower'. For the US itself, recent experience in the Middle East has repercussions throughout the world, not least with America's traditional allies asking themselves about the solidity of American commitment. America now shares global commercial and financial power with Europe, yet it is in Asia that the largest trade surpluses and foreign exchange reserves now lie. China in particular is demonstrating an ability to integrate into the world economy muh more quickly and successfully than many had anticipated with India not far behind.

Yet it is significant that in the global political economy both China and India are playing a game whose rules were 'written' by the European–American relationship. The structure of the global economy, from its liberalized capital flows to its increasing constitutionalization in the form of the World Trade Organization, owes everything to Euro-American diplomacy, business and conceptions of how world affairs ought to be conducted. Even patterns of business–government interactions in forums like ASEAN are imitations of consultative practices that have been hallmarks of Euro-American relations for years. In sum, Europe and America remain central to the global political economy, though not always in ways that are appreciated. In the global diplomatic system, the EU and the US are still near to the core of world events, and their diplomatic dealings with each other are still influential. In terms of global security, we can see that the US remains more central than the EU, if only on the basis of its 'hard power' credentials, but its position is challenged by new or sometimes resurgent powers, not all of them states.

A theme raised throughout this book has been the relative willingness of the EU to adopt multilateral approaches to international relations in both security and economic spheres. For some observers, the evolution of a multipolar world will suit Europe much more than America, for the latter is seen as a unilateralist first, using international organizations or coalitions only as a last resort. Such views are not so much wrong as lacking in nuance. For many developing states, the EU is not a paragon of 'give-and-take' multilateralism; it is a bully that uses its market dominance to gain policy preferences, just like the United States. The EU's fondness for regulation and standards, though highly successful in some spheres, is deeply opposed by some states, who despair at the demands this would place on their governments and societies. Though the EU's internal market is large and affluent, on most measures of productivity, innovation and wealth, it still trails the United States. The United States has indeed been highly unilateralist in recent years, but this period may draw to a close. The world's most sophisticated armed forces backed by the world's largest military budget show no signs of being able to quell unrest in Iraq and Afghanistan. The American public, no less than the European, seems completely unwilling to contemplate the kind of protracted conflict, demanding a combination of military resources with diplomacy and economic or social interventions, that might defeat the insurgents. Such conflicts are not easily sustainable either in Europe or America – at least not when their territories remain relatively unthreatened.

Overview and conclusion: what kind of 'Euro-American system'?

At the end of Chapter 2, we argued that it is possible to see EU–US relations in (at least) four ways: as a system based on 'power and security', on 'dominance and resistance', on 'interdependence and integration' and on 'institutions and cooperation'. From the discussion above, it can be seen that each of these elements is present in the current 'Euro-American system'. Rather than separate systems, they represent four coexisting tendencies within one complex system of relations, responding both to change within the EU and the US and to change within the broader world arena. This coexistence of qualities and tendencies is what helps us to understand the functioning of the system, and to evaluate the impact of change in any of its components or in its broader environment. The very point of this book is to equip the reader with a set of analytical questions with which they can penetrate the complexities of the system and its significance for the world arena. It is possible, though, to arrive at some broad conclusions from this final discussion:

- First, there is evidence to support the argument that the 'Euro-American system' is one in which economic, political and security issues occur at a number of intersecting levels, and in which both the EU and the US are effectively part of each other's policymaking processes. State policies and 'state functions' remain important if not central, but they are surrounded by a constellation of other actors and factors.
- Second, the system does show the presence and the interaction of markets, hierarchies and networks, and policymakers are at their most effective when they recognize the varying configurations these elements can take. Many of the areas we have looked at demonstrate these interactions and configurations, but the key word is 'varying'; we have provided evidence for at least some of the ways in which this variation occurs, and for some of its consequences both for the EU and the US and for the rest of the world.
- Third, the system has generated an increasingly dense set of institutions, many of which have become dominated by the EU–US relationship as the EU has expanded to become in some ways synonymous with the 'Euro-American system'. Increasingly, the key transatlantic institutions and practices are those

generated around the EU and the US, with other organizations such as NATO and the OSCE occupying reduced roles. But here again, there are variations, especially between the political economy of EU–US relations and the diplomatic or security dimensions of the relationship.

- Fourth, the system has been crucially impacted by change: change within the EU and the US, and change within the broader world arena. Many of the areas we have explored in this book show the significant impact of processes such as globalization or the ending of the cold war. More specifically, they suggest that the world around the 'Euro-American system' is changing in ways that present major challenges as well as major opportunities for policymakers, and that are likely to impact on the mutual EU and US understandings of the changes taking place.

- Finally, the system is not one of 'either/or'. It is not one that can be turned on or off by policymakers either in the EU or in the US. Its extended history, its institutional density, the shared experiences of transatlantic elites, and the sheer self-interest embodied in the world's closest economic and security relationship mean that it is robust and resilient. But it is not immortal. It is not impossible to conceive of circumstances in which the boundaries of the system are exceeded, and in which the conventions of crisis management that have grown up over fifty or more years might be discarded. In this case, we would be talking not of 'competition and convergence' but of 'confrontation and conflict'.

We hope that this book has enabled the reader to sharpen their appreciation of what lies behind the EU–US relationship, how it relates to the institutions and policy processes of both the EU and the US, and how the 'Euro-American system' relates to the broader world arena. We have aimed to show the complexity of the relationship, the variations that occur within it and the ways in which the relationship is managed through good times and bad. Analytically, it is our conviction that an appreciation of different perspectives on the relationship, and their links to different narratives of its development and future course, is the best way in which to construct a rich view of what matters in EU–US relations. But the result is a series of more sharply defined and well illustrated questions, not a single answer to the question 'what kind of Euro-American system?'

Bibliography

Aggarwal, V. and Fogarty, E. (eds) (2004) *EU Trade Strategies. Between Regionalism and Globalism* (New York: Palgrave Macmillan).

Ahearne, A. and Eichengreen, B. (2007) 'Europe's External Monetary and Financial Relations Since the Euro: A Review and a Proposal', paper presented at the conference, Bruegel Project on Europe and the Global Economy, 12–13 October 2006, http://www.nuigalway.ie/staff/alan_ahearne/documents/ahearne_eichengreen.pdf, accessed 15 June 2007.

Albert, M. (1992) *Capitalisme contre capitalisme* (Paris: Seuil).

Albright, M. (1998) Statement to the North Atlantic Council, Brussels, 8th December 1998. Found at http://secretary,state,gov/www/statements/1998/981208.html, accessed 20 July 2007.

Alcácer, J. and Chung, W. (2007) 'Location Strategies and Knowledge Spillovers', *Management Science*, 53(5): 760–76.

Alecu de Flers, N. and Regelsberger, E. (2005) 'The EU and Inter-Regional Cooperation', in C. Hill and M. Smith (eds), *International Relations and the European Union* (Oxford: Oxford University Press).

Aliboni, R. (2005) 'The Geopolitical Implications of the European Neighbourhood Policy', *European Foreign Affairs Review* 10(1): 1–16.

Allen, D. (1997),'EPC/CFSP, the Soviet Union and the Former Soviet Republics: Do the Twelve have a Coherent Policy?', in E. Regelsberger, P. de Schoutheete de Tervarent and W. Wessels (eds), *Foreign Policy of the European Union: From EPC to CFSP and Beyond* (Boulder, CO: Rienner).

Allen, D. (1998) 'Who Speaks for Europe? The Search for an Effective and Coherent External Policy', in J. Peterson and H. Sjursen (eds), *A Common Foreign Policy for Europe? Competing Visions of the CFSP* (London: Routledge).

Allen, D. and Pijpers, A. (eds) (1984) *European Foreign Policies and the Arab-Israeli Dispute* (The Hague: Nijhoff).

Allen, D. and Smith, M. (1982) 'Europe, the United States and the Middle East: A Case Study in Comparative Policy-making', *Journal of Common Market Studies*, 22(2): December: 125–46.

Allen, D. and Smith, M. (1989) 'Western Europe in the Atlantic System of the 1980s: Towards a New Identity?', in S. Gill (ed.), *Atlantic Relations: Beyond the Reagan Era* (Brighton: Harvester Wheatsheaf).

Allen, D. and Smith, M. (1991–2) 'The European Union in the New Europe: Bearing the Burden of Change', *International Journal*, 47 (1, Winter): 1–28.

Allen, D. and Smith, M. (2000) 'External Policy Developments', in G. Edwards and G. Wiessala (eds), *The European Union: Annual Review of Activities, 1999* (Oxford: Blackwell).

Allen, D. and Smith, M. (2001) 'External Policy Developments' in G. Edwards and G. Wiessala (eds), *The European Union: Annual Review of Activities, 2000* (Oxford: Blackwell).

Allen, D. and Smith, M. (2002) 'External Policy Developments', in G. Edwards and G. Wiessala (eds), *The European Union: Annual Review of Activities, 2001/2002* (Oxford: Blackwell).

Allen, D. and Smith, M. (2003) 'External Policy Developments' in L. Miles (ed.), *The European Union: Annual Review of Activities, 2002/2003* (Oxford: Blackwell).

Allen, D. and Smith, M. (2004) 'External Policy Developments', in L. Miles (ed.), *The European Union: Annual Review of Activities, 2003/2004* (Oxford: Blackwell).

Allen, D. and Smith, M. (2005) 'External Policy Developments', in L. Miles (ed.), *The European Union: Annual Review 2004/2005* (Oxford: Blackewell).

Allen, D. and Smith, M. (2006) 'Relations with the rest of the World', in U. Sedelmeier and A. Young (eds), *The European Union Annual Review 2005/2006* (Oxford: Blackwell).

Allen, D. and Smith, M. (2007) 'Relations with the Rest of the World', in U. Sedelmeier and A. Young (eds), *The European Union Annual Review 2006/2007* (Oxford: Blackwell).

Allen, D. and Wallace, W. (1977) 'European Political Cooperation: Procedure As a Substitute for Policy?', in H. Wallace, W. Wallace and C. Webb (eds), *Policy-Making in the European Communities*. (Chichester: Wiley).

Alting von Geusau, F. (1993) *Beyond Containment and Division: Western Cooperation from a Post-Totalitarian Perspective* (The Hague: Nijhoff).

Andrews, D. (ed.) (2005) *The Atlantic Alliance Under Stress: US–European Relations after Iraq* (Cambridge: Cambridge University Press).

Archibugi, D. and Coco, A. (2005) 'Is Europe Becoming the Most Dynamic Knowledge Economy in the World?', *Journal of Common Market Studies*, 43(3): 433–59.

Ashbaugh, H. (2001) 'Non-US Firms' Accounting Standard Choices', *Journal of Accounting and Public Policy*, 20(2): 129–53.

Asmus, R. (1997) 'Double Enlargement: Redefining the Atlantic Partnership After the Cold War', in D. Gompert and S. Larrabee (eds) *America and Europe: A Partnership for a New Era* (Cambridge: Cambridge University Press).

Baily, M.N. (2007) 'Testimony Prepared for the Hearing: the Globalization of R&D, United States House of Representatives, Committee on Science And Technology, 12 June, http://democrats.science.house.gov/Media/File/Commdocs/hearings/2007/full/12jun/baily_testimony.pdf, accessed 20 August 2007.

Baily, M.N. and Kirkegaard, J.K. (2004) *Transforming the European Economy* (Washington: Institute for International Economics).

Baily, M.N. and Lawrence, R. (2006) 'Can America Still Compete or Does It Need a New Trade Paradigm?' Policy Brief PB06–9, Peterson Institute for International Economics.

Baldwin, M., Peterson, J. and Stokes, B. (2003) 'Trade and Economic

Relations', in J. Peterson and M. Pollack (eds), *Europe, America, Bush: Transatlantic Relations in the Twenty-First Century* (London: Routledge).

Batt. J., Lynch, D., Missiroli, A., Ortega, M. and Triantaphyllou, D. (2003) *Partners and Neighbours: A CFSP for a Wider Europe*. Chaillot Paper 64 (Paris: EU Institute for Security Studies).

Baun, M. (2000) *A Wider Europe* (Lanham, MD: Rowman & Littlefield).

Becker, W. (2007) 'Euro Riding High as an International Reserve Currency', EU Monitor 46, Deutsche Bank Research, May 4, http://www.dbresearch.com/PROD/DBR_INTERNET_EN-PROD/PROD0000000000209994.   pdf, accessed 1 July 2007.

Beloff, M. (1976) *The United States and the Unity of Europe* (Westport, CT: Greenwood).

Berger, S. and Dore, R. (eds) (1997) *Convergence or Diversity? National Models of Production and Distribution in a Global Economy*, (Ithaca, NY: Cornell University Press.)

Bergsten F. (1998) 'Competition Policy and the World Economy', speech to the World Economic Forum, Davos, Switzerland, 30 January, http.//peter-soninstitute.org/publications/print.cfm?doc=pub&ResearchIC=303, accessed 2 January 2007.

Bergsten, F. (2005) 'The Euro and the World Economy', paper given at the European Central Bank, Frankfurt, 27 April, http://www.iie.com/publications/papers/bergsten0405.pdf, accessed 11 July 2007.

Bergsten, F. (2007) 'The Dollar and the Renminbi', Statement before the Hearing on US Economic Relations with China: Strategies and Options on Exchange Rates and Market Access, Subcommittee on Security and International Trade and Finance, Committee on Banking, Housing and Urban Affairs, United States Senate, 23 May, http://www.iie.com/publications/papers/paper.cfm?ResearchID=747, accessed 17 June 2007.

Bhattacharjea, A. (2006) 'The Case for a Multilateral Agreement on Competition Policy: A Developing Country Perspective', *Journal of International Economic Law*, 9 (2, June): 293–324.

Blinder, A. (2006) 'Offshoring: the Next Industrial Revolution?', *Foreign Affairs*, 85(2): 113–28.

Blinder A. (2007) 'Testimony of Alan S. Blinder, Gordon Renschler Memorial Professor of Economics, Princeton University', House of Representatives, Committee on Science and Technology, 12 June, http://democrats.science.house.gov/Media/File/Commdocs/hearings/2007/full/12jun/blinder_testimony.pdf, accessed 20 August 2007.

Bodansky, D. (2003) 'Transatlantic Environmental Relations', in J. Peterson and M. Pollack (eds), *Europe, America, Bush: Transatlantic Relations in the Twenty-First Century* (London: Routledge).

Bora, B. (2004) 'Investment Issues in the WTO', in B. Hocking and S. McGuire (eds), *Trade Politics*, 2nd edn (London: Routledge).

Branscomb, L. (ed.) (1993), *Empowering Technology: Implementing a US Strategy* (Cambridge, MA: MIT Press).

Bremer, H. (2001) 'The First Two Decades of the Bayh–Dole Act as Public Policy', National Association of State Universities and Land Grant

Colleges, 11 November, http://www.nasulgc.org/COTT/Bayh-Dohl/ Bremer_speech.htm, accessed 7 January 2007.

Bretherton, C. and Vogler, J. (2006) *The European Union as a Global Actor* (London: Routledge).

Brusoni, S. and Geuna A. (2003) 'An International Comparison of Sectoral Knowledge Bases: Persistence and Integration of the Pharmaceutical Industry', *Research Policy*, 32(2): 1897–912.

Bugaski, J. and Teleki, I. (eds) (2007) *Atlantic Bridges: America's New European Allies* (Lanham, MD: Rowman & Littlefield).

Burtless, G. (2007) 'Globalization and Income Polarization in Rich Countries', Issues in Economic Policy, Paper no. 5 (Washington, DC: The Brookings Institution).

Busch, M. and Reinhardt, E. (2006) 'Three's a Crowd: Third Parties and WTO Settlement', *World Politics*, 58(4): 446–77.

Busse, M., Huth, M. and Koopmann, G. (2000) 'Preferential Trade Agreements: The Case of EU-Mexico', HWWA Discussion Paper 103, Hamburg Institute of International Economics, http://opus.zbw-kiel.de/voll-texte/2003/680/pdf/103.pdf, accessed 21 August 2007.

Buzan, B. and Diez, T. (1999) 'The European Union and Turkey', *Survival*, 41(1): 41–57.

Cafruny, A. and Ryner, M. (eds) (2003) *A Ruined Fortress? Neoliberal Hegemony and Transformation in Europe* (Lanham, MD: Rowman & Littlefield).

Calingaert, M. (1996) *European Integration Revisited: Progress, Prospects and US Interests* (Washington, DC: Brookings Institution Press).

Calleo, D. (1970) *The Atlantic Fantasy: The US, NATO and Europe* (Baltimore, MD: Johns Hopkins University Press).

Calleo, D. (1981) *The Imperious Economy* (Cambridge, MA: Harvard University Press).

Calleo, D. and Rowland, B. (1973) *America and the World Political Economy: Atlantic Dreams and National Realities* (Bloomington: Indiana State University Press).

Cameron, F. (2007) *An Introduction to European Foreign Policy* (London: Routledge).

Camps, M. (1960) 'Britain, the Six and American Policy', *Foreign Affairs* 39(1): 112–22.

Camps, M. (1967) *European Unification in the Sixties: From the Veto to the Crisis* (Oxford: Oxford University Press for the Royal Institute of International Affairs).

Cannady, C. (2004) 'North-South Trade in Intellectual Property: Can it be Fair?', *World Trade Review*, 3(2): 317–28.

Capling, A. (2004) 'The Politics of Intellectual Property', in B. Hocking and S. McGuire (eds), *Trade Politics*, 2nd edn (Routledge: London) 179–93.

Capling A. and Nossal, K.M. (2006) 'Blowback: Investor-State Dispute Mechanisms in International Trade Agreements', *Governance*, 19(2): 157–72.

Chase, J. and Ravenal, E. (eds) (1976) *Atlantis Lost: The United States and*

Europe after the Cold War (New York: New York University Press for the Council on Foreign Relations).

Chernow, R. (2004) *Alexander Hamilton* (New York: Penguin).

Chesbrough, H. (2003) 'The Era of Open Innovation', *MIT Sloan Management Review*, 44(3): 35–41.

Cleveland, H. (1966) *The Atlantic Idea and its European Rivals* (New York: McGraw-Hill for the Council on Foreign Relations).

Cohen, B.(2003) 'Global Currency Rivalry: Can the Euro Ever Challenge the Dollar?', *Journal of Common Market Studies*, 41(4): 575–95.

Cohen L. and Noll, R. (2001) 'Is US Science Policy at Risk? Trends in Federal Support for R&D', *The Brookings Review*, 19(1): 10–15, http://www.brook.edu/press/review/winter2001/cohen.htm, accessed 19 August 2007.

Cooper, R. (1968) *The Economics of Interdependence: Economic Policy in The Atlantic Community* (New York: McGraw-Hill for the Council on Foreign Relations).

Cornish, P. and Edwards, G, (2001) 'Beyond the NATO/EU Dichotomy: The Beginnings of a European Strategic Culture', *International Affairs*, 77(3), July: 587–605.

Council of the European Union (2003) *A Secure Europe in a Better World: European Security Strategy*. Brussels, 12th December.

Cowles, M. (1996) 'The EU Committee of AmCham: The Powerful Voice of American Firms in Brussels', *Journal of European Public Policy* 3(3): 339–58.

Cowles, M. (2001a) 'Private Firms and US-EU Policy-Making: The Transatlantic Business Dialogue', in E. Philippart and P. Winand (eds), *Ever-Closer Partnership: Policy-Making in US-EU Relations* (Brussels: PI.E.-Peter Lang).

Cowles, M. (2001b) 'The Transatlantic Business Dialogue: Transforming The New Transatlantic Dialogue', in M. Pollack and G. Shaffer (eds), *Transatlantic Governance in the Global Economy* (Lanham, MD: Rowman & Littlefield).

Cox, M. (2003) 'Commentary: Martians and Venutians in the New World Order', *International Affairs* 79(3): 523–32.

Crawford, B. (1996) 'Explaining Defection from International Cooperation: Germany's Unilateral Recognition of Croatia', *World Politics*, 48(4): 482–521.

Cromwell, W. (1969) *Political Problems of Atlantic Partnership: National Perspectives* (Bruges: College of Europe).

Crowe, B. (2003) 'A Common European Foreign Policy After Iraq?', *International Affairs*, 79(3): 533–46.

Czempiel, E.-O. and Rustow, D. (eds) (1976) *The Euro-American System* (Frankfurt: Campus).

Daalder, I. and Lindsay, J. (2003) *America Unbound: The Bush Revolution in Foreign Policy* (Washington, DC: Brookings Institution Press).

Damro, C. (2001) 'Building an International Identity: The EU and

Extraterritorial Competition Policy', *Journal of European Public Policy*, 8(2): 208–26.

Damro, C. (2004) 'Multilateral Competition Policy and Transatlantic Compromise', *European Foreign Affairs Review*, 9(2): 269–87.

Damro, C. (2006) 'The New Trade Politics and EU Competition Policy: Shopping for Convergence and Cooperation', *Journal of European Public Policy*, 13(6): 867–86.

Dannreuther, D. (ed.) (2003) *European Union Foreign and Security Policy: Towards a Neighbourhood Strategy* (London: Routledge).

Dannreuther, R. and Peterson, J. (eds) (2006) *Security Strategy and Transatlantic Relations* (London: Routledge).

Daveri, F. (2002) 'The New Economy in Europe, 1992–2001', *Oxford Review of Economic Policy*, 18(3): 345–62.

De Bièvre, D. (2006) 'The EU Regulatory Trade Agenda and the Quest for WTO Enforcement', *Journal of European Public Policy*, 13(6): 851–66.

Den Boer, M. and Monar, J. (2002) '11 September and the Challenge of Global Terrorism to the EU as a Security Actor', in G. Edwards and G. Wiessala (eds), *The European Union: Annual Review of the EU 2001/2002* (Oxford: Blackwell).

DePorte, A. (1986) *Europe between the Superpowers: The Enduring Balance*, 2nd edn (New Haven CT: Yale University Press).

Devuyst, Y. (2001) 'Transatlantic Competition Relations', in M. Pollack and G. Shaffer (eds) *Transatlantic Governance in the Global Economy* (Oxford: Rowman & Littlefield).

Diebold, W. (1959) *The Schuman Plan* (New York: Praeger).

Diebold, W. (1960) 'The Changed Economic Position of Western Europe: Some Implications for US Policy and International Organizations', *International Organization* 14(1): 1–19.

Diebold, W. (1972) *The United States and the Industrial World: American Foreign Economic Policy in the 1970s* (New York: Praeger for the Council on Foreign Relations).

Ding Y., Hope, O. C., Jeanjean, T. and Stolowy, H. (2007) 'Differences Between Domestic Accounting Standards and IAS: Measurement, Determinants and Implications', *Journal of Accounting and Public Policy*, 26(1): 1–38.

Doctor, M. (2007) 'Why Bother with Inter-Regionalism? Negotiations for an EU-Mercosur Agreement', *Journal of Common Market Studies*, 45(2): 281–314.

Dosi, G., Llerena, P. and Sylos Labini, M. (2005) 'Evaluating and Comparing the Innovation Performance of the United States and European Union', paper prepared for the TrendChart Policy Workshop, 2005, http://www.trendchart.org/scoreboards/scoreboard2005/pdf/EIS%202005%20EU%20versus%20US.pdf, accessed 10 June 2006.

Drahos, P. (2007) 'Weaving Webs of Influence: The United States, Free Trade Agreements and Dispute Resolution', *Journal of World Trade*, 41(1): 191–207.

Drejer, I. (2004) 'Identifying Innovation in Surveys of Services: A Schumpeterian Perspective', *Research Policy*, 33: 551–62.

Duckenfield, M. (1999) 'From GEMU to EMU: Bundesbank–Government Relations in Germany in the 1990s', *West European Politics*, 22(3); 87–108.

Edwards, G. and Regelsberger, E. (eds) (1990) *Europe's Global Links: The European Community and Inter-Regional Cooperation* (London: Pinter).

Eichengreen, B. (ed.) (1998) *Transatlantic Economic Relations in the Post-Cold War Era* (New York: Council on Foreign Relations).

Eichengreen, B. (2004) 'The Dollar and the New Bretton Woods System', Thornton Lecture, Cass Business School, City University, London, December.

Eichengreen, B. and Ghironi, R. (1998), 'European Monetary Integration and International Monetary Cooperation', in Eichengreen B. (1998) *Transatlantic Economic Relations in the Post-Cold War Era* (New York: Council on Foreign Relations).

Elgström, O. and Smith, M. (2000) 'Introduction: Negotiation and Policy-Making in the European Union – Processes, System and Order', *Journal of European Public Policy* 7(5): 673–83.

Ellwood, D. (1992) *Rebuilding Europe: Western Europe, America and Postwar Reconstruction* (London: Longman).

European Central Bank (2005) *Review of the International Role of the Euro*, Frankfurt: ECB, December, http://www. ecb.int/pub/pdf/other/euro-international-role200512en.pdf, accessed 10 June 2007.

European Commission (1994b) *Towards a New Asia Strategy*. Communication from the Commission to the Council.

European Commission (1997) 'Capital for Exploiting Research Results', *innovation and Technology Transfer*, Brussels, DGXII, April.

European Commission (2004a) 'A Proactive Competition Policy for a Competitive Europe', Communication from the Commission, 20 April, COM(2004) 293 final, accessed 15 August 2006.

European Commission (2004b) 'Accomplishing a Sustainable Agricultural Model for Europe Through CAP Reform – Sugar Sector Reform', Communication from the Commission, COM(2004) 499 final, 14 July, http://europa.eu.int/comm/agriculture/capreform/sugarprop_en.pdf.

European Commission (2004c) *Facing the Challenge: The Lisbon Strategy For Growth and Employment*, report of the High-Level Group Chaired by Wim Kok, http://ec.europa.eu/growthandjobs/pdf/kok_report_en.pdf, accessed 22 August 2007.

European Commission (2005a) *A Stronger EU-US Partnership and a More Open Market for the 21st Century*, COM(2005) 196 final, Brussels 18 May.

European Commission (2005b) *Review of the Framework for Relations Between the European Union and the United States: An Independent Study*, report of an academic team led by Professor John Peterson, Brussels, 18 April.

European Commission (2005c) *Bilateral Trade Relations – USA*, http://ec.europa.eu/trade/issues/bilateral/data.htm, accessed 6 January 2007.

European Commission (2005d) *Key Figures 2005: Towards a European Research Area*, Directorate for Research, ftp://ftp.cordis.lu/pub/indicators/docs/2004_1857_en_web.pdf, accessed 10 June 2006.

European Commission (2006) 'Vienna Summit Declaration', 21 June, http://www.eu2006.at/includes/Download_Dokumente/2106EUUDeclaration.pdf, accessed 15 May 2007.

European Commission (2007a) African, Caribbean, Pacific: Economic Partnership Agreements: Questions and Answers', 'http://ec.europa.eu/trade/issues/bilateral/regions/acp/memo010307_en.htm, accessed 4 June 2007.

European Commission (2007b) 'European Competition Policy in a Changing World and Globalised Economy: Fundamentals, New Objectives and Challenges Ahead', speech by Commissioner Neelie Kroes at the GCLC/College of Europe conference, '50 Years of EC Competition Law', Brussels, 5 June.

European Commission (2007c) 'Low business R&D a major threat to the European Knowledge-Based Economy', IP-07–790, 11 June, http://europa.eu/rapid/pressReleasesAction.do?reference=IP/07/790&format=HTML&aged=0&language=EN&guiLanguage=en, accessed 22 August 2007.

Eurostat (2005) 'First Preliminary Results: Research and Development in the EU', press release, 6 December 2005, http://epp.eurostat.ec.europa.eu/pls/portal/docs/PAGE/PGP_PRD_CAT_PREREL/PGE_CAT_PREREL_YEAR_2005/PGE_CAT_PREREL_YEAR_2005_MONTH_12/9–06122005–EN-AP.PDF, accessed 7 January 2007.

Evenett, S., Lehmann, A. and Steil, B. (2000) 'Antitrust Policy in an Evolving Global Marketplace', in S. Evenett, A. Lehmann and B. Steil (eds), *Antitrust Goes Global* (Washington and London: Brookings and RIIA).

Everts, S. (2004) *Engaging Iran: A Test Case for European Union Foreign Policy* (London: Centre for European Reform).

Faini, R. and Portes, R. (eds) (1995) *European Union Trade with Eastern Europe: Adjustment and Opportunities* (London: Centre for Economic Policy Research).

Fassbender, H. (2007) 'Europe's Productivity Challenge', *McKinsey Quarterly*, issue 2, June 2007.

Faust, J. (2004) 'Blueprint for an Inter-Regional Future? The European Union and the Southern Cone', in V. Aggarwal and E. Fogarty (eds), *EU Trade Strategies: Between Regionalism and Globalism* (Basingstoke: Palgrave Macmillan).

Featherstone, K. and Ginsberg, R. (1996) *The United States and the European Union in the 1990s: Partners in Transition* (London: Macmillan).

Federal Reserve (2006) *Monetary Policy Report to Congress*, Washington: Federal Reserve, 19 May, http://www.federalreserve.gov/boarddocs/hh/2006/july/fullreport.pdf, accessed 10 January 2007.

Feinberg, R. (2003) 'The Political Economy of the United States' Free Trade Agreements', *World Economy*, 26(7): 1019–040.

Foot, R., MacFarlane, N. and Mastanduno, M. (eds) (2003) *US Hegemony and International Organizations* (Oxford: Oxford University Press).

Forsberg, T. and Herd, G. (2006) *Divided West: European Security and the*

Transatlantic Relationship (Oxford: Blackwell for the Royal institute of International Affairs).

Forster, A. (1999) 'EU and Southeast Asia Relations: A Balancing Act', *International Affairs*, 75(4): 743–58.

Forster, A. (2000) 'Evaluating the EU–ASEM Relationship: A Negotiated Order Approach', *Journal of European Public Policy*, (95): 787–805.

Forster, A. and Wallace, W. (2000) 'Common Foreign and Security Policy: From Shadow to Substance?', in H. Wallace and W. Wallace (eds), *Policy-Making in the European Union*, 4th edn (Oxford: Oxford University Press).

Fox, E. (2006a) 'The WTO's First Antitrust Case – Mexican Telecom: A Sleeping Victory for Trade and Competition', *Journal of International Economic Law*, 9(2): 271–92.

Fox, E. (2006b) 'Testimony before the Antitrust Modernisation Commission', Hearing on International Issues, 15 February, http://www.kcl.ac.uk/depsta/law/research/cel/events/05_06/lectures/efpaper.pdf, accessed January 15, 2007.

Fox, E., Rudolf P. and Lawrence S. (2004) *US Anti-Trust in a Global Context*, *'Cases and Materials*, Appendix A. (Rochester, NY: Thomson West).

Freeman, C. (2004) 'Technological Infrastructure and International Competitiveness', *Industrial and Corporate Change*, 13(3): 541–69.

Freedman, L. (1982) 'The Atlantic Crisis', *International Affairs*, 58(3): 395–412.

Freedman, L. (ed.) (1983) *The Troubled Alliance* (London: Heinemann for the Royal Institute of International Affairs).

Frelleson, T. (2001) 'Processes and Procedures in EU–US Foreign Policy Cooperation: From the Transatlantic Declaration to the New Transatlantic Agenda', in E. Philippart and P. Winand (eds), *Ever Closer Partnership: Policy-Making in US–EU Relations* (Brussels: P.I.E.-Peter Lang).

Frieden, J., Gros, D. and Jones, J. (eds) (1998) *The New Political Economy of EMU* (Boston: Rowman & Littlefield).

Friis, L. and Murphy, A. (2000) '"Turbo-Charged Negotiations": The EU and the Stability Pact for South Eastern Europe', *Journal of European Public Policy* 7(5): 767–86.

Funke, M. and Rahn, J. (2005) 'Just How Undervalued is the Chinese Renminbi?', *World Economy*, 28(4): 465–90.

Fursdon, E. (1980) *The European Defence Community: A History* (London: Macmillan).

GAAP.web (2007) 'SEC Allows Choice Between IFRS or US GAAP', http://www.gaapweb.com/News/171–SEC-allows-choice-between-IFRS-or-US-GAAP.html, accessed 1 August 2007.

Gagne, G. and Morin, J-F. (2006) 'The Evolving American Policy on Investment Protection: Evidence from Recent FTAs and the 2004 Model BIT', *Journal of International Economic Law*, 9(2): 357–82.

Gallagher, P. (2007) *Inquit Database of SPS Notifications*, http://www.petergallagher.com.au/index.php/site/article/inquit-database-of-sps-notifications/, accessed 7 August 2007.

Gamble, A. and Payne, A. (eds) (1996) *Regionalism and World Order* (Basingstoke: Macmillan).

Gann, L. and Duignan, P. (1998) *Contemporary Europe and the Atlantic Alliance: A Political History* (Oxford: Blackwell).

Gardner, A. (2001) 'From the Transatlantic Declaration to the New Transatlantic Agenda: The Shaping of institutional Mechanisms and Policy Objectives by National and Supranational Actors', in E. Philippart and P. Winand (eds), *Ever Closer Partnership: Policy-Making in US- EU Relations* (Brussels: P.I.E.-Peter Lang).

Gehrig, T. and Menkhoff, L. (2005) 'The Rise of Fund Managers in Foreign Exchange: Will Fundamentals Ultimately Dominate?', *World Economy*, 28(4): 519–40.

General Accounting Office (1998) *Technology Transfer: Administration of the Bayh-Dole Act by Research Universities*, Washington DC: GAO-RCED 98–126, http://www.gao.gov/archive/1998/rc98126.pdf, accessed 7 January 2007.

Giesecke, S. (2000) 'The Contrasting Roles of Government in the Development of Biotechnology Industry in the US and Germany', *Research Policy*, 29: 205-23.

Gilson, J. (2004) 'Weaving a new Silk Road: Europe Meets Asia', in V. Aggarwal and E. Fogarty (eds), *EU Trade Strategies: Between Regionalism and Globalism* (Basingstoke: Palgrave Macmillan).

Ginsberg, R. (1989) *Foreign Policy Actions of the European Union* (Boulder, CO: Rienner).

Ginsberg, R. (2001) *The European Union in International Politics: Baptism by Fire* (Lanham, MD: Rowman & Littlefield).

Gnesotto, N. (ed.) (2004) *EU Security and Defence Policy: The First Five Years* (Paris: European Union Institute for Security Studies).

Goldstein, J. (2000) 'The United States and World Trade: Hegemony by Proxy?', in T. Lawton, J. Rosenau and A. Verdun (eds), *Strange Power: Shaping the Parameters of International Relations and International Political Economy* (Aldershot: Ashgate).

Gompert, D. and Larrabee, S. (eds) (1997) *America and Europe: A Partnership for a New Era* (Cambridge: Cambridge University Press).

Gordon, P. and Shapiro, J. (2004) *Allies at War: America, Europe, and the Crisis over Iraq* (New York: McGraw-Hill for the Brookings Institution).

Gordon, R. (2003) 'Exploding Productivity Growth: Context, Causes and Implications', *Brookings Papers on Economic Activity*, 34(2): 207–98.

Gourevitch, P. (1996) 'The Macro Politics of Micro-Institutional Differences in the Analysis of Comparative Capitalism', in Berger, S. and R. Dore (eds), *Convergence or Diversity? National Models of Production and Distribution in a Global Economy* (Ithaca, NY: Cornell University Press).

Gow, J. (1997) *Triumph of the Lack of Will: International Diplomacy and the Yugoslav War* (London: Hurst).

Grosser, A. (1980) *The Western Alliance: European–American Relations since 1945* (London: Continuum).

Grugel, J. (2004) 'New Regionalism and Modes of Governance – Comparing

US and EU Strategies in Latin America', *European Journal of International Relations*, 10(4): 603–26.

Guay, T. (1999) *The United States and the European Union: The Political Economy of a Relationship* (Sheffield: Sheffield Academic Press).

Guzman, A. (1998) 'Is International Antitrust Possible?', *New York University Law Review*, 73(5): 1507.

Haftendorn, H. and Tuschhoff, C. (eds) (1993) *America and Europe in an Era of Change* (Boulder, CO: Westview).

Hakim, P. (2006) 'Is Washington Losing Latin America?', *Foreign Affairs*, 85(1): 39–53.

Halliday, F. (2001) *Two Hours That Shook the World – Causes and Consequences*, (London: Saqi Books).

Halper, S. and Clarke, J. (2004) *America Alone: The Neo-Conservatives and the Global Order* (Cambridge: Cambridge University Press).

Ham, R.M. and Mowery, D. (1995) 'Enduring Dilemmas in US Technology Policy', *California Management Review*, 37(4): 89–107.

Hanrieder, W. (ed.) (1974) *The United States and Western Europe: Political, Economic and Strategic Perspectives* (Cambridge, MA: Winthrop).

Hanrieder, W. (ed.) (1982) *Economic Issues and the Atlantic Community* (New York: Praeger).

Harrison, M. (1982) *The Reluctant Ally: France and European Security* (Baltimore, MD: Johns Hopkins University Press).

Hart, D. (2001) 'Antitrust and Technological Innovation in the US: Ideas, Institutions, Decisions and Impacts, 1890–2000', *Research Policy*, 30(6): 923–36.

Held, D. and Koenig-Archibugi, M. (eds) (2004) *American Power in the 21st Century* (Cambridge: Polity).

Henderson, K. (ed.) (1999) *Back to Europe: Central and Eastern Europe and the European Union* (London: UCL Press).

Henning, C.R. (2006) 'Organizing Foreign Exchange Intervention in the Euro Area', *Journal of Common Market Studies*, 42–5(2): 315–42.

Hettne, B., Inotai, A. and Sunkel, O. (eds) (1999) *Globalism and the New Regionalism* (Basingstoke: Palgrave Macmillan).

Hill, C. (ed.) (1995) *The Actors in Europe's Foreign Policy* (London: Routledge).

Hill, C. (1998) 'Closing the Capability-Expectations Gap?', in J. Peterson and H. Sjursen (eds), *A Common Foreign Policy for Europe? Competing Visions of the CFSP* (London: Routledge).

Hill, C. (2004) 'Renationalising or Regrouping? European Foreign Policy Since 11 September 2001', *Journal of Common Market Studies* 42(1): 143–63.

Hill, C. and Smith, M. (eds) (2005) *International Relations and the European Union* (Oxford: Oxford University Press).

Hocking, B. and Smith, M. (1997) *Beyond Foreign Economic Policy: The United States, the Single European Market and the Changing World Economy* (London: Cassell/Pinter).

Hoffmann, S. (1968) *Gulliver's Troubles, or the Setting of American Foreign Policy* (New York: McGraw-Hill for the Council on Foreign Relations).

Hoffmann, S, (1978) *Primacy or World Order: American Foreign Policy since The Cold War* (New York: McGraw-Hill).

Hoffmann, S. (1996) 'Yugoslavia: Implications for Europe and for European Institutions', in R. Ullman (ed.), *The World and Yugoslavia's Wars* (New York: Council on Foreign Relations Press).

Hoffmann, S. and Maier, C. (eds) (1984) *The Marshall Plan: A Retrospective* (Boulder, CO: Westview).

Hogan, M. (1987) *The Marshall Plan: America, Britain, and the Reconstruction of Western Europe, 1947–1952* (Cambridge: Cambridge University Press).

Holland, M. (2000) 'Resisting Reform or Risking Revival? Renegotiating the Lomé Convention', in M. Green Cowles and M. Smith (eds), *The State of the European Union Volume 5: Risks, Reform, Resistance and Revival* (Oxford: Oxford University Press).

Holland, M. (2002) *The European Union and the Third World* (Basingstoke: Palgrave Macmillan).

Hong Kong Stock Exchange (2007) *The Year in Review, 2006*, http://www.hkex.com.hk/data/factbook/2006/e/01.pdf, accessed 17 May 2007.

Howorth, J. (2003) 'Foreign and Defence Policy Cooperation', in J. Peterson and M. Pollack (eds), *Europe, America, Bush: Transatlantic Relations In the Twenty-First Century* (London: Routledge).

Howorth, J. (2005) 'From Security to Defence: The Evolution of the CFSP', in C. Hill and M. Smith (eds), *International Relations and the European Union* (Oxford: Oxford University Press).

Howorth, J. (2007) *Security and Defence Policy in the European Union* (Basingstoke: Palgrave Macmillan).

Hufbauer, G. (ed.) (1990) *Europe 1992: An American Perspective* (Washington, DC: Brookings Institution).

Hufbauer, G. and Neumann, F. (2002) 'US-EU Trade: An American Perspective', Peterson Institute for International Economics, Washington, DC, http://www.iie.com/publications/papers/paper.cfm?ResearchID=460, accessed 24 December 2006.

ICN (2007b) 'Competition Authorities Agree to Develop Merger and Unilateral Conduct Guidance, Emphasize Co-operation, Outreach and Guidance', news release, 1 June, http://www.internationalcompetitionnetwork.org/index.php/en/newsroom/2007/06/1/28, accessed 15 June 2007.

Ikenberry, J. (ed.) (2002) *America Unrivaled: The Future of the Balance of Power* (Ithaca, NY: Cornell University Press).

Ikenberry, J. (ed.) (2006) *Liberal Order and Imperial Ambition* (Cambridge: Polity).

International Competition Network (ICN) (2007a) 'About the ICN', http://www.internationalcompetitionnetwork.org/index.php/en/about-icn, accessed 15 June 2007.

International Organization of Securities Commissions (IOSCO) 'IOSCO

Membership and Committees List', http://www.iosco.org/lists/, accessed 21 June 2007.

Janow, M. (2000) 'Transatlantic Cooperation on Competition Policy', in S. Evenett, A. Lehmann and B. Steil (eds), *Antitrust Goes Global*, (Brookings and RIIA: Washington and London).

Jervis, R. (2005) *American Foreign Policy in a New Era* (London: Routledge).

Jervis, R. (2006) 'The Remaking of a Unipolar World', *Washington Quarterly*, 29(3): 7–19.

Joffe, J. (1987) *The Limited Partnership: Europe, the United States, and the Burdens of Alliance* (Cambridge, MA: Ballinger).

Jones, E. (2006) 'Europe's Market Liberalisation is a Bad Model for a Global Trade Agenda', *Journal of European Public Policy*, 13(6): 943–57.

Kagan, R. (2003) *Of Paradise and Power: America and Europe in the New World Order* (New York: Knopf).

Kaiser, K. (1973) *Europe and America: The Future of the Relationship* (Washington, DC: Columbia Books).

Kaiser, K. (1974) 'Europe and America: A Critical Phase', *Foreign Affairs*, 52(4): 725–41.

Kaiser, K. and Schwartz, H-P. (eds) (1977) *America and Western Europe: Problems and Prospects* (Lexington, MA: Heath).

Kaldor, M. (2004) 'American Power: From "Compellance" to Cosmopolitanism?', in D. Held and M. Koenig-Archibugi (eds), *American Power in the 21st Century* (Cambridge: Polity).

Kaldor, M., Martin, M. and Selchow, S. (2007) 'Human Security: A New Strategic Narrative for Europe', *International Affairs*, 83(2): 273–88.

Keohane, R. (1979) 'American Policy Toward Advanced Industrial Countries: The Struggle to Make Others Adjust', in K. Oye, R. Rothchild and R. Lieber (eds), *Eagle Entangled: U.S. Foreign Policy in a Complex World* (New York: Longman).

Keohane, R. (2003) 'Ironies of Sovereignty: The EU and the US', in J. Weiler, I. Begg and J. Peterson (eds), *Integration in an Expanding European Union: Reassessing the Fundamentals* (Oxford: Blackwell).

Keohane, R. and Hoffmann, S. (eds) (1993) *After the Cold War: International Institutions and State Strategies in Europe, 1989–92* (Cambridge, MA: Harvard University Press).

Keukeleire, S. (2003) 'The European Union as a Diplomatic Actor: Internal, Traditional and Structural Diplomacy', *Diplomacy and Statecraft*, 14(3): 31–56.

Knodt, M. (2004) 'International Embeddedness of European Multi-Level Governance', *Journal of European Public Policy*, 11(4): 701–19.

Kolodziej, E. (1980–81) 'Europe: The Partial Partner', *International Security*, 5(3): 104–31.

Krause, L. (1968) *European Economic Integration and the United States* (Washington, DC: Brookings Institution).

Krugman, P. (1994) 'Competitiveness: A Dangerous Obsession', *Foreign Affairs*, 73(2): 28-44.

Kuhlmann, S. (2001) 'Future Governance of Innovation Policy in Europe – Three Scenarios', *Research Policy*, 30: 953–976.

Kupchan, C. (2002) *The End of the American Era: US Foreign Policy and the Geopolitics of the Twenty-First Century* (New York: Vintage).

Laatikainen, K. and Smith, K. (eds) (2004) *The European Union at the United Nations: Intersecting Multilateralisms* (Basingstoke: Palgrave Macmillan).

Laffan, B., O'Donnell, R. and Smith, M. (2000) *Europe's Experimental Union: Rethinking Integration* (London: Routledge).

Lamy, P., *Trade Policy in the Prodi Commission, 1999–2004: An Assessment*, Brussels, 19 November 2004, http://trade.ec.europa.eu/doclib/docs/2006/september/tradoc_120087.pdf, accessed 10 June 2007.

Lardy, N. (2005) 'China: The Great New Economic Challenge?', in F. Bergsten (ed.), *The United States and the World Economy: Foreign Economic Policy for the Next Decade* (Washington, DC: Institute for International Finance).

Larrabee, S. (1997) 'Security Challenges on Europe's Eastern Periphery', in D. Gompert and S. Larrabee (eds), *America and Europe: A Partnership for a New Era* (Cambridge: Cambridge University Press).

Lawton, L. and McGuire, S. (2005) }Adjusting to Liberalization: Tracing the Impact of the WTO on European Textiles and Chemicals Industries', *Business and Politics*, 7(3), www.bepress.B&P, article 4.

LeBlond, P. (2006) 'The Political Stability and Growth Pact is Dead: Long Live the Economic Stability and Growth Pact', *Journal of Common Market Studies*, 44(5): 969–90.

Leiserson, G. and Rohaly, J. (2006) The Distribution of the 2001–2006 Tax Cuts: Updated Projections, November, Tax Policy Centre, Washington, http://www.urban.org//UploadedPDF/411378_tax_cuts.pdf, accessed 10 January 2007.

Lieber, R. (1979) 'Europe and America in the World Energy Crisis', *International Affairs*, 55(4): 552–7.

Lieber, R. (2007) *The American Era: Power and Strategy for the 21st Century* (Cambridge: Cambridge University Press).

Lieven, A. (2002) 'The End of the West?', *Prospect*, September: 20–25.

Lieven, A. (2004) *America Right or Wrong: An Anatomy of American Nationalism* (Oxford and New York: Oxford University Press).

Light, M. (2003) 'US and European Perspectives on Russia', in J. Peterson and M. Pollack (eds), *Europe, America, Bush: Transatlantic Relations in the Twenty-First Century* (London: Routledge).

Light, M., White, S. and Lowenhardt, J. (2000) 'A Wider Europe: The View From Moscow and Kyiv', *International Affairs* 76(1): 77–88.

Lindeque, J. and McGuire, S. (2007) 'The United States and the WTO: Hegemony Constrained or Confirmed?', *Management International Review*, 47(5): 725–44.

Lindberg, T. (ed.) (2005) *Beyond Paradise and Power: Europe, America, and the Future of a Troubled Partnership* (London: Routledge).

Lindstrom, G. (ed.) (2003) *Shift or Rift? Assessing EU-US Relations After Iraq* (Paris: EU Institute for Security Studies).

Lindstrom, G. (2005) *EU-US Burdensharing: Who Does What?* Chaillot Paper 82, (Paris: European Union Institute for Security Studies).

Lindstrom, G. and Schmitt, B. (eds) (2004) *One Year On: Lessons from*

Iraq Chaillot Paper 68, (Paris: European Union Institute for Security Studies).

Lister, M. (ed.) (1999) *New Perspectives on European Union Development Cooperation* (Boulder, CO: Westview).

Little, R. and Smith, M. (eds) (2005) *Perspectives on World Politics*, 3rd edn (London: Routledge).

Luce, E. 'Out on a Limb: Why Blue-Collar Americans See Their Future as Precarious', *Financial Times*, 3 May 2006.

Ludlow, P. (1982) *The Making of the European Monetary System: A Case Study of the Politics of the European Community* (London: Butterworth).

Lundestad, G. (1998) *"Empire" By Integration: The United States and European Integration, 1945–1997* (Oxford: Oxford University Press).

Lundestad, G. (2005) *The United States and Western Europe Since 1945: From "Empire" by Integration to Transatlantic Drift* (Oxford: Oxford University Press).

MacKinnon, R. (2004) 'Optimum Currency Areas and Key Currencies: Mundell I versus Mundell II', *Journal of Common Market Studies*, 42(4): 689–715.

Mahnke, D., Rees, W. and Thompson, W. (2004) *Redefining Transatlantic Security Relations: The Challenge of Change* (Manchester: Manchester University Press).

Manger, M. (2005) 'Competition and Bilateralism in Trade Policy: the Case of Japan's Free Trade Agreements', *Review of International Political Economy*, 12(5): 804–28.

Manners, I. (2006) 'Normative Power Europe Reconsidered: Beyond the Crossroads', *Journal of European Public Policy*, 13(2): 182–99.

Manners, I. and Whitman, R. (2003) 'The "Difference Engine": Constructing and Representing the International Identity of the European Union', *Journal of European Public Policy*, 10(3): 380–404.

McCormick, J. (2007) *The European Superpower* (Basingstoke: Palgrave Macmillan).

McCowan, L. and Cini, M. (1999) 'Discretion and Politicization in EU Competition Policy: the Case of Merger Control', *Governance*, 12(2): 176–7.

McCreevy, C. (2007) 'Update on Financial Services', Speech delivered to the European Parliament's Open ECON Coordinators meeting, SPEECH/07/482, Strasbourg, 10 July.

McGuire, S. (1997) *Airbus Industrie: Cooperation and Conflict in US-EC Trade Relations* (Basingstoke: Macmillan).

McGuire, S. (2004) 'Firms and Governments in International Trade', in B. Hocking and S. McGuire (eds), *Trade Politics*, 2nd edn (London: Routledge).

McGuire, S. (2006) 'No More Euro-Champions: The Interaction of EU Industrial and Trade Policies', *Journal of European Public Policy*, 13(6): 887–905.

McMahon, J. (1998) 'ASEAN and the Asia-Europe Meeting: Strengthening the

European Union's Relationship with Southeast Asia', *European Foreign Affairs Review*, 3(2): 233–51.

McNamara, K. (2006) 'Economic Governance, Ideas and EMU: What Currency Does Policy Consensus Have Today?', *Journal of Common Market Studies*, 44(4): 803–21.

Mee, C. (1984) *The Marshall Plan: The Launching of the Pax Americana* (New York: Simon & Schuster).

Melamed, D. (1998) 'Antitrust Enforcement in the Global Economy', speech at the Fordham Corporate Law Institute, New York, 22 October, http://www.usdoj.gov/atr/public/speeches/2043.htm, accessed 21 August 2006.

Meunier, S. (2005) *Trading Voices: The European Union in International Commercial Negotiations* (Princeton: Princeton University Press).

Meunier, S. and Nicolaïdis, K. (2006) 'The European Union as a Conflicted Trade Power', *Journal of European Public Policy*, 13(6): 906–25.

Milward, A. (1984) *The Reconstruction of Western Europe, 1945–1951* (London: Methuen).

Monar, J. (2004) 'The European Union as an International Actor in the Domain of Justice and Home Affairs', *European Foreign Affairs Review* 9(3): 395–416.

Morgan, E. and McGuire, S. (2004) 'Transatlantic Divergence: GE-Honeywell and the EU's Merger Policy', *Journal of European Public Policy*, 11(1): 39–56.

Mowery, D. (1998) 'The Changing Structure of the US National Innovation System: Implications for International Conflict and Cooperation in R&D', *Research Policy*, 27: 639–54.

Mowery, D. and Rosenberg, N. (1989) *Technology and the Pursuit of Economic Growth*, (Cambridge: Cambridge University Press).

Mowery, D. and Rosenberg, N. (1998) 'Introduction', in D. Mowery and N. Rosenberg, *Paths of Innovation* (Cambridge: Cambridge University Press), 1–10.

Mowle, T. (2004) *Allies at Odds? The United States and the European Union* (Basingstoke: Palgrave Macmillan).

Muller, K. (2005) 'Nationalist Currents in German Economic Liberalism', in Eric Helleiner and Andreas Pickel (eds), *Economic Nationalism in a Globalizing World* (Ithaca: Cornell University Press: 141–63).

Müller-Brandeck-Bocquet, G. (2000) 'Perspectives for a New Regionalism: Relations Between the EU and the MERCOSUR', *European Foreign Affairs Review*, 5(4): 561–79.

Musu, C. and Wallace, W. (2003) ' The Middle East: Focus of Discord?', in J. Peterson and M. Pollack (eds), *Europe, America, Bush: Transatlantic Relations in the Twenty-First Century* (London: Routledge).

Narlikar, A. (2004) 'The Ministerial Process and Power Dynamics in the World Trade Organisation: Understanding Failure from Seattle to Cancún', *New Political Economy*, 9(3): 413–28.

Narlikar A. and Tussie, D. (2004) 'The G20 at the Cancún Ministerial:

Developing Countries and their Evolving Coalitions in the WTO', *World Economy*, 27(7): 947–66.

National Science Foundation (2005) *National Patterns of Research and Development Resources, 2003* (Washington, DC: NSF, Division of Science Resources Statistics, February).

National Science Foundation (2007a) *Why Did They Come to the United States: A Profile of Immigrant Scientists and Engineers*, NSF Policy Brief 07–324, June. http://www.nsf.gov/statistics/infbrief/nsf07324/, accessed July 11 2007.

National Science Foundation (2007b) 'R&D Expenditures', Division of Science Resources Statistics, http://www.nsf.gov/statistics/nsf07319/content.cfm?pub_id=1874&id=4#multinational, accessed 20 August 2007.

National Science Foundation (2007c) 'President's FY 2008 Budget Requests 1% Increase in R&D Funding', NSF-07–327, http://www.nsf.gov/statistics/infbrief/nsf07327/, accessed 22 August 2007.

National Science Foundation (2007d) *Asia's Rising Science and Technology Strength: Comparative Indicators for Asia, the European Union and the United States*, (Washington: National Science Foundation), http://www.nsf.gov/statistics/nsf07319/pdf/nsf07319.pdf, accessed 22 August 2007.

Navarro, L. (2003) *Industrial Policy in the Economic Literature: Recent Theoretical Work and Its Implications for EU Policy*, EU Enterprise paper 12, http://ec.europa.eu/enterprise/library/enterprise-papers/pdf/enterprise_paper_12_2003.pdf, accessed 24 May 2006.

Nello, S. and Smith, K. (1998) *The European Union and Central and Eastern Europe* (Aldershot: Ashgate).

Niblett, R. and Wallace, W. (eds) (2001) *Rethinking European Order: West European Perspectives, 1989–1997* (Basingstoke: Palgrave Macmillan).

Nugent, N. (ed.) (2004) *European Union Enlargement* (Basingstoke: Palgrave Macmillan).

Nuttall, S. (1994) 'The EC and Yugoslavia: *Deus ex Machina* or *Machina Sine Deo*?', in N. Nugent (ed.), *The European Union 1993: Annual Review of Activities* (Oxford: Blackwell).

Nye, J. (2002) *The Paradox of American Power: Why the World's Only Superpower Can't Go It Alone* (New York: Oxford University Press).

Nye, J. (2004a) *Soft Power: The Means to Succeed in World Politics* (New York: Public Affairs Press).

Nye, J. (2004b) 'Hard Power, Soft Power, and "The War on Terrorism"', in D. Held and M. Koenig-Archibugi (eds), *American Power in the 21st Century* (Cambridge: Polity).

Olsen, G. (2002) 'Promoting Democracy, Preventing Conflict: The European Union and Africa', *International Politics* 39 (3): 311–28.

Organisation for Economic Co-operation and Development (2005) *OECD Science, Technology and Industry Scoreboard*, Paris: OECD.

Organisation for Economic Co-operation and Development (2006a) 'China Will Become the World's Second Highest Investor in R&D by the End of 2006, Finds OECD', press release, OECD, Paris, 4 December 2006, http://www.oecd.org/document/0,3455,en_2649_37417_37770522_1_1_1_37417,00.html, accessed 14 June 2007.

Organisation for Economic Co-operation and Development (2006b), *OECD Science, Technology and Industry Outlook, Highlights* (Paris).

Ortega, M. (ed.) (2003) *The European Union and the Crisis in the Middle East* Chaillot Paper 62. (Paris: European Union Institute for Security Studies).

Ortega, M. (ed.) (2007) *Building the Future: The EU's Contribution to Global Governance.* Chaillot Paper 100, April (Paris: EU Institute for Security Studies).

Ostry, S. (1997) *The Post-Cold War Trading System: Who's on First?* (Chicago: University of Chicago Press).

Oye, K., Lieber, R. and Rothchild, R. (eds) (1983) *Eagle Defiant: US Foreign Policy in the 80s* (Boston: Little, Brown).

Oye, K., Lieber, R. and Rothchild, R. (eds) (1987) *Eagle Resurgent? The Reagan Era in American Foreign Policy* (Boston: Little, Brown).

Paeman, H. and Bensch, A. (1995) *From the GATT to the WTO: The European Community in the Uruguay Round* (Leuven: University of Leuven Press).

Papaioannou, E., Portes, R. and Siourounis, G. (2006) 'Optimal Currency Shares in International Reserves: the Impact of the Euro and the Prospects for the Dollar', European Central Bank working paper 694, November, http://www.ecb.int/pub/pdf/scpwps/ecbwp694.pdf, accessed 17 July 2007.

Pape, R. (2005) 'Soft Balancing Against the United States', *International Security*, 30(1): 7–45.

Payne, A. (ed.) (2004) *The New Regional Politics of Development* (Basingstoke: Palgrave Macmillan).

Pelkmans, J. and Winters, A. (1988) *Europe's Domestic Market* (London: Routledge & Kegan Paul for the Royal Institute of International Affairs).

Perez, R. (2006) 'Are Economic Partnership Agreements a First-Best Optimum for the African, Caribbean and Pacific Countries?', *Journal of World Trade*, 40(6): 999–1019.

Petersmann, E-U. (2003) 'Prevention and Settlement of Transatlantic Economic Disputes: Legal Strategies for EU/US Leadership', in E-U. Petersmann and M. Pollack (eds), *Transatlantic Economic Disputes: The EU, the US and the WTO* (Oxford: Oxford University Press, 3–64).

Peterson, J. (1996a) 'Research and Development Policy', in H. Kassim and A. Menon (eds), *The European Union and National Industrial Policy* (London: Routledge).

Peterson, J. (1996b) *Europe and America in the 1990s: The Prospects for Partnership*, 2nd edn (London: Routledge).

Peterson, J. (2003) 'The US and Europe in the Balkans', in J. Peterson and M. Pollack (eds), *Europe, America, Bush: Transatlantic Relations in the Twenty-First Century* (London: Routledge).

Peterson, J. (2004a) 'Europe, America, Iraq: Worst Ever, Ever Worsening', in L. Miles (ed.) *The European Union: Annual Review 2003–2004* (Oxford: Blackwell).

Peterson, J. and Pollack, M. (eds) (2003), *Europe, America, Bush: Transatlantic Relations in the Twenty-First Century* (London: Routledge).

Pfaltzgraff, R. (1969) *The Atlantic Community: A Complex Imbalance* (New York: Van Nostrand Reinhold).

Philippart, E. and Winand, P. (eds) (2001) *Ever Closer Partnership: Policy-Making in US–EU Relations* (Brussels: P.I.E./Peter Lang).

Pigman, G. (2004) 'Continuity and Change in US Trade Policy, 1993–2003', in B. Hocking and S. McGuire (eds), *Trade Politics*, 2nd edn (London: Routledge).

Piketty, T. and Saez, E. (2006) 'The Evolution of Top Incomes: A Historical and Institutional Perspective', NBER Working Paper, #11955, January.

Pinder, J. (1983) 'Interdependence: Problem or Solution?', in L. Freedman (ed.), *The Troubled Alliance* (London: Heinemann for the Royal Institute of International Affairs).

Pollack, M. (2003a) 'Unilateral America, Multilateral Europe?', in J. Peterson and M. Pollack (eds), *Europe, America, Bush: Transatlantic Relations in the Twenty-First Century* (London: Routledge).

Pollack, M. (2003b) 'Managing System Friction: Regulatory Conflicts and Transatlantic Relations in the WTO', in E-U. Petersmann and M. Pollack (eds), *Transatlantic Economic Disputes: The EU, the US and the WTO* (Oxford: Oxford University Press).

Pollack, M. (2005) 'The New Transatlantic Agenda at Ten: Reflections on an Experiment in International Governance', *Journal of Common Market Studies*, 43(5): 899–919.

Pollack, M. and Shaffer, G. (eds) (2001) *Transatlantic Governance in the Global Economy* (Lanham, MD: Rowman & Littlefield).

Pond, E. (2004) *Friendly Fire: The Near-Death of the Transatlantic Alliance* (Washington, DC: Brookings Institution Press for the European Union Studies Association).

Porter, T. (2005) 'The United States in International Trade Politics: Liberal Leader or Heavy-Handed Hegemon?', in D. Kelly and W. Grant (eds), *The Politics of International Trade in the 21st Century: Actors, Issues and Regional Dynamics* (Basingstoke: Palgrave Macmillan).

Posch, W. (ed.) (2006) *Iranian Challenges*, Chaillot Paper 89. (Paris: European Union Institute for Security Studies).

Posen, A. (2005) *The Euro at Five: Ready for a Global Role?* (Washington, DC: Institute for International Economics).

Posen, B. (2006) 'European Security and Defense Policy: Response to Unipolarity?', *Security Studies*, 15(2): 149–86.

Potočnik, J. (2007) 'Research and the Structuring of the Lisbon Vision', speech delivered at the conference, Coordinating Framework Programme and Structural Funds to Support R&D, Brussels, 3 May.

Ravenhill, J. (2004) 'Back to the Nest? Europe's Relations with the African, Caribbean and Pacific Group of Countries', in V. Aggarwal and E. Fogarty (eds), *EU Trade Strategies: Between Regionalism and Globalism* (Basingstoke: Palgrave Macmillan).

Rees, W. (2006) *Transatlantic Counter-Terrorism Cooperation: The New Imperative* (London: Routledge).

Rees, W. and Aldrich, R. (2005) 'Contending Culture of Counterterrorism: Transatlantic Divergence or Convergence?', *International Affairs*, 81(5), October: 905–24.

Robertson, P. and Patel, P. (2007), 'New Wine in Old Bottles: Technological Diffusion in Developed Economies', *Research Policy*, 36: 708–21.

Rosecrance, R. (ed.) (1976) *America as an Ordinary Country: US Foreign Policy and the Future* (Ithaca, NY: Cornell University Press).

Rosecrance, R. (1986) *The Rise of the Trading State: Commerce and Conquest in the Modern World* (New York: Basic Books).

Rosecrance, R. (1993) 'Trading States in a New Concert of Europe', in H. Haftendorn and C, Tuschhoff (eds), *America and Europe in an Era of Change* (Boulder, CO: Westview).

Sally, R. (2004) 'The WTO in Perspective', in B. Hocking and S. McGuire (eds), *Trade Politics*, 2nd edn (London: Routledge).

Santiso, J. (2007) 'The Emergence of Latin Multinationals' *Deutsche Bank Research*, March.

Sandholtz, W. and Zysman, J. (1989) '1992: Recasting the European Bargain', *World Politics*, 42(1): 95–128.

Sbragia, A. (1998) 'Institution-Building from Above and Below: The European Community in Global Environmental Politics', in W. Sandholtz and A. Stone Sweet (eds), *European Integration and Supranational Governance* (Oxford: Oxford University Press).

Scheve, K. and Slaughter, M. (2007) 'A New Deal for Globalisation', *Foreign Affairs*, 86(4): 34–48.

Schirm, S. (2002) *Globalization and the New Regionalism* (Cambridge: Polity).

Scholte J.A. (2002) 'International Finance', in D. Held and T. McGrew (eds) *Governing Globalisation* (Cambridge: Polity).

Schumpeter, J. (1942) *Capitalism, Socialism and Democracy* (New York: Knopf).

Schwok, R. (1991) *U.S.–EC Relations in the Post-Cold War Era: Conflict or Partnership?* (Boulder, CO: Westview).

Sedelmeier, U. (2004) 'Eastern Enlargement', in H. Wallace, W. Wallace and M. Pollack (eds), *Policy-Making in the European Union*, 5th edn (Oxford: Oxford University Press).

Segal, A. (2004) 'Is America Losing Its Edge?', *Foreign Affairs*, 83(6): 2–8.

Sell, S. (2003) *Private Power, Public Law: The Globalization of Intellectual Property Rights* (Cambridge: Cambridge University Press).

Sen G. (2003) 'The United States and the GATT/WTO System', in R. Foot, S.N. McFarlane and M. Mastanduno (eds), *US Hegemony and International Organizations* (Oxford: Oxford University Press).

Servan-Schreiber, J-J. (1968) *The American Challenge* (London: Hamish Hamilton).

Shaffer, G. (2003) *Defending Interests: Public–Private Partnerships in WTO Litigation* (Washington, DC: Brookings Institution).

Shambaugh, D. (2005) 'The New Strategic Triangle: US and European Reactions to China's Rise', *Washington Quarterly*, 28(3): 7–25.

Sharp, M. (1998) Competitiveness and Cohesion – Are the Two Compatible?', *Research Policy*, 27: 569–88.

Shiroyama, H. (2007) 'The Harmonisation of Automobile Environmental

Standards Between Japan, the United States and Europe: The "De-Politicising Strategy" by Industry and the Dynamics Between Firms And Governments in a Transnational Context', *Pacific Review*, 20(3): 351–70.

Shonfield, A. and Oliver, H. (eds) (1976) *International Economic Relations of the Western World, 1959–1971* (London: Oxford University Press for the Royal Institute of International Affairs).

Sloan, S. (2005) *NATO, the European Union and the Atlantic Community: The Transatlantic Bargain Challenged*, 2nd edn (Lanham, MD: Rowman & Littlefield).

Smith, A. (2000) *The Return to Europe: The Reintegration of Eastern Europe into the European Economy* (Basingstoke: Macmillan).

Smith, H. (1995) *European Union Foreign Policy and Central America* (Basingstoke: Macmillan).

Smith, H. (1998) 'Actually Existing Foreign Policy – Or Not? The EU in Latin and Central America', in J. Peterson and H. Sjursen (eds), *A Common Foreign Policy for Europe? Competing Visions of the CFSP* (London: Routledge).

Smith, K. (1999) *The Making of European Union Foreign Policy: The Case of Eastern Europe* (London: Macmillan).

Smith, K. (2000) 'The End of Civilian Power EU: A Welcome demise or Cause for Concern?', *International Spectator*, 35(2): 11–28.

Smith, K. (2003) *European Union Foreign Policy in a Changing World* (Cambridge: Polity).

Smith, K. (2005a) 'Enlargement and European Order', in C. Hill and M. Smith (eds), *International Relations and the European Union* (Oxford: Oxford University Press).

Smith, K. (2005b) 'The Outsiders: The Neighbourhood Strategy', *International Affairs*, 81(4): 757–74.

Smith, K. (2005c) 'Beyond the Civilian Power EU Debate', in B. Irondelle (ed.), *A la Recherché de la politique étrangère européenne* (Paris: L'Harmattan).

Smith, K. (2006a) 'The European Union, Human Rights and the United Nations', in K. Laatikainen and K. Smith (eds), *The European Union at the United Nations: Intersecting Multilateralisms* (Basingstoke: Palgrave Macmillan).

Smith, K. (2006b) 'The Limits of Proactive Cosmopolitanism: The EU and Burma, Cuba and Zimbabwe', in O. Elgström and M. Smith (eds), *The European Union's Roles in International Politics: Concepts and Analysis* (London: Routledge).

Smith, M. (1978) 'From the "Year of Europe" to a Year of Carter: Continuing Patterns and Problems in Euro-American Relations', *Journal of Common Market Studies*, 17(1): 26–44.

Smith, M. (1992) '"The Devil You Know": The United States and a Changing European Community', *International Affairs*, 68(1): 103–20.

Smith, M. (1998) 'Competitive Cooperation and EU-US Relations: Can the EU be a Strategic Partner for the US in the Global Political Economy?', *Journal of European Public Policy*, 5(4): 561–77.

Smith, M. (2000) 'Negotiating New Europes: The Roles of the European Union', *Journal of European Public Policy*, 7(5): 806–22.

Smith, M. (2001) 'European Foreign and Security Policy', in S. Bromley (ed.), *Governing the European Union* (London: Sage).

Smith, M. (2004) 'Between Two Worlds? The European Union, the United States and World Order', *International Politics*, 41(1): 96–117.

Smith, M. (2005a) 'Taming the Elephant? The European Union and the Management of American Power', *Perspectives on European Politics and Society*, 6(1): 129–54.

Smith, M. (2005b) 'The European Union and the United States of America: The Politics of "Bi-Multilateral" Negotiations', in O. Elgström and C. Jönsson (eds), *European Union Negotiations: Processes, Networks and Institutions* (London: Routledge).

Smith, M. (2005c) 'European Union Enlargement and the United States: 2004 in Perspective', paper presented to the Annual and Research Conference of the University Association for Contemporary European Studies, Zagreb, Croatia, September.

Smith, M. (2005d) Crises and Crisis Management in the Euro-American System: Past, Present and Future', paper presented at the biennial conference of the European Union Studies Association, Austin TX, April.

Smith, M. (2006a) 'European Foreign Policy in Crisis? EU Responses to the George W. Bush Administration', *European Political Science*, 5(1): 41–51.

Smith, M. (2006b) 'The Shock of the Real? Trends in European Foreign and Security Policy Since September 2001', *Studia Diplomatica*, 59(1): 27–44.

Smith, M. (2008) 'The European Union and International Order: European and Global Dimensions', *European Foreign Affairs Review*.

Smith, M. and Steffenson, R. (2005) 'The EU and the United States', in C. Hill and M. Smith (eds), *International Relations and the European Union* (Oxford: Oxford University Press).

Smith, M. and Woolcock, S. (1993) *The United States and the European Community in a Transformed World* (London: Pinter for the Royal Institute of International Affairs).

Smith, M. and Woolcock, S. (1994) 'Learning to Cooperate: The Clinton Administration and the European Union', *International Affairs*, 70(3): 459–76.

Soderbaum, F., Stalgren, P. and van Langenhove, L. (2005) 'The EU as a Global Actor and the Dynamics of Inter-Regionalism: A Comparative Analysis', *Journal of European Integration*, 27(3): 365–80.

Spence, D. (1991) *Enlargement Without Accession: The EC's Response to German Unification*. Discussion Paper 36 (London: Royal Institute for International Affairs).

Steffenson, R. (2005) *Managing EU–US Relations: Actors, Institutions and the New Transatlantic Agenda* (Manchester: Manchester University Press).

Story, J. (ed.) (1993) *The New Europe* (Oxford: Blackwell).

Teló, M. (ed.) (2001) *European Union and New Regionalism* (Aldershot: Ashgate).

Thurbon, E. and Weiss, L. (2006) 'From Player to Pawn: Howard's Trade

Legacy', *Australian Review of Public Affairs*, 26 February, http://www.australianreview.net/digest/2006/02/thurbon_weiss.html, accessed 14 March 2007.

Todd, E. (2003) *After the Empire: The Breakdown of the American Order* (New York: Columbia University Press).

Todorov, F. and Valke, A. (2006) 'Judicial Review of Merger Control Decisions in the European Union', *The Anti-Trust Bulletin*, 51(2): 339–81.

Treverton, G. (1985) *Making the Alliance Work: The United States and Western Europe* (London: Macmillan).

Treverton, G. (ed.) (1991) *The Shape of the New Europe* (New York: Council on Foreign Relations).

Tsoukalis, L. (ed.) (1986) *Europe, America and the World Economy* (Oxford: Blackwell).

Tsoukalis, L. (2000) 'Economic and Monetary Union: Political Conviction and Economic Uncertainty', in H. Wallace and W. Wallace, *Policy Making in the European Union* (Oxford: Oxford University Press): 149–78.

Tyson, L. (1992) *Who's Bashing Whom? Trade Conflict in High Technology Sectors*, (Washington, DC: Institute for International Economics).

UNCTAD (2006) *World Investment Report, 2006*, Geneva.

UNICE (2006) 'UNICE Position Paper on Cohesion Policy and Competitiveness', Brussels: UNICE, 16 November, http://www.unice.org/DocShareNoFrame/Common/GetFileURL.asp?FileURL=F_4, accessed 7 January 2007.

United Nations Conference on Trade And Development (2006) *World Investment Report: FDI from Developing and Transition Economies: Implications for Development* (Geneva: UNCTAD).

United States Congress (2002) *Trade Promotion Authority Act*, Public Law 107-210, http://www.govtrack.us/congress/billtext.xpd?bill=h107-3005, accessed 15 May 2007.

United States Congress (2007) Legislative Highlights: The America Creating Opportunities to Meaningfully Promote Excellence in Technology, Education, and Science Act (COMPETES), House Committee on Science and Technology, United States Congress, 31 July 2007, http://science.house.gov/legislation/leg_highlights_detail.aspx?NewsID=1938, accessed 20 August 2007.

United States Department of State (2006), 'US Bilateral Investment Treaty Program', Fact Sheet, http://www.state.gov/e/eeb/rls/fs/2006/22422.htm, accessed 23 May 2007.

United States Trade Representative (2004) 'United States and Morocco Sign Historic Free Trade Agreement', press release, 18 June 2004, http://www.ustr.gov/Document_Library/Press_Releases/2004/June/United_States_Morocco_Sign_Historic_Free_Trade_Agreement.html, accessed 14 March 2007.

United States Trade Representative (2005) US – Central America – Dominican Republic Free Trade Agreement, statement of acting US Trade Representative Peter Allgeier, Committee on Finance, United States Senate, 13 April 2005.

United States Trade Representative (2006) 'Trade Compliance Centre', http://tcc.export.gov/Trade_Agreements/Bilateral_Investment_Treaties/index.asp, accessed 7 January 2007.

United States Trade Representative (2007) 'Bilateral trade Agreements', http://www.ustr.gov/Trade_Agreements/Bilateral/Section_Index.htmi, accessed 16 August 2007.

Vanhoonacker, S. (2001) *The Bush Administration (1989–1993) and the Development of a European Security Identity* (Aldershot: Ashgate).

Vanhoonacker, S. (2005) 'The Institutional Framework', in C. Hill and M. Smith (eds), *International Relations and the European Union* (Oxford: Oxford University Press).

Veljanovski, V. (2004) 'EC Merger Policy After GE/Honeywell and Airtours', *The Anti-Trust Bulletin*, 49(2): 153–93.

Vernon, R. (1973) 'Rogue Elephant in the Forest: An Appraisal of Transatlantic Relations', *Foreign Affairs* 52(2): 163–79.

Vogler, J. (2005) 'The European Union's Contribution to Global Environmental Governance', *International Affairs*, 81(4): 835–50.

Vogler, J. and Bretherton, C. (2006) 'The European Union as a Protagonist to the United States on Climate Change', *International Studies Perspectives* 7: 1–22.

Wallace, W. (2000) 'From the Atlantic to the Bug, form the Arctic to the Tigris? The Transformation of the EU', *International Affairs* 76(3): 475–94.

Walter, A. (1993) *World Power and World Money* (London: Harvester Wheatsheaf).

Wan, M. (2007) 'The United States, Japan and the European Union: Comparing Political Economy Approaches to China', *Pacific Review*, 20(3): 397–421.

Warnecke, S. (ed.) (1972) *The European Community in the 1970s* (New York: Praeger).

Webber, M. (1996) *The International Politics of Russia and the Successor States* (Manchester: Manchester University Press).

Webber, M. (ed.) (2000) *Russia and Europe Conflict or Cooperation?* (Basingstoke: Macmillan).

Webber, M. (2001) 'Third Party Inclusion in European Security and Defence Policy: A Case Study of Russia', *European Foreign Affairs Review*, 6(4): 407–26.

Webber, M. (2007) *Inclusion, Exclusion and the Governance of European Security* (Manchester: Manchester University Press).

Weller, M. (1999) 'The Rambouillet Conference on Kosovo', *International Affairs*, 75(2): 211–52.

Whalley, J. and Leith, C. (2003) 'Competitive Liberalisation and a US-SACU FTA'. National Bureau of Economic Research, working paper 10168, December.

White, S., McAllister, I. and Light, M. (2002) 'Enlargement and the New Outsiders', *Journal of Common Market Studies*, 40(1): 135–54.

Whitman, R. (1998) *From Civilian Power to Superpower? The International Identity of the European Union* (Basingstoke: Macmillan).

Wiener, J. (2005) 'GATS and the Politics of "Trade in Services"', in D. Kelly and W. Grant (eds), *The Politics of International Trade in the 21st Century: Actors, Issues and Regional Dynamics* (Basingstoke: Palgrave Macmillan).

Wilkinson, R. (2005) 'The World Trade Organization and the Regulation of International Trade', in D. Kelly and W. Grant (eds), *The Politics of International Trade in the 21st Century: Actors, Issues and Regional Dynamics* (London: Palgrave Macmillan).

Wilks, S. (2005) 'Agency Escape: Decentralisation or Dominance of the European Commission in the Modernisation of Competition Policy?', *Governance*, 18(3): 431–52.

Winand, P. (1993) *Eisenhower, Kennedy and the United States of Europe* (London: Macmillan).

Woodward, B. (2006) *State of Denial Bush at War, Part III* (New York: Simon & Schuster).

Woolcock, S. and van der Ven, H. (eds) (1986) *International Trade in the Post-Multilateral Era* (Cambridge, MA: Harvard University Press).

World Trade Organization (2000) *Trade Policy Review – the European Union*, 14 July.

World Trade Organization (2001) 'Ministerial Declaration', 14 November, http://www.wto.org/english/thewto_e/minist_e/min01_e/mindecl_e.htm# relationship, accessed 7 January 2007.

World Trade Organization (2004) WT/DS265/R, European Communities – Export Subsidies on Sugar, 15 October 2004.

World Trade Organization (2006) *World Trade Report 2006*, WTO: Geneva, 2006, Appendix Table 1, p.11

World Trade Organization (2007) 'Regional Trade Agreements', http:// www.wto.org/english/tratop_e/region_e/region_e.htm, accessed 20 August 2007.

Young, A. (2004) 'The Incidental Fortress: The Single European Market and World Trade', *Journal of Common Market Studies*, 42(2): 393–414.

Young, A. and Peterson, J. (2006) 'The EU and the New Trade Politics', *Journal of European Public Policy*, 13(6): 795–814.

Young, O. (1972) 'The Actors in World Politics', in J. Rosenau, V. Davis and M. East (eds), *The Analysis of International Politics* (New York: Free Press).

Youngs, R. (2006) *Europe and the Middle East: In the Shadow of September 11* (Boulder, CO: Rienner).

Zabarowski, M. (ed.) (2006a) *Friends Again? EU-US Relations After the Crisis* (Paris: EU Institute for Security Studies).

Zabarowski, M. (ed.) (2006b), *Facing China's Rise: Guidelines for an EU Strategy*. Chaillot Paper 94, December (Paris: EU Institute for Security Studies).

Zelikow, P. and Rice, C. (1995) *Germany Unified and Europe Transformed: A Study in Statecraft* (Cambridge, MA: Harvard University Press).

Zhou, P. and Leydesdorff, L. (2006) 'The Emergence of China as a Leading Nation in Science', *Research Policy*, 35: 83–104.

Zucconi, M. (1996) 'The EU in the Former Yugoslavia', in A. Chayes and A. Chayes (eds), *Preventing Conflict in the Post-Communist World: Mobilizing International and Regional Organizations* (Washington, DC: Brookings Institution).

Index